IN THE SHADOW OF MIGRATION

WITHDRAWN

VERHANDELINGEN
VAN HET KONINKLIJK INSTITUUT
VOOR TAAL-, LAND- EN VOLKENKUNDE

174

JANET RODENBURG

IN THE SHADOW OF MIGRATION

RURAL WOMEN AND THEIR HOUSEHOLDS IN
NORTH TAPANULI, INDONESIA

1997
KITLV Press
Leiden

EXCLUSIVE DISTRIBUTORS:
THE CELLAR BOOK SHOP
18090 WYOMING
DETROIT, MICH. 48221
U.S.A.

Published by:
KITLV Press
Koninklijk Instituut voor Taal-, Land- en Volkenkunde
(Royal Institute of Linguistics and Anthropology)
P.O. Box 9515
2300 RA Leiden
The Netherlands

DS
632
.T62
R63
1997

Cover: Youetta de Jager and Rita DeCoursey

ISBN 90 6718 108 0

© 1997 Koninklijk Instituut voor Taal-, Land- en Volkenkunde

No part of this publication may be reproduced or transmitted in any form or by any means, electronic or mechanical, including photocopy, recording, or any information storage and retrieval system, without permission from the copyright owner.

Printed in the Netherlands

Contents

Preface		vii
I	Introduction; Gender, households, and migration	1
II	The villages	15
III	Men and women in the migration process	43
IV	The moral economy of kinship	75
V	The value of land	101
VI	The education syndrome	143
VII	Wives, sisters, and mothers	171
VIII	Conclusion	199
Glossary		207
Bibliography		209
Index		233

Preface

During the years of research that culminated in the writing of this book a number of people and institutions have made direct or indirect contributions to my work. Financial support for the research and the writing of this book was provided by the University of Amsterdam. Fieldwork in Indonesia was carried out under the supervision of the Lembaga Ilmu Pengetahuan Indonesia (LIPI), and sponsored by Professor Dr Ahmudi Pasaribu, then rector at the Universitas HKBP Nommensen in Medan. I want to thank the members of the Regional Planning Team of this university, Chris Eijkemans, Jan Piet van der Mijl, and Roy Timmer, for their stimulating discussions and for providing me with a Dutch home on my visits to Medan.

It is impossible to thank adequately the people of Simatupang and Simarmata, most of whom gave generously and good-naturedly of their time. Their continuous questioning of the fruits they could reap from the research forced me to consider my own role critically. Sharing daily events with the women gave me an intimate insight into village living. Special thanks go to Ompu Tuanhuta Sianturi, the late *kepala negeri* in Simatupang, who enjoyed sharing his knowledge with me. He was expecting his second grandchild during my stay, and when it was born just before I left the field, he named her after me – Janet.

My research assistants Manotar, Roida, and Kinne cheerfully hiked with me to remote fields. Their sense of humour kept me going through rain and difficult conditions. Marlise, who cooked my daily meals in Simatupang, was another close friend and confidante. I am grateful to the friends at KSPPM in Siborong-borong with whom I could share my insights and experiences whenever I dropped in.

I should like to thank my supervisors Otto van den Muijzenberg and Loes Schenk-Sandbergen for their patience and guidance. Their comments continually forced me back to the issues that prompted my interest in migration, namely rural development and its effects on the livelihood options of women and men. At various times during the past five years or so, each of them has spent hours with me going over questions that led to the point of view I finally developed. Toon Pennings helped me to process the bulk of quantitative data. When the time came that a complete manuscript could be read, Frans Hüsken and Daniël van Aken were particularly helpful. I also benefited from the comments and suggestions of Mies Grijns, Juliette Koning, Joke van Reenen, and Indira Simbolon. Rita DeCoursey, my editor at the KITLV, was patient, understanding, and helpful.

Finally, my special appreciation and thanks go to Peter Bosch for sharing six months of fieldwork with me. His study on land quality and land use proved a vital complement to my own research. He meticulously drew the maps and edited most of the tables. I also want to mention our children Reinout and Jolijt, whose births during the writing of the book were not only a joy to us but also – because 'Anak do hatuaon' – a relief to the Toba Batak villagers. By their very presence they continually reminded me that there is more to life than writing a dissertation.

During the research I discovered that my own rural family background bore many similarities to the Toba Batak situation. I thank my parents for educating me to university level and for encouraging my search for independence. Their visit to North Tapanuli (their first flight!) meant much to me.

CHAPTER I

Introduction
Gender, households, and migration

On a Sunday afternoon, as I walk through Simarmata village, several men in the roadside coffee shop try to attract my attention. They want to know about my research, what I am doing, and how the villagers will benefit. Then they give a concise analysis of present-day Toba Batak village society: *semua pergi* (everyone moves out).

One of the men, Ama[1] Meli, tells me he had been a hawker in East Sumatra for many years. When he married, his wife remained in the village, cultivating the family land and raising the children, while he travelled back and forth. Two years ago, he stopped trading and retired to his home community of Simarmata. He has eight children: three sons and five daughters. The two eldest sons are also engaged in commerce and live with their families in West Sumatra. The youngest son studied in Medan and recently obtained a position in a government office. Two daughters have become farmers elsewhere in Tapanuli, another is a housewife in Medan, and two are still single and living at home.

Ama Meli's account of migration is one of many that could be told by the villagers, and probably by Toba Batak throughout North Tapanuli. His story illustrates a point made in other studies[2], namely that Toba Batak men play a leading role in migration. While I eagerly listened to the often colourful accounts of the migrants' trips, and the hardships they encountered in a strange and sometimes hostile environment, my main interest was in the other side of the picture: the women who keep the rural economy running, thereby enabling their menfolk to migrate.

I would suggest that the underrepresentation of Toba Batak women in migration calls for a deeper understanding of women's roles in rural areas. What are the economic and cultural conditions that have fostered the mobility of men rather than women? How is mobility related to the dominant gender ideology? Explaining gender-specific migration, however,

---

[1] Ama (father of) and Nai (mother of) are used before the name of one's first child, in this case Meli (a pseudonym).
[2] Bruner 1961; Cunningham 1958; Leinbach and Suwarno 1983; Röll 1984; Sherman 1990.

is only one side of the coin. A subsequent question is: if the majority of the migrants are male, what about the women 'staying behind'? What is their role in decision-making? Do women act on their own behalf or do they merely wait and see? With husbands, brothers, or children migrating, how do women perceive their own lives and their labour? How can one explain the contradiction between the high number of young men sitting idly in the coffee shop complaining about unemployment, and women working hard for an average of sixteen hours a day? What does it mean for a woman to be a farmer in a society in which the status of agriculture is declining? To what extent does she have control over revenues from the land? Does her work on the land result in economic independence, or only in an aching back as a result of her double burden? How does migration affect patrilineal kinship relations and women's roles within them?

This study explores the relationship between out-migration and gender roles in two villages in North Tapanuli, where out-migration has been part of the way of life for at least a century. I will show that socio-economic changes on the macro level do not necessarily lead to changes in social structures, such as patriarchy and gender roles in the family. Toba Batak women perform the lion's share of the work in the rural economy, toiling longer hours and often contributing more to family income than their male relatives – but are viewed as 'unproductive' by government statisticians, economists, development experts, and even by the males in their own household. I will highlight the unrecognized contribution of rural women, the often invisible partners in migration ventures. The main purpose is to throw light on the options faced by the women staying behind and the adjustments they make, as well as their reasons for making them. The 'invisible' nature of women's contributions generally reinforces the social perception that they are 'dependents' rather than 'producers'. The empirical findings of my research, however, challenge a number of common assumptions about the 'fate' of women left behind. I suggest that the picture of men gaining from migration at the expense of women is grossly oversimplified and needs modification.

There is much variation in the situation of women staying behind. Some maintain close ties with their absent relatives and receive regular remittances. Others may finally find themselves abandoned. Migration of male household members entails risks and uncertainty. For the women in the village there is not only the uncertainty whether the migrant will find a job, but also whether he will support the rural household. Who are these women staying behind? Why do they not migrate themselves? Are their problems compensated for by remittances and other non-material benefits? These are the issues that are investigated in this book. But I will start with a brief discussion of current theoretical approaches which view migration from a gender and household perspective, followed by the approach chosen for the present study.

Household and kinship as mediators in the migration process

In the late 1970s and early 1980s the primary concern among migration scholars was to overcome the limitations of micro and macro perspectives which had dominated migration studies. It was increasingly recognized that the study of population movement should cover both individual and structural factors influencing migration behaviour. This approach led various authors (Pessar 1982; Trager 1984; Wood 1981) to search for analytical bridges that related individual behaviour to the overall process of macro-economic change. The approach taken, then, represented an effort to integrate two different levels of analysis into a single conceptual framework.

In the studies mentioned above, the household (or in some cases social networks of family and kinship) emerged as an intermediate variable, which would bridge the gap between individual and social levels of analysis, between 'the overly individualistic focus of social-psychological attributes, on the one hand, and structural determinism, which views people as passive victims, on the other' (D. Wolf 1992:13). As Radcliffe (1990) demonstrates in her study of migration in the Andes, the household is an important mediator between the demands and opportunities of the labour market and individual decisions to migrate. Decisions to migrate are seldom either an individual affair or wholly dictated by processes from outside, but usually take place within a household or kinship context (Dinerman 1978; Schmink 1984; Trager 1988). The composition of the household and one's position in it – based on gender, birth order, or marital status – influence one's opportunity to migrate. In this way, internal relations within the family and the household provide the basis for understanding potential differences in the patterns and characteristics of male and female migration. We shall see that women's dual roles as producers and reproducers in the household division of labour are key components in shaping and defining migration patterns. In the case of male migration, a man's decision to migrate is conditional on the presence of someone at home who will carry out the essential tasks connected with production and reproduction. In North Tapanuli, as in many other rural settings, the gender division of labour calls for women and elderly people to continue and intensify their work in the agricultural sector, while men seek additional income as traders or labourers (Standing 1985).

Household strategies of migration

Having identified the household as an important intermediary unit in migration behaviour, several studies have specifically focused on 'household strategies of migration' directed to improving the average well-being of the household or family unit (Harbison 1981; Trager 1984; Wood 1981). In these studies it is assumed that people make long-term plans on the basis of a set of conscious choices, weighing up the costs and benefits of their activities. The notion of household strategies views people not as passive victims of modernization but as agents[3] shaping their own lives within larger structures and institutions. It focuses on the imaginative way in which the poor manage to obtain and keep access to the essentials of life (Redclift 1986:218). Another merit is that by viewing people as agents it has provided new insights into the work of women and children (Schmink 1984; White 1980). The concept of household strategies has been used in relation to migration in particular, describing the way households adapt themselves to external structural changes (Arizpe 1982; Findley 1987; Trager 1988).

The significance of migration as a household strategy has also been demonstrated by research on the rural exodus in Europe in the eighteenth and nineteenth centuries (Brettell 1986; Redclift 1986). These studies show that there is a direct link between population density and limited access to resources on the one hand, and out-migration on the other. In the context of rural impoverishment, of tiny households inadequate for the support of all members, children became increasingly vital resources. Migration was used as part of a household strategy of risk diversification wherein a member of the household was encouraged to migrate in order to send back remittances.

The course pursued by Mexican peasants in the late 1970s was referred to by Arizpe (1982) as 'relay migration'. Relay migration is defined as a household-based strategy in which the goal is to keep one or more family members in the city earning a cash income for as long a period as possible. Fathers go to the city while the children are young, but when they get older, sons and daughters are also able to participate, contributing their income to the household budget until they marry. Arizpe relates the high value placed on children in the villages she studied to the need to increase the family's available labour force for this purpose.

The concept of household strategies presumes that there is consensus and cooperation between household members. It is usually believed that the household pursues one collective goal based on a set of common interests.

---

[3] In the context of this study 'agency' refers to the creative mechanisms which household members use to reach certain goals, for example new patterns of cooperation within the community or inter- and intra-household support, but it may also include the splitting up of households or families.

The household is also understood as a unit of production and reproduction which shares among its members the income derived from the available means of production and family labour. The adult members of the household decide collectively on all major issues. The notion of migration as a household strategy implies that the migrant – although absent – remains part of the household as long as he or she contributes to the family income.

As will be discussed below, what is often presented as *the* strategy of a household can also be conceived as the outcome of a struggle for domination between male and female, old and young, powerful and powerless.

Intra-household and extra-household relations

It is a significant step forward to recognize that migration decisions are made by the household or kinship group and not simply by the individual. But, as Murray (1981:167) rightly states, it does not follow from this that the household necessarily exhibits internal harmony of interests. As others have demonstrated (Roldán 1988; D. Wolf 1990), reference to 'household strategies' and 'household decisions' obscures the advantages for some members at the expense of others. Viewing migration behaviour as a collective strategy often conceals the dissent, resistance, and tensions around decisions which are made by the most powerful family members but which affect all members of the household: 'Contrary to the neoclassical view of the consensual household, we find that it is an arena of social relations organized along generational, gender, and kinship lines' (Pessar 1988:196-7).

There is ample evidence from feminist anthropological, sociological, historical, and economic studies to show that the household is a locus of tensions and conflict, but also of cooperation – a locus of inequality but also of mutuality.[4] By stressing intra-household relations instead of the household as a unit, the voices, decisions, desires, and acts of resistance of all members become apparent. Acknowledgement of this is central to understanding the meaning and consequences of migration for women staying behind.

Focusing on households does not mean that households are seen as restricted or autonomous entities. Not only should attention be paid to relations within households, but also to inter-household relations (economic and social ties with other households). Another focus should be the household's relation to wider social and economic conditions. Male-dominated political, educational, and religious institutions, for instance, tend to reinforce existing gender inequalities (Folbre 1988).

In the context of this study, kinship ties extending beyond household boundaries also play an important role, regulating the inheritance of goods

---

[4] Beneria and Roldán 1987; Bruce and Dwyer 1988; Folbre 1988; D. Wolf 1990.

and titles, but also guaranteeing loyalty, support, and mutual assistance (Moore 1988:60). In small-scale societies, such as traditional Toba Batak society, kinship ties were the basis for political and economic cooperation. Today, kin relations can still be important in thwarting institutionalized economic and political structures. As we shall see in Chapter V, Toba Batak women can use kin ties to gain access to resources outside the household and, in this way, are able to utilize the land of relatives who have migrated.

The women who stay behind

Having rejected the notion of a collective household strategy of migration and having recognized that multiple voices exist, we may now turn to the different roles of men and women in the migration process. Numerous case studies have shown how male and female migrants play different roles in the rural economies they leave, as well as in the labour markets they enter (Trager 1984; Wilkinson 1987). Hence, gender is a crucial concept for understanding the organization of migration, because people organize their participation in agricultural production and in external labour markets by using gender-based criteria in the allocation of labour.

While great progress has been made in both conceptual and empirical terms on the subject of women as migrants (Ong 1987; Trager 1988), relatively little attention has been paid to the experiences of non-migrant women in households from which other members, particularly men, migrate. For example, a study by Guest (1989) on migration strategies of Central Javanese households scarcely acknowledges the role of gender. Not only does this study ignore gender differences, but the author reduces women's role in the decision that men should migrate to one of passive acquiescence. As in most other studies, there is an implicit assumption that when women remain at home they are not active in the migration process.

In their study on gender and migration in developing countries, Chant and Radcliffe (1992:16) list four reasons why men have often been the first to migrate: a. because they are considered breadwinners, b. because men have better access to work in destination areas, c. because women generally have to care for children and are therefore less mobile, and d. because of socio-cultural restrictions on the independent movement of women. Below, I shall discuss these reasons one by one. However, I shall start with the most decisive factor – related to the others but not mentioned by Chant and Radcliffe – that is, the gender division of labour in production.

In many Third World societies the gender division of labour in pre-colonial and colonial times was a major influencing factor triggering male migration (Hay 1976; Murray 1981). Traditionally, men were active in warfare, trading, hunting, and herding, all of which required some mobility.

Women had the complementary roles of cultivator and caretaker. The introduction of taxes and labour recruitment in the colonial period reinforced the existing pattern of male migration. In the meantime, the women kept things going at home. Women continue to play a crucial role in daily farming activities. Many of them can do without men.[5]

Despite their sometimes marginal participation in farm activities, it is the men who have traditionally controlled productive resources and who – as Chant and Radcliffe argue – were considered breadwinners. This meant that when basic needs were not met, it was their duty to seek other income-generating activities to supplement the farm income.[6] In North Tapanuli, where non-farm employment is scarce, this has resulted in out-migration of male household members. Since wages in urban areas are insufficient to support a wife and children, taking their family with them is beyond the means of most men. Therefore, the wife and children remain behind in the countryside, working the land or engaging in petty trade to earn their share of the family's livelihood.

Another reason why fewer women migrate than men is the fact that men have more privileged access to jobs. In southern Africa, for instance, only men are recruited by Europeans for plantations or mines. The latter take advantage of the prevailing methods of food production which are such that women can carry out nearly all the operations unaided by men. It is therefore possible to economize on labour costs in the destination areas by employing only male workers, leaving children, and old people to be supported in the home village by able-bodied women. The men migrate in search of alternative employment in mainly urban areas, leaving their wives behind for seasons or even years. Thus, the segmented urban labour markets also contribute to decisions by women to stay behind.

Even where women have no farm responsibilities or where the supply of jobs for women is sufficient, many women are still constrained by reproductive responsibilities. With the low wages women normally earn in the city, they cannot afford the costs of child care. Men are at an advantage because of their ability to migrate over longer distances for a job, without the burden of children or the fear of sexual exploitation that women may face.

---

[5]   In other areas of Indonesia, such as parts of Java, agricultural intensification through improved seeds and production technology has resulted in a decline in labour demand, forcing people to look for work elsewhere. Depending on which activity is mechanized, the redundant workers could be either men or women (see, for instance, Collier, Wiradi and Soentoro 1973). In North Tapanuli, however, agricultural modernization did not lead to an expulsion of labourers but instead induced male circular migrants to stay at home (see Chapter V for further details).

[6]   Interestingly, in the matrilineal societies of West Sumatra, traditional migration patterns are also male-dominated but it is the women who control vital economic resources. Male migration is attributed to the marginal role of men in the kinship system (Kato 1982).

An additional reason for the migration of adolescent men in some societies was to evade parental authority and to show that they were competent to look after themselves (Hay 1976; Kato 1982). In some situations, the young men might also use their migration to earn money to pay a bride-price for their future wife. In the end, the situation of women staying in the village while their husbands migrate is the result of strong economic as well as cultural factors.

Notwithstanding their apparent marginal role in actual movements, adult women staying behind often have scope to influence 'family decisions'. They may have a say in deciding whether and when a family member will migrate and where to, and how to compensate for his or her absence (Arizpe 1982; Colfer 1983; Corner 1981; Laguerre 1978). A case study in Kalimantan found that in less than five percent of the cases in one village and in less than fifteen percent in another village, the wife had not participated in the decision on her husband's migration (Colfer 1983).

The wife continues to carry out her work in an autonomous fashion, while her husband goes his own way and contributes to the household budget as before. If the husband has migrated only a short distance, he can return weekly to see his wife and children. In general, women staying behind appear to cope fairly well when men have relatively weak roles in the rural economy.[7]

If the migrant husband is able to send sufficient remittances, his wife can hire seasonal labourers to compensate for his absence. However, if the absent husband does not remit regularly and the wife does not have independent control over rural resources, she may have difficulty in making ends meet. Such women staying behind may find themselves in a marginalized position as a result of growing socio-economic inequality when compared to their male counterparts who operate in the 'modern' sector of the economy (Grijns 1986:67). It is not only economic marginalization which may put pressure on women's livelihood, but also a growing non-material insecurity and loss of status and self-respect: the process of migration itself devalues the spheres now left to women, namely agriculture and local affairs; in other words, women become marginalized relative to migrant men. This marginalization of women often goes hand in hand with the prevailing gender ideology. The ideology legitimizes the marginalization process, while at the same time further reinforcing existing ideas of gender inequality (Schrijvers 1985:13).

Instead of finding a growing marginalization of women, studies in various countries[8] have argued that male out-migration results in women

---

[7] Bourque and Warren 1981:125-33; Colfer 1983; Huston 1979:42-3; MacGaffey 1983.
[8] Chaney 1983; Connell 1984; Gordon 1981; Massiah 1986; Murray 1981.

acquiring greater de facto independence in household management. This may translate into more 'economic power', 'autonomy', or 'status' at the family level, and even the community level. However, what these authors fail to consider is the possible 'traditional' strength of women and their fairly autonomous position in action and decision-making. At the same time, one can question the applicability of the conclusions of these studies to other areas. It is no coincidence that most studies on the effects of male mobility on women have been carried out in regions with a marked history of seasonal unemployment, international migration, or contract labour, for example the Caribbean (Chaney 1983:53; Momsen 1987) and southern Africa (Gordon 1981; Murray 1981). We should be aware that the strong position of Caribbean women in their families is related not only to male out-migration, but also to the matrilineal kinship system and to the legacy of slavery. Such locally specific circumstances make it difficult to pursue a comparison with other, non-matrilineal, societies.

Nor are the issues facing women in southern Africa very relevant to women in North Tapanuli. Semi-proletarian migrants in the South African mines have little in common with migrant husbands from Tapanuli who set up their own enterprises, mainly as itinerant traders. Because revenue from trade is uncertain, most Toba Batak wives do not count on their husband's remittances, but resort to private strategies – most notably trying as far as possible to maintain control over their own earnings, private savings, and so forth – in order to protect themselves and their children.

The problem of unravelling ethnic and cultural traditions from male out-migration, together with the relative scarcity of information about North Tapanuli, makes it especially worthwhile to consider the implications for gender roles and relations in this region. Studies of de jure female-headed households in Indonesia suggest that these women have relatively more freedom than women living in male-headed households. They are often found to have a ready tongue and to enjoy relative economic independence (see for example Hetler 1986; Jayawardena 1977). It is an interesting question to what extent temporary female headship in North Tapanuli, resulting from male migration, yields similar results.

Approach of this study

In this study I am primarily interested in rural women whose immediate family members have migrated – women who stay behind to raise children, to run their households and, quite often, to manage agricultural activities. Rather than just assessing the 'impact' of male migration, as do most studies which focus on 'women left behind' (Gordon 1981; Grawert 1992; Jetley 1984; Palmer 1985), I shall argue that the out-migration of Toba Batak males is compatible with the historical gender-specific division of labour. Instead of measuring 'worsening' or 'improving' conditions in the life of Toba Batak women, this study focuses on how gender relations in rural Tapanuli are affected by historically specific migration patterns.

From the studies cited so far it has become clear that there is a paucity of information on non-migrant women staying behind in Southeast Asia generally and in Indonesia in particular. It is by and large acknowledged that mobility patterns, employment opportunities, and education are differentiated along gender lines: women usually define and pursue their interests as wives, sisters, and mothers, whereas men continue to adopt a far more individual stance in pursuing their goals. Yet, the few studies available on women staying behind in the Asian countryside fail to 'engender' the migration process. They do not show how macro processes intersect with those in the local community and the household, and how gender meanings shape the bargaining power of men and women on these interconnected sites (Hart 1991:95).

Part of my purpose in this book is to redress the rather androcentric focus of most migration studies by according a more central role to non-migrant women. As I shall try to show, a gender-informed analysis of migration requires a fundamental rethinking of 'the fate of women left behind'. The women left behind are generally portrayed as vulnerable in relation to vital resources, such as health and education, without attention being paid to the potential strength of this group in keeping their families and communities going under difficult conditions.

Although it is not to be denied that Toba Batak women are less mobile than men, they are active participants in the migration process through their influence on the choices made within the family (Findley and Williams 1991; Wiest 1973), through their participation in the decisions about the migration of men (Baca and Bryan 1985) and through their acceptance and even creation of new roles as de facto household heads while their husbands are away. By focusing only on the (male) migrants and their moves, many researchers have overlooked the fact that we are dealing with a gendered process of migration and thus squarely missed the roles of (non-migrant) women within it (Riley and Gardner 1993:197).

Apart from emphasizing gender specificity and its consequences, any discussion of migration must be seen within its wider social context. Such a perspective requires first obtaining insight into the local history and economy of North Tapanuli in order to understand the conditions under which migration occurs. In rural Tapanuli, a large majority of farmers are poor and have difficulty making ends meet through farming alone. Others can live from the land but are unable to provide their children with sufficient land in the future. These developments are due to population growth, land fragmentation, and rural stagnation. Accompanying these factors are expectations of earning a better living in urban areas, as a response to an increased level of education.

Second, it is important to investigate the role of cultural values in shaping the activities of migrants and stayers. The Toba Batak have a patrilineal society, in the sense that it emphasizes descent from father to son. This has consequences for inheritance rights, for social and political organization, and for settlement patterns. A patrilineal system is also frequently associated with the term 'patriarchy', which assumes men are in the dominant position. In such a setting, women are often viewed as objects, while men are readily depicted as actors who hold the key to really important matters. Marriage systems, for example, are analysed in terms of the exchanges men make (as 'wife givers' and 'wife receivers'), using women to weave their kin network (Vergouwen 1964). Besides the risk of male bias, an exclusive focus on kinship is not sufficient to explain the complex gender relations among the Toba Batak. I shall therefore turn to the household as one of the places where power relations between genders and generations can be observed (Postel-Coster 1985). For the study of rural out-migration in particular, the household constitutes an important level of analysis, for it is at this level that decisions are made regarding the generation of income, education, and migration. Following Roldan, I view the rural Toba Batak household as an essentially contradictory institution:

> 'While it is a locus of gender and age hierarchies, it is also – and most often – a source of economic, psychological, and emotional/affective support. As such, any analysis of intra-household processes must be sensitive to the contradictory pressures exerted by the supportive and the oppressive elements involved in family interaction.' (Roldán 1988:229-30.)

An analysis of contradictions and potential conflicts in decision-making may reveal the complex interrelationships between migrants and stayers, as well as between households and broader economic and socio-cultural systems. I shall show that Toba Batak women pursue personal goals in the context of stronger forces: powerful family systems that use women as instruments for patriarchal or kinship ends; discriminatory customs and laws surrounding divorce and widowhood; inheritance rules that deprive women outright of assets or undermine their economic rights; and norms that confine women's roles to reproduction and the nurturing of dependents.

When discussing migration and gender relations, the concept of power is of paramount importance. Following Schrijvers (1985:199), I will use a definition of power as 'the possibility of determining one's own as well as other people's thoughts and actions', or the ability to get things done. Although in the context of the patrilineal kinship system I find it hard to maintain that Toba Batak women have formal power (or authority), they do exert a kind of behind-the-throne power in order to achieve desired goals. Power and changes in power relations include the less visible or even invisible mechanisms influencing people's actions and ideas. It is more than imposing one's will. Power is often exerted without force; it is something that goes without saying, legitimized by internalized ideas about masculinity and femininity (Komter 1989).

A Toba Batak woman who stays behind is not necessarily powerless. She may be of the opinion that the migration of a husband or son may be the best or only way for her family or herself to achieve economic or social goals. The division of labour and responsibilities by gender makes migration a more difficult and socially less acceptable process for women than men. In such cases, women who do not migrate themselves may strongly encourage their husbands or children to migrate. Even in areas such as North Tapanuli, where there are fewer opportunities for women to migrate, migration can be seen by women as a deliberate choice: they are actively involved in the movements of the men around them, both economically and emotionally.

Throughout the book I have tried not to depict rural women as a homogeneous group. Women differ as a result of variation in age, class, and marital status, but also in their relationship with the migrant. While most studies on the 'women left behind' assume that only husbands migrate (for example, Palmer 1985; Shaheed 1981), husband migration is not (or no longer) the dominant pattern in North Tapanuli. Rather, in both villages studied, migration of sons and daughters in search of further education is the common trend.

The exclusive focus of some studies on wives who remain behind while their husbands migrate has confirmed prevailing stereotypes of the position of women in rural areas. It has led to a portrayal of rural women as solely engaged in subsistence agriculture, while men participate in the modern urban economy (Moore 1988:76). In this book I try not to depict rural women as a marginal, residual population. I argue that women are 'actors' or 'agents' and not just spectators in the process of out-migration. Within the limits of the prevailing gender ideology they may be lesser actors, but they are certainly not excluded from decision-making and are indispensable in providing the support needed for their relatives to migrate. Their work in agriculture and their management skills provide the household with a dependable source of income throughout the year. Indeed, the availability of an agricultural base allows male heads of households to migrate, knowing that basic needs are being met in the interim before their remittances arrive. Their wives grow crops, raise pigs, visit markets, nurture children, and perpetuate the cycles of kinship, linking ancestors and descendants. In short, in the villages studied here, women's activities ensure the ongoing economic as well as social reproduction of the domestic unit, whether their husbands are present or not.

The approach adopted is an anthropological one and aims to combine an examination of actor-oriented insights and strategies with an understanding of the structural forces which formed the context of migration as it evolved from the late nineteenth century through the colonial era until the present day. Using this model, I hope to shed some light on an actor who has hitherto only been glimpsed, hovering in the shadows somewhere over the shoulder of a male migrant: the Toba Batak woman.

Hamlet with two opposing rows of traditional houses, Simarmata

Simatupang men chatting in a roadside café

CHAPTER II
The villages

In this chapter I describe some of my fieldwork experiences and discuss how the two villages were selected and what methodology was used. This is followed by an overview of contemporary and demographic characteristics of North Tapanuli, leading to a description of the research sites. I conclude with a brief impression of the everyday life of Toba Batak men and women.

Research methods and site selection

To select two villages from the hundreds of rural villages in the Batak highlands, I first went through the available statistical data at the district office in Tarutung. This provided some quantitative data on rates of out-migration, sex ratios, and employment opportunities. I subsequently made a number of trips through the area and had talks with several subdistrict and village heads about the local situation. I was lucky to come across a non-governmental organization, Kelompok Studi Pengembangan Prakarsa Masyarakat (KSPPM), which, with staff members working at the grassroots level, proved to be a valuable source of information and offered a welcome 'refuge' during fieldwork.

Kecamatan Muara, a subdistrict south of Lake Toba, was selected as a first study site. Apart from location near the lake, which gave extra flavour to the whole enterprise, this subdistrict had a relatively high rate of out-migration. *Desa* Simatupang was chosen because it met the requirements of workable size and location and because the inhabitants were hospitable to strangers. As we learned later, some people in Simatupang initially took us for 'hippies', but within a few days this rumour had faded away. One Sunday shortly after our arrival we were invited by the parson to give a speech in front of the full church. After that, hundreds of people knew who we were and why we were there. The village elders competed in 'adopting' us into the Sianturi and Togatorop clans, relationships which paved the way to participating in most village ceremonies, to taking part in ritual dances, and to sharing in the *jambar* (ritual division of meat). Even in Medan, identifying my association with a Toba Batak clan turned out to be advantageous when haggling over the price of a pedicab ride.

During the first six months of fieldwork I was accompanied by my partner, Peter Bosch, who carried out separate but related research on land quality and land use (Bosch 1990) – a topic which, I regret to admit, appealed more to the villagers' imagination than did my anthropological inquiries. I presented myself as what I was, a student from the Netherlands who had come to Indonesia to study the life of the people there. This was quite easily accepted by the villagers, as many were familiar with Indonesian students who were sent to the countryside for practical fieldwork, and some even had relatives who had studied abroad.

Instead of living with a local family, we preferred to live on our own, thereby avoiding a possible bias in favour of one particular family or *marga* (clan). Housing was easily obtained since one of the results of migration was an ample supply of vacant dwellings. We were offered a house in the *perumahan sekolah* (teachers' accommodation), typical of the whole of Indonesia but an unnecessary facility in Simatupang where most teachers originate from the village and have their own homes that better suit an average Toba Batak family. Later on, we moved to a house on the other side of the village owned by an *ompu* (grandmother) who had migrated to join her son in Medan. Directly next to the house was one of the rice mills, which gave me the opportunity to drop in every now and then to chat with the women waiting for their rice to be processed. The disadvantage, of course, was that for several hours a day I had to put up with the roaring of the machine.

Since migration in Simatupang appeared to be dominated by young people moving out permanently, halfway through my stay I decided to look for a second research site with a larger number of husbands migrating, in order to gather supplementary data. I assumed that, because of men's key position in the household, migration of husbands would result in more visible shifts in labour division, authority patterns, and control over resources. After Peter had left for the Netherlands to resume his job, I moved to the village of Simarmata on Samosir Island, where circular migration of husbands was more common. Here I stayed from September until January. Through the intervention of the local parson I was able to occupy the old parsonage. While the back of the house was wrecked, the front had a large veranda with a splendid view over the village square.

Much has been written about the pros and cons of doing fieldwork with a spouse and I will not dwell on the matter long. Apart from the pleasure of each other's company, a clear advantage was that Peter's presence in Simatupang gave me the opportunity to participate in the male domain. For instance, when we walked through the village we were often invited into one of the coffee shops where local men would typically gather in the late afternoon. Although the men would initially direct their attention to Peter,

I soon joined in the conversation as well, if only because I spoke Indonesian more fluently. These chats, especially those with the village elders, were often very informative. After some time, it was no longer a problem dropping in once in a while with my assistant or alone. In this way I acquired a number of important male informants, the first and most significant being Ompu Tuanhuta. Another man, a retired schoolteacher, taught me the Batak language, and was also willing to spend hours discussing land tenure and Simatupang's settlement history. In Simarmata, on the other hand, where I lived alone, I seldom mixed with the coffee-shop-goers. The other side of the coin was that, living on my own, the women felt less hesitant about coming to my house, assuming that I felt lonely.

In both villages, I started fieldwork by visiting all the households, while simultaneously taking a census. The data concerned sex, age, education, marital status, occupation, access to land, and migration histories of all resident household members. For absent members, questions were asked about reasons for leaving, present residence, frequency of return, and frequency and amount of remittances. I also asked adult women their opinions on the migration of their children or husband. While the censuses yielded a considerable amount of quantitative data on the migrants who had left their subdistrict (*kecamatan*) to work or study elsewhere, this method, of course, seriously underestimates actual migration rates. For example, entire households that had left did not figure in the census unless there was still an ageing parent in the village.[1] Elderly people who had moved away to join children who had migrated also failed to appear in the census. Although the total number of migrants is certainly underreported, the large proportion of sons, daughters, husbands, and brothers who have migrated from the villages is nonetheless impressive.

Throughout the census, and later during the interviews, I was assisted by three local women: Manotar in Simatupang, and Roida and Kinne in Simarmata. They introduced me to the villagers, acted as interpreters from Indonesian to Toba Batak and vice versa, and became my friends. In everyday life people speak their own language, Toba Batak, which is quite different from Indonesian. I could follow a simple conversation in Toba Batak and could understand the gist of an interview, but because of the limited time available I did not become fluent in the language. Unfortunately, the use of a tape recorder proved too much of a distraction during interviews, so I decided not to use one.

The qualitative part of my study was to ask questions about women's lives in the village, and to gain insight into the complex of circumstances, experiences, and ideas playing a part in the migration process. I delved into

---

[1] This methodological problem is also mentioned in a review article by Lipton (1982:191).

women's attitudes towards the migrants, how they spent the meagre remittances, the women's feelings towards their absent husbands, and their relationship with children who had migrated. As far as possible, I tried to visit the same woman several times. But getting information was not always easy. Questions considered too intimate were often turned back on me, or simply ignored (see also Hart 1991). Especially on visits to relatively well-off households (containing, for example, an educated adult male), it often happened that the man sent his wife to the kitchen while he took over the conversation, assuming that I was more interested in talking to him. Even women who were very outspoken and opinionated allowed their husbands to intrude. My talks with women from poorer households often took place outside or on the doorstep, thus attracting several neighbours. Everyone was keen to answer a question, and many seemed to know more about the life of a particular woman than she herself did. These group discussions took far more time than personal interviews, but they were often very lively and much more useful than individual questionnaires. To someone who is not fluent in the local language, however, such discussions are not easy to follow.

I must admit that my relationship with the women was often not as intimate as I wished. It was only after continuous questioning and through indirect suggestions that the women ventured to express their personal feelings, but even then they were quite ambivalent. Illiterate women were sometimes especially afraid that I would misuse their information. They made it very clear when they did not want to talk. Information on sensitive matters, such as personal feelings or financial affairs, was sometimes obtained simply by observing people's actions or expressions and listening to their comments. In a few instances, I was confronted with distrust and reservation due to the villagers' bad experiences with the Dutch in the colonial period. Once, in response to my question on land and yields, one elderly woman began wailing loudly, fearing that the Dutch colonialists had returned to collect taxes.

Another problem I faced was that the women were busy most of the time. Our conversations were repeatedly interrupted by the demands of small children. The women were occupied either with household work or field work, especially during the peak seasons of transplanting and harvesting rice. The alternative was for me to accompany them to their fields or to the local market. Sharing in these activities, as well as attending clan rituals, participating in the weekly churchgoing, and chatting here and there gave me insight into the daily lives of village women.

Besides extensive talks with village women, I had opportunities to meet visiting migrants whenever they showed up in the village. On several trips to Medan, I was able to interview a handful of villagers who had migrated.

Although the study would have been more complete if the perspectives of the migrants had been included, it was impossible to 'follow' the migrants to their destination areas in the time available. Sometimes the villagers were reluctant to give a relative's address, or they simply did not know where he or she lived. In these cases I did not press them, because the main focus of the research was on the village and I did not want to risk my relationships there. Anyway, tracing a person in Medan through an address turned out to be a very difficult job.

My research approaches in the two villages were slightly different. Peter's presence in Simatupang enabled me to compare his information on land and labour gathered in the field with my data from the census, and to cross-check. Landholding data proved the most difficult to collect, and throughout our field research we were constantly revising the amount of land each household controlled. Too many parcels of land were simply 'forgotten' by the respondents, thus making it impossible to guarantee complete retrieval and reconstruction of land arrangements. Because there was no possibility of cross-checking in the second location (Simarmata), I decided to pay less attention to land questions in favour of more intensive interviews on issues directly related to migration and household relations.

As mentioned above, villagers were not very frank in talking about their material conditions. They pathetically duelled upon their poverty, but were much more reluctant to reveal the size and source of their household income. To most people, detailed questions on financial affairs involved too great an invasion of privacy – a problem also mentioned by Clauss (1982) for the Simalungun Batak – so I refrained from asking. Moreover, there is a high seasonal variation in agricultural income and expenditures. The migrants do not earn a fixed income, nor do they send regular remittances to their families.

A budget study of ten selected households in Simatupang covering a period of four months helped somewhat to overcome this lack of information. It should be stressed that it was only after considerable familiarity had been established that some of this information emerged; even so, I suspect that several households did not provide information on all financial affairs, and there are probably additional intricacies of which I was not aware.

To guarantee a sufficient number of circular migrants in the second location, I decided to study three adjacent villages which I have called the 'Simarmata region', after one of them. In one of the villages, a census was carried out which was more or less similar to the one held in Simatupang but, for reasons cited above, focused less on the land situation and more on family relations.

To form an idea of migration intentions, a questionnaire was distributed among some 200 third-year students in their late teens who were in senior

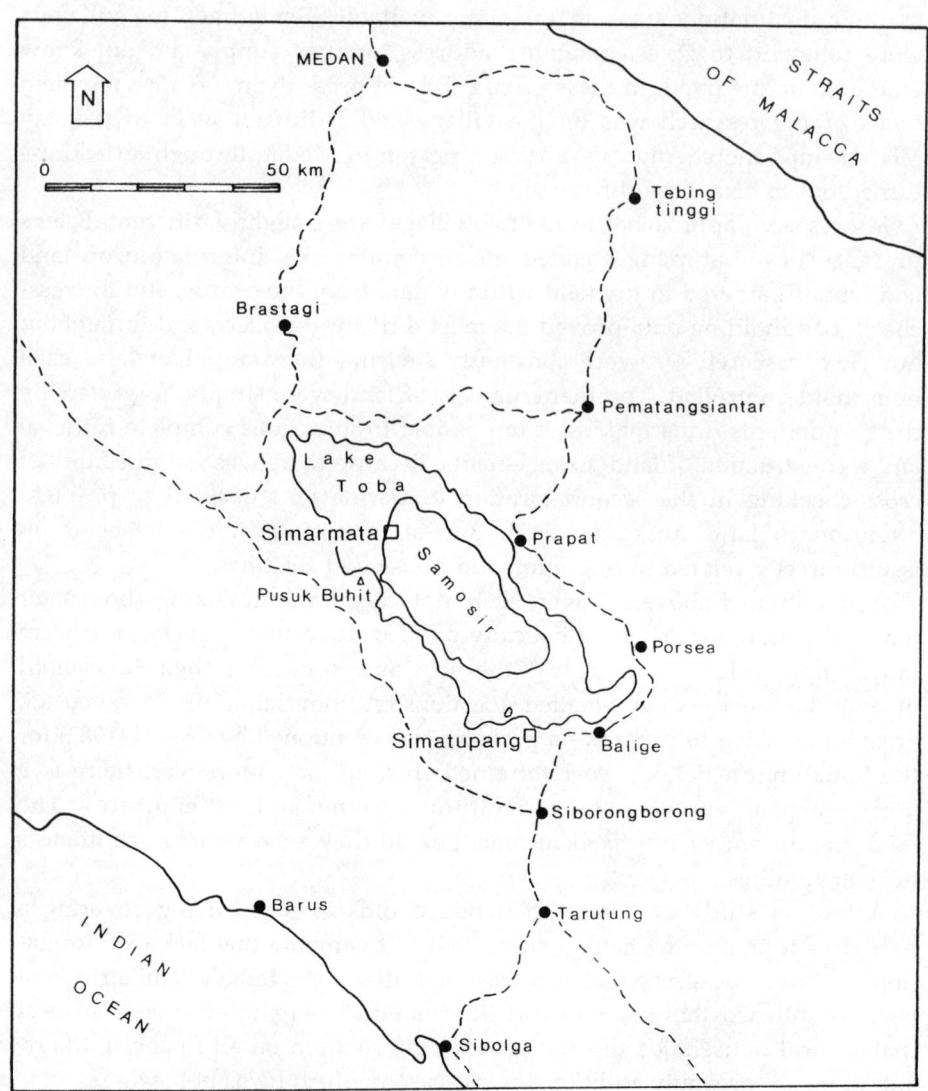

Map 1. North Tapanuli, showing the location of the research sites

high school in Muara. Questions were asked about their future plans (to migrate or stay in the village), and how these related to the composition of the household, to the socio-economic situation of their parents, and to their urban connections. More detailed information on this questionnaire is given in Chapter VI.

Having indicated the methodological setting of the study and my role as researcher, I shall now turn to a description of the physical setting: North Tapanuli and the two research sites.

The Toba Batak area

The villages of Simatupang and Simarmata are located in the area which today is called *kabupaten* (district) North Tapanuli. This is the homeland of the Toba Batak, one of six Batak groups[2] occupying contiguous areas of North Sumatra, the westernmost and second largest island of Indonesia. The eastern part of Batak territory is a mountainous area, part of the Bukit Barisan range which runs the length of Sumatra. The western part is a gently sloping high plain of volcanic origin. In the heartland is Lake Toba and on the northwest bank of the lake lies the mountain Pusuk Buhit, which the Toba Batak believe marks the point of origin of all the Batak people (see Map 1).

Social organization of the Toba Batak is patrilineal and patrilocal, with named exogamous clans. The key group is the localized lineage, which controls land and constitutes the primary political and ceremonial unit. The next level below the tribal patrilineage is the clan (*marga*), each of which traces its descent back to a particular male ancestor and shares the same name. The Toba Batak traditionally[3] had a decentralized political organization characterized by many local chiefs and endemic inter-village warfare (Vergouwen 1964).

In pre-colonial times, the Batak highlands used to be a rather isolated part of Indonesia, although there were several influences from outside, for example the impact of Hindu culture between the second and fifteenth centuries (Cunningham 1958:5; Loeb 1935:20-1) and the Padri movement at the turn of the nineteenth century, which brought militant Muslim Minangkabau, neighbours to the south, as far north as Lake Toba (Dobbin 1983). Social contacts between the main Batak groups in North Sumatra were

---

[2] The other Batak groups include Karo, Pakpak-Dairi, Simalungun, Angkola, and Mandailing. Although the groups are related, each has its own customs and language and they conceive of themselves as separate units.

[3] I will use the concepts 'tradition' and 'change' as they are used by most authors in order to clarify some basic features of Toba Batak social organization. 'Tradition' in this sense usually refers to the situation before the end of the nineteenth century.

limited to small-scale barter and occasional warfare across the borders.

Western contact began in the 1860s with the arrival of German Protestant missionaries and Dutch government officials, although complete administrative control was not achieved until 1907 (Viner 1979).[4] Very few foreigners actually lived in the Batak highlands, as no plantations, industry, or European settlements were established there. The land remained under the control of local village and kin groups. In the meantime the East Coast of Sumatra (Sumatra's Oostkust) emerged as one of the most lucrative export ventures of the Western colonial empires. Dutch, Chinese, and Javanese migrated in large numbers to the East Coast, which became a vast estate area for such commercial crops as tobacco, rubber, palm oil, tea, and coconut. A colonial network of roads and railways was built to serve the estates, so that eastern Sumatra was reasonably well provided with transport facilities (Bruner 1972). As an area of economic boom, eastern Sumatra attracted the most migrants, while the subsistence-oriented Batak hinterland lost the most people. North Tapanuli is the third poorest of North Sumatra's eleven districts, with one of the lowest average incomes per capita. Apart from the main connections, roads are scarce and often in a bad state, so that few villages in the interior can be reached by motor vehicles. Often, the *huta* (hamlets) are linked only by narrow footpaths.

Until this century, the interior highlands had much higher population densities than the coastal lowlands.[5] This may be due to the fact that tropical epidemics were more prevalent in the lowland areas. In contrast to much of eastern Sumatra, where marshes and slow muddy rivers predominated, water flow in Tapanuli was rapid and clean, an important factor for hygiene. Moreover, the drier environment of the highlands may have been favour-

---

[4] The Verenigde Oost-Indische Compagnie (Dutch East Indies Company) had trade relations with Toba Batak dating from 1694 but traded via couriers and did not enter the heartland areas (Cunningham 1958:8; Pedersen 1970:18).

[5] The following table (based on *Volkstelling 1930*, I:156) summarizes differences in population densities between the Batak highlands and some other parts of North Sumatra:

Area	Population density (persons/km² land)	
	1930	1985
Batak highlands:		
Dairi	17	
Samosir	123	166
Barus	25	
Toba	44	
Toba Plateau	32	
Silindung	52	
Average for Batak highlands	37	77*
lowlands:		
Gouvernement Sumatra's Oostkust	18	
Gouvernement Atjeh	18	54

* North Tapanuli in 1988

able to deforestation, which facilitated the exploitation of agricultural land, and thus its occupation.[6] The highest population densities can be found in flat, fertile areas which have been occupied for a long time. These are the deltas around Lake Toba, the coasts of Samosir Island, and the Silindung valley. The Toba Batak plateau, the area around Dolok Sanggul, with its poor-quality soils, has been less densely populated.

Unfortunately, exact population figures are not available. Dutch population data are probably an underestimate since they are based on the reports of local chiefs who had to collect taxes from their subjects. One source estimated the population in 1914 of what is today called North Tapanuli to be 385,000 (Barth, cited in Castles 1972:41). By the time of the 1930 population census it had grown to 523,000. If these statistics are correct, then the Batak population increased by 36 percent in sixteen years, or 1.8 percent annually, an indication of both a low mortality rate and a high fertility rate. Until the twentieth century, population figures had remained low (although higher than in the lowlands) because of frequent diseases, like cholera and smallpox (Janssen 1924:360). Due to improved health care, child mortality was significantly reduced.[7] It has been estimated that the number of children per mother in 1930 was around eight. Crude birth rates from the *Jahresbericht* of the Rheinische Mission in 1931-32, which refer to the Christian population only, varied between 35 and 60 per 1000 inhabitants. The number of children in relation to adults in North Tapanuli was the highest of Sumatra.

From very early times migration has been a significant means of redistributing Toba Batak population. As we shall see in the next chapter, migration was the main mechanism of lineage fission and a prime means of reducing local tensions due to population pressure (Tobing 1956:21).

> 'As a result of population pressure, the steep slopes of the valley were terraced, and cassava and fruit trees were grown there. [...] The hutas themselves were jammed full; each one had ten to twenty-five families, living in houses which filled the space within the huta walls. [...] The tiny valley of Meat was filled beyond its capacity to support the population.' (Cunningham 1958:77.)

After independence, Toba Batak migration expanded enormously. The Toba Batak did not leave their homeland only because of the scarcity of rice fields, but rather because they chose not to remain farmers – at least not in the highlands. At the same time the spread of mass media and education have made new opportunities elsewhere in North Sumatra widely known and

---

[6] Another reason, given by Sherman (1990:22-3) to explain the relatively high population densities in the Batak highlands, is the possibility that in the past, lowland citizens may have moved to the interior of Sumatra to evade taxes by coastal patrols coming from Srivijaya and other naval powers. However, I did not find any traces of such movements.

[7] Nevertheless, according to L.R. van Bemmelen (1931:18), Samosir Island, which at that time had some 96,000 inhabitants, did not have a single doctor.

easily accessible. Transport facilities have expanded enormously, encouraging people to *mangaranto* (migrate); villagers have become used to travelling frequently.

Despite steady out-migration, North Tapanuli today still includes the most densely populated areas of North Sumatra. Among them are *kecamatan* Muara and Simanindo, the subdistricts in which my research sites are located, the villages of Simatupang and Simarmata.

Table 1. Population density in Muara and Simanindo subdistricts

	persons/km^2		persons/km^2 of arable land	annual growth rate
	1961	1985	1985	1961-85
Muara	174	198	582	0.5
Simanindo	98	105	482	0.3
North Tapanuli	96	76	121	1.1

Notes: Arable land constitutes settlements and fields. The actual population increase in North Tapanuli was from 558,553 in 1961 to 724,982 in 1985 (Source: Van der Mijl 1988:15-22).

Judging by the terraces lying fallow in Samosir and Muara, the population may have been higher at times in the past (Scholz 1983). This would explain the exaggerated claim, often made by educated urban Batak, that North Tapanuli has been deserted by all but the very old and the very young. The notion of near-total abandonment of the Toba homeland strongly persists, because many inhabitants do indeed migrate permanently. Yet, as will become clear in the following chapters, those who remain in the village maintain a firm foothold and in various ways support the migration endeavours of their relatives.

The major productive activity of the Toba Batak is irrigated and dry agriculture supplemented by an extensive trade network and cyclical markets. Given the limited industrialization, it is hardly surprising that the district supports no significant urban centre. Prospects for attracting large-scale industrial or commercial establishments are not bright, owing to the remote location and to possible conflicts over *adat* land.[8] One of the largest towns is the district capital of Tarutung, where the district authorities are seated, local development plans and programmes are coordinated, and the courts and the main police office are located. Compared to other *kabupaten*, North Tapanuli has few employment opportunities outside agriculture. Even the tourist hotels, which have mushroomed on the shores of Lake Toba in

---

[8] A notable exception is the much contested P.T. Indorayon pulp and rayon factory in Porsea subdistrict, which started to take over land for commercial eucalyptus plantations in 1986. For more information, see Simbolon 1992.

places like Parapat, Tomok, Tuktuk, and Pangururan, are all in the hands of urban owners. They hardly employ local people, and if they do it is only as unskilled labourers receiving rather low wages. As a result, those villagers seeking employment have to travel to other districts or provinces to find a job.

The two villages

Simatupang

Just between the townships of Balige and Siborong-borong on the Trans-Sumatra Highway, a small wooden sign directs the unsuspecting tourist to Huta Ginjang, which provides one of the most beautiful panoramas of the Batak highlands. On a clear day the altitude of about 1600 metres offers an overwhelming view of Lake Toba and its surroundings. Towards the left, a green valley gives the area a lush appearance. Located on a plain between Lake Toba and the central plateau of Humbang, this valley receives sufficient water for irrigation, making wet-rice cultivation possible. The fields are interspersed with dark-green spots, representing small settlements with mango trees. In the centre of the valley, the village of Simatupang is easily discernible as a cluster of hamlets (*huta*), with three church towers rising above the houses. Towards the south, a steep crater wall separates the area from the Humbang plateau. To reach Simatupang, one follows the road winding down towards Lake Toba.

Desa Simatupang falls within the administrative subdistrict (*kecamatan*) of Muara. It covers an area of more than four square kilometres and is the third most populous village (*Kecamatan Muara dalam angka* 1986:8-10). The centre of the subdistrict is a small township called Pasar Muara, some four kilometres to the northwest. There the subdistrict office, the police station, the post office, and a health centre can be found. On Thursday the weekly market (*onan*) is held and the shops and coffee shops surrounding the market place do good business. The other days of the week Muara is a sleepy collection of dirt roads leading to a deserted landing stage on the shore of Lake Toba.

The village of Simatupang consists of a conglomeration of *huta*, some of which were built as long as seven generations ago. Most of them are occupied by descendants of the founding Simatupang clan, bearing the names of Togatorop, Sianturi, and Siburian. A typical *huta* was described by Vergouwen (1964:105) as

> 'a small square with a fine, hard, bare courtyard in the centre of it. On one side of this square there is a small group of houses, usually set in a row; each house has its own kitchen-garden at the back. Opposite the row of houses there is a row of rice granaries. There is usually a mud wallow or two. The whole is enclosed by a wall on

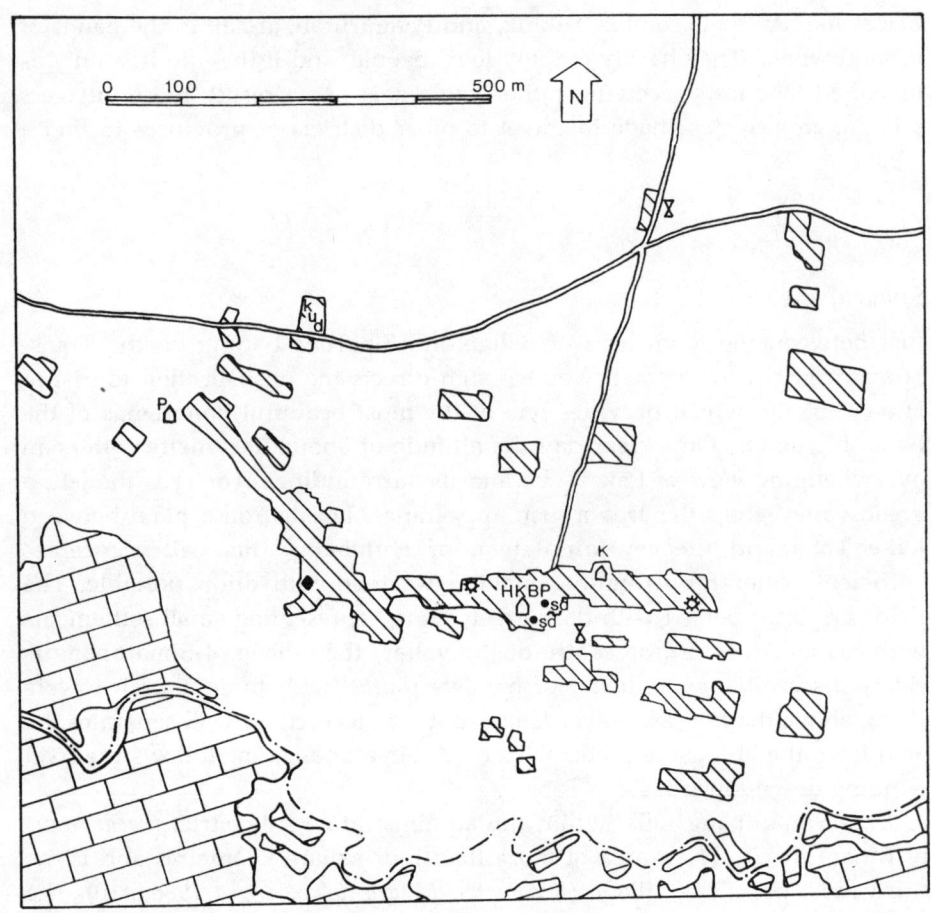

Map 2. The village of Simatupang

Legend

- ▨ village
- ▱ wet-rice fields
- ○ church
  - HKBP = Lutheran
  - K = Catholic
  - P = Pentecostal
- • school
- sd = primary school
- ♦ balai desa/kantor kepala desa (village hall)
- ◌ rice mill
- ⊗ tugu
- kud = village cooperative

which there are tall bamboos [...]. One will find pigs rooting under the houses, dogs nosing about, chickens scratching the ground [...]. A woman will be sitting at her loom in front of one of the houses while a young girl stamps rice in a large stamping-block.'

Today the appearance of most Batak hamlets has changed significantly. The walls and bamboo hedges have fallen down for lack of upkeep. The original Batak houses, with their boat-shaped sugar-palm roofs, are increasingly being replaced by more modern houses covered with corrugated iron.

Notwithstanding its physical decay, the *huta* still retains most of its social functions. The courtyard (*alaman*) is a perfect meeting place and working area. Harvested rice is dried in the sun while women chase off chickens and chat with their neighbours. Others cut wood for daily cooking or tie their harvested onions, and children play around. On festive occasions big meals are prepared for the kinsmen and kinswomen who attend *adat* ceremonies in front of the house of married or deceased residents. The courtyard may be filled with hundreds of guests, and loudspeakers are used to make sure that no one misses the slightest detail. At weddings a microphone is often used to give a running commentary that can be heard throughout the village.

Apart from the traditional *huta,* several houses near the main street have been built haphazardly, according to no traditional pattern. On the roadside are small shops (*kode*) carrying a limited stock of daily necessities such as cooking oil, matches, soap, kerosene, cigarettes, and tinned fish. Public buildings – two primary schools, and three churches – can also be found here. With no exception, everyone in Simatupang is a Christian. The majority attend the brick HKBP church,[9] which is Lutheran, another group is Catholic, and a minority belong to the Pentecostal church. The final official building in Simatupang is the village hall (*balai desa*). This meeting place is a symbol of village democracy, but I never witnessed it functioning. To catch up on local and national news the village men generally gather in one of six local coffee shops.

Each morning two buses leave from Muara for Medan. Its passengers include middle-aged villagers paying a visit to relatives in Pematang Siantar or Medan. The men wear formal trousers, ironed shirts, and shiny shoes. The women are dressed in their best skirts and, for this occasion, wear some jewellery. Several youngsters take the bus to resume their studies after a holiday, or to seek a job in the city. On market days transport facilities are broader. Minibuses are loaded with sacks of farm produce (mangoes, onions, peanuts, rice) to be sold at the regional market (*onan*) or to private mer-

---

[9] HKBP stands for Huria Kristen Batak Protestan, which is the Batak Protestant Association. In 1930 it was constituted as a legally independent church. For more details, see Pedersen 1970.

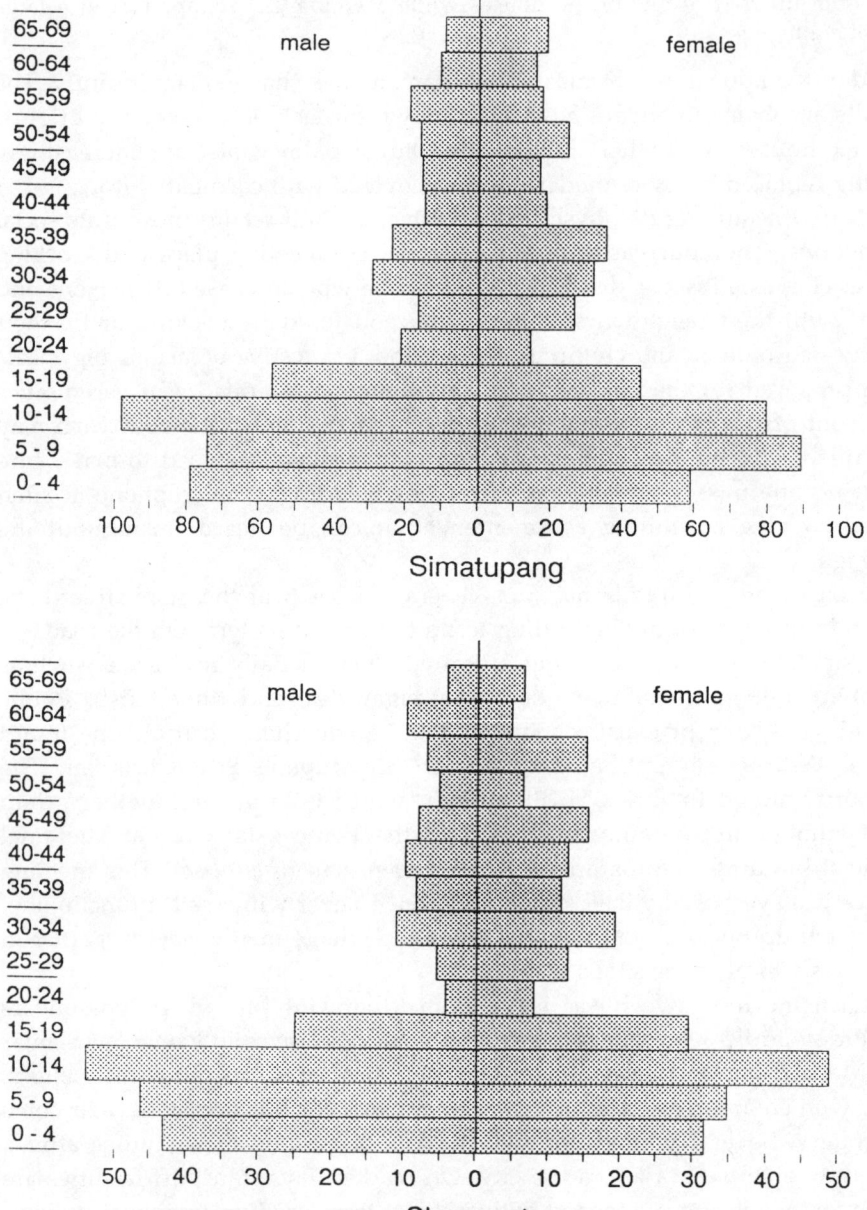

Figure 1. Population by age and sex (in absolute figures; 70+ category not included)

chants in Balige, Siborong-borong, or Tarutung. It is women who do this trading, and through their frequent trips into regional centres they maintain connections outside the village.[10] If men travel, it is more often for leisure – to escape, so they say, the 'monotony of village life' – or for official transactions.

According to the census I carried out in February 1988, the village of Simatupang had 1,018 inhabitants, spread over 206 households. Data from the district office in Tarutung, revealed that annual population growth in Simatupang was 0.9 percent between 1976 and 1986; for Muara subdistrict as a whole it was 1.1 percent.[11] There were 47 houses unoccupied (19 percent), which indicates considerable emigration from the village – although, of course, some dwellings in remote *huta* were vacant just because the former inhabitants preferred a newly-built house near the road. Aside from a handful of resident professionals (nurses, teachers, vicar), all 206 households rely on agriculture, operating their own or other people's land. Most cultivated land is dependent on rainfall only, although runoff water from the nearby crater wall is directed onto strategically located rice fields through small weirs. Farmers raise a variety of crops; about half of the farm land is used for wet rice; this is the main staple and surpluses are sold. The rest of the fields are devoted to dry crops, such as peanuts, onions, cassava, and cloves. The land is highly fragmented. The average farm household operated 0.38 ha, and 68 percent cultivated even less than this.

It is difficult to support the argument that the upper limit of population density has been reached. On the one hand the apparent swelling of the hamlet cluster to its present size occurred because it is possible to harvest two rice crops a year and to raise cash crops rather profitably. On the other hand there is a relatively high rate of out-migration, although due to high fertility this has not resulted in a continuing decline in population. This will be discussed further in the next chapter.

Figure 1 gives the distribution of the population by age and sex. Although there are no reliable figures for estimating population growth for the village, the age breakdown presented here suggests a high birth rate. More than half the total population is under the age of twenty. Apart from a high birth rate, the population graph also shows the extent of out-migration. The underrepresentation of the 20–34 age group is remarkable. Clearly it is the young adults, those with the greatest urban job opportunities, who have left (and continue to leave) the village in the highest numbers. The 25–34

---

[10] For most Simatupang dwellers, using a bus is the only way to cover a long distance. However, the mobility of certain villagers (teachers and civil servants) has increased because of the use of motorbikes, which are used exclusively by men.
[11] In the period 1971–1980 annual population growth in North Tapanuli was 1.0 percent versus 2.6 percent for the whole province of North Sumatra (Ginting and Daroesman 1982:54).

Bus transport to and from regional markets, Simatupang

Simatupang's main road with women selling and buying
garden surpluses and home-made snacks

category constitutes only nine percent of males and eleven percent of females. This reflects the situation in North Tapanuli as a whole, where in 1985 this category constituted nine percent of the population (for both men and women). At the national level in 1986 this age group constituted fourteen percent of males and fifteen percent of females (Van der Mijl 1988:14). Surprisingly, in Simatupang in 1988 the sex ratio in the age group 15–24 was 130 men per 100 women, while the 1986 population census for Simatupang showed a male deficiency (96 men per 100 women) (*Kecamatan Muara dalam angka* 1986). These sex ratios are based on relatively small numbers and we can therefore question their reliability. Nevertheless, they do indicate a trend of increasing out-migration of young women, a relatively recent development which will be discussed further in Chapter III. When we have a look at the 25–59 age group, however, there is a considerable preponderance of females: 76 men per 100 women.

Table 2. Main occupations of Simatupang villagers (age 15–64) in 1988

	Men		Women		Total		Sex ratio (males per 100 females)
Farmer	119	54%	165	68%	284	62%	72
Civil servant	43	20%	19	8%	62	13%	226
Student	39	18%	32	13%	71	15%	122
Other	18	8%	28	11%	46	10%	47
Total	219	100%	244	100%	463	100%	90

The significance of the sex ratios becomes evident when we compare the main occupations by gender of the economically active population. Table 2 shows that the majority of the villagers are engaged in farming. Most holdings combine irrigated and dry cultivation and consequently require considerable labour input from women and men all year long. Nevertheless, the table shows that women outnumber men in agriculture by fourteen percent.[12] Rather than choosing farming as a profession, most women enter (or remain in) farming by marrying men who are farmers. Women usually pull and plant the rice seedlings and are responsible for the weeding afterwards, while land preparation and repairing rice terraces are considered men's work. A considerable number of the male population (20 percent) work as civil servants – the majority outside the village – while only eight percent of females do. Quite a few women have their main occupation in

---

[12] A similar calculation made by Sherman (1990:199) for an area just south of Samosir demonstrated that farming females outnumbered farming males by 17 percent, with married women and widows outnumbering married men and widowers by 13 percent.

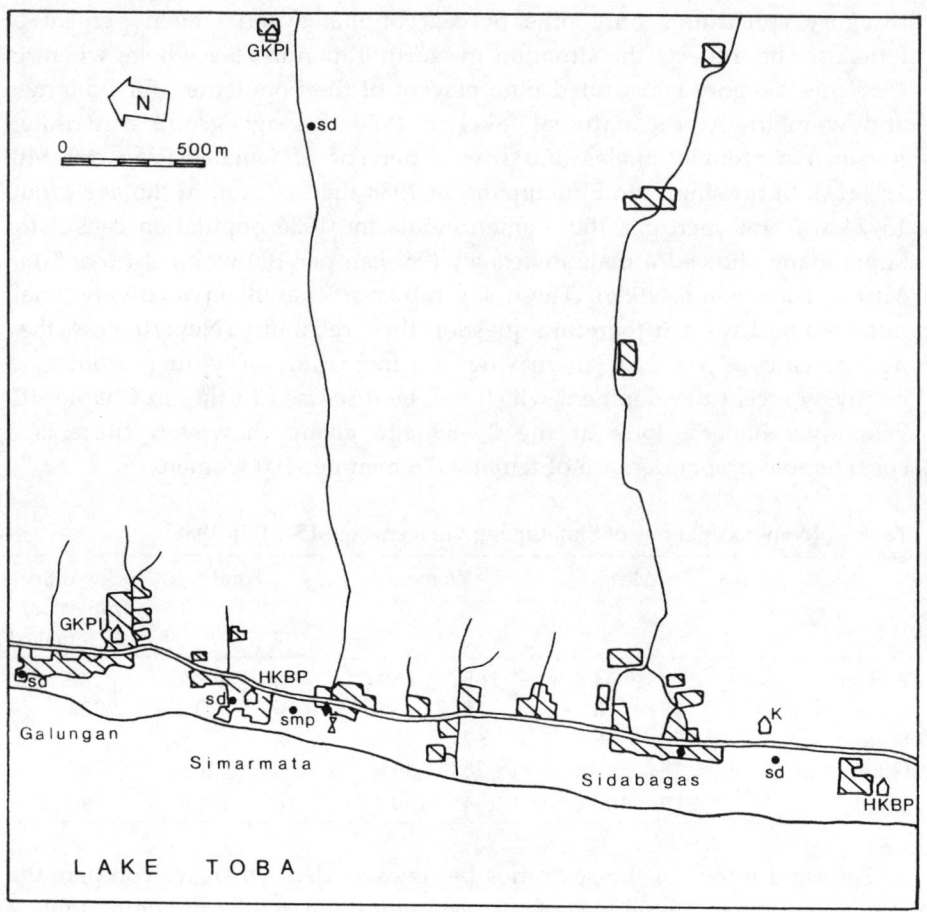

Map 3. The region of Simarmata

Legend

⌧ village

○ church
HKBP = Lutheran
K = Catholic
GKPI = Protestant

♦ balai desa/kantor kepala desa (village hall)
⚒ tugu

• school
sd = primary school
smp = lower secondary school

local petty trade (*martiga-tiga*), either running a coffee shop or a small store, or selling agricultural produce at regional markets. But even the households with off-farm income still rely heavily on agricultural production to meet their own food needs, mainly through unpaid female family labour. However, as is often the case with this kind of data, they give an incomplete picture of the actual occupational situation, since many villagers carry out more than one activity. Even the secondary school teacher could be seen spraying his rice fields after school. All in all, the table shows that women make up 54 percent of the total labour force in *desa* Simatupang.

Simarmata

As mentioned before, the area I shall refer to as Simarmata in fact covers three neighbouring villages which merge into one another without any visible boundary (see Map 3). To get there from Medan one travels for four hours by bus to the tourist centre of Parapat on the shore of Lake Toba. From there, a ferry and numerous smaller motorboats carry vehicles and people to the other side. Once on the island, minibuses continue on the asphalted ring road, stopping on their way westward at Simarmata. The distance between Simatupang and Simarmata is about 125 km and I did not come across any direct kinship connections between the two villages.

The main road in Simarmata is lined with wooden Western-style houses. As in Simatupang, we find several shops in between, selling essentials like soap, cooking oil, and biscuits. A number of *lapo* (coffee shops) take advantage of their roadside location and sell drinks and cigarettes to the men who gather there in the late afternoons. A bit more off the road are the clustered *huta*. This typical Batak settlement pattern manifests itself even better here than in Muara. Single *huta* lie amidst fields and fallow land. In most *huta* we find two rows of houses opposite each other, often with beautiful decorative woodcarving on the front. Another salient feature in Simarmata, as on Samosir as a whole, is the large number of newly constructed monuments (*tugu*) for ancestor worship. Some of these concrete buildings are five to ten metres high, with life-size figures of the clan founder on top (Bruner 1987:133; Schefold 1988). Each of the three villages has its own church and its own primary school. A common experience for a visitor is to pass some undistinguished off-white structure and overhear the refrain of children's voices chanting in unison the multiplication tables or the five basic principles of Indonesia (Pancasila). The centre village has a junior high school which serves the neighbouring villages.

The landscape in Simarmata is somewhat different from that in Muara. It gradually rises from the lake to the central Samosir plateau. It is more barren and rocky than the flat river deltas of Muara and Balige and especially the plateau is sparsely populated. Cultivation is concentrated on the narrow strip of land between Lake Toba and the slopes of the plateau. More than half of the farms are smaller than 0.25 ha. The soil, especially in the upland area, has a low humus content and is easily eroded.[13] The scarcity of water hampers irrigation, which means that agricultural opportunities are more limited than in Simatupang. People can grow dry rice and red shallots if there is enough rainfall. If not, they must resort to less appealing crops such as maize and cassava. Under the glaring sun, the cracked soil with thorny shrubs contrasts sharply with the deep blue lake below. In the dry season the people uphill (three *huta* or 33 households) often have to walk a long way to obtain drinking water or to bathe.

The mobility of people during my stay was striking. Simarmata is on the paved road with regular jeepney (*motor sewa*) service between the ferry at Tomok on the east coast and Pangururan on the west coast of the island. Samosir is a typical emigration area, with many adolescents and adults studying or working temporarily in one of Sumatra's urban areas. There are many connections with regions on the mainland, such as Simalungun and Dairi, through business, education, or kinship relations.

In one of the three adjacent villages, where most circular migrants were found, a census was carried out, according to which the population of this village was 517 persons, divided over 115 households. Data from the village head, revealed that annual population growth over the period 1977-1987 was slightly negative (− 0.1), which indicates considerable permanent out-migration. This is also reflected in the 62 unoccupied houses (16 percent) in the three villages, which is comparable to the situation in Simatupang.

The data on which Figure 1 is based show that more than 50 percent of the village population are under 15 years of age, while only 8 percent are 60 years or older. As in Simatupang, the average number of living children is six per mother. There is a preponderance of females in Simarmata which, as discussed in the following chapter, is related to gender-specific migration. This is especially evident in the 20–34 age group. The latter makes up only 8 percent of the male population and 15 percent of the females. Likewise, the census shows a sex ratio of 56 men for every 100 women in the age group 25–59 (compared to 76 in Simatupang).[14]

Those who stay in the village have little choice about how to support themselves. The rural economy is hardly diversified and farming one's own or other people's land is the major activity of most inhabitants. See Table 3, which gives the main occupations of Simarmata villagers in 1988.

---

[13] The danger of soil erosion was mentioned long ago by Tideman (1934).
[14] In the two villages in Pangururan subdistrict studied by Wolfs (1988), there was a surplus of unmarried women who, according to the villagers, had difficulty in finding a suitable spouse. Although in Simarmata there were also more single women than men in the age group 20–34, finding a marriage partner was not mentioned as a problem.

Table 3. Main occupations of Simarmata villagers (age 15–64) in 1988

	Men		Women		Total		Sex ratio (males per 100 females)
Farmer	67	73%	111	82%	178	78%	60
Civil servant	6	7%	2	1%	8	4%	300
Student	17	18%	17	13%	34	14%	100
Other	2	2%	6	4%	8	4%	33
Total	92	100%	136	100%	228	100%	68

As can be seen in Table 3, the proportion of farmers is considerably higher than in Simatupang (which had 68 percent female and 54 percent male farmers). Although I did not notice a clear-cut gender division in dry agriculture, it was women and girls, more often than men, who could be seen bent over their hoes, shaking soil from the tubers. Women were most active in planting, weeding, and processing, including the tedious peeling and binding of shallots. Apart from farming, a number of households fish on the side. Although it is the man who usually goes out on the lake, both husband and wife will mend old nets or make new ones. Moreover, it is the women who take care of the fish once the catch has been brought ashore. They sell small quantities of fresh fish in the village and sometimes take them to the regional market in Pangururan. Another typical female activity in Simarmata is weaving mats made of *pandanus* (a reed-like grass). In the afternoon, during slack periods between planting and harvesting, the women sit in the shade to cut and dry the leaves to be processed later. The mats are used in the house, but surpluses are taken to the market in Haranggoal in Simalungun district (on the north side of Lake Toba) and to other regional markets. Depending on size and quality, a mat yields Rp 500 to Rp 5000 (US$ 0.25–2.50). For a number of women the small-scale trade (*martiga-tiga*) of mats is an important source of income. On the whole, women's contribution to the labour force is remarkably high: according to the census they constitute 60 percent of the total labour force.[15]

Village livelihood

In contrast to the 'occupational multiplicity' found in lowland Javanese communities (see, for example, White 1976), farming is the primary means of subsistence in Toba Batak villages. Other work opportunities are limited. Of course, there have always been a handful of villagers working part-time

---

[15] In Indonesia as a whole, the labour participation rate for women in 1988 was reported to be only 37 percent (UNICEF 1989:88).

as petty traders, carpenters, or bricklayers. Primary school teachers, religious teachers, and civil servants can also be found in the village. But, on the whole, most inhabitants of Simatupang and Simarmata cultivate their own land and derive most of their income from what they can grow. To a large extent, farming has retained a subsistence character. Any surpluses are sold to co-villagers, or to urban lorry drivers who act as middlemen. The overall scarcity of fertile land has been a major factor inducing the Toba Batak to migrate, either to supplement their agricultural income on a temporary basis or to stay away permanently.

Apart from being an agricultural area, the Batak highlands are frequently – and justifiably – portrayed as a perfect vacation setting for both Indonesians and foreigners. The slow pace of life, hot springs, beautiful scenery, and Batak folklore combine to make the area attractive to tourists. Batak villages are indeed picturesque when the sky is blue, the breeze cool, and the surrounding fields and hills a soothing green after the monsoon rains. But closer observation reveals that this idyllic first impression does not correspond with daily village life. Most villagers have to drudge in the fields from sunrise to sunset in order to feed their children. They have to make do with cassava, rice, and salted dry fish, sometimes accompanied by vegetables (usually cassava leaves). Meat is served only on festive occasions, for which a pig, or sometimes a water buffalo, is slaughtered. If a migrant husband returns he makes sure there is good food, and usually a chicken will be sacrificed. Or, as one child in Simarmata put it, 'When my father comes home it is a party; then there is meat, sweets, and money'. In many Batak homes furniture is scarce, sometimes without beds or chairs, so that the inhabitants simply stretch out on their *pandanus* mats. Housing is primitive, lacking water and sanitary facilities. People have to go outside to relieve themselves, their excrement immediately being swallowed by stray pigs.

Clean water is a major problem. The water table in both research sites is very low, which makes it difficult and expensive to dig wells, and forces the villagers to make use of surface water. Simarmata families near the roadside usually collect water from Lake Toba. Those living in the upland *huta*, however, have to use small streams that disappear altogether in the dry season. In Simatupang, water is obtained from a small river winding through the rice fields, which is abundant but muddy in the rainy season and seemingly clean but small in the dry period. Due to the increased use of agricultural fertilizers and pesticides, the water has become polluted, thereby threatening the villagers' health. During my stay in Simatupang, and in cooperation with a regional non-governmental organization, water pipes were installed to provide clean drinking water for the entire village. The system pumps water from a well in the crater wall, and distributes it to eight communal taps scattered throughout the village. Apart from providing clean water, the new system has considerably lightened women's daily tasks of collecting and storing water.[16]

Use of electricity for household lighting is not widespread. In Simatupang only about a quarter of the households have invested in electrical connections, provided by the state electric company (PLN). Simarmata, on the other hand, has not yet been reached by PLN, but electricity from private diesel engines is used by almost half of the households. The others have not invested in electricity, as they feel they cannot afford the installation or the monthly charges.

Despite the similarities, my general impression is that Simatupang households, on the whole, are somewhat better off than those in Simarmata, probably due to the more diversified farming in the first village. Simatupang women were usually quick to offer me drinks during visits, while in Simarmata this seldom happened (although the villagers were certainly not less hospitable). Another difference was that only in Simatupang did I hear of women participating in an *arisan*, or rotating savings club, which may be an indication of having enough money to put some aside. Moreover, although the HKBP congregation in Simarmata has recently built a new church, it is no more than a brick skeleton, without ceiling or stucco. Since few churchgoers in Simarmata can afford a hymnbook, someone reads the hymns aloud, line by line; while in Simatupang most people bring their own hymnbooks.

On the whole, amenities and services in both villages, as in the subdistrict as a whole, are rudimentary. This helps explain why better-educated teachers tend to dislike village life, and why urban-trained doctors are reluctant to settle in the countryside. In an effort to make modern medicine and health care available to all villagers, the Indonesian government has set up primary health care centres (*puskesmas*). The clinic closest to Simatupang is in the township of Muara. The health centre attended by Simarmata villagers is in Pangururan. The nearest post offices are in the regional centres of Muara and (for Simarmata) Ambarita or Pangururan, and mail is delivered in the village several times a week. To buy stamps or to cash a money order, villagers have to go to the post office. Both men and women travel beyond the village, but men have more 'outside' contacts.

---

[16] Clean drinking water had been promised several times by the ruling Golkar party in order to win votes in Simatupang since there had been a considerable number of adherents of the Partai Demokrasi Indonesia (Indonesian Democratic Party) before. These promises, however, had never been lived up to. Therefore, in consultation with the Simatupang villagers, the non-governmental organization KSPPM (Kelompok Studi dan Pengembangan Prakarsa Masyarakat) took steps to bring clean water to the people.

Woman weaving a *pandanus* mat while chatting with a neighbour, Simarmata

Space, speech, and gender

When I first entered Simatupang and Simarmata, my initial contacts were with adult men. They were sitting in the roadside coffee shops, or in front of their houses, always ready for a chat. Meeting women was much harder in the beginning, a problem also mentioned by Krause (1981:60). Not that women stayed inside their houses. On the contrary, they were frequently outside in the courtyard or in the fields, but often they were either too busy to have lengthy conversations or somewhat suspicious of my nosing around. Moreover, relations among women are limited to a more private sphere, spatially confined to the house and the *huta*, or when they are on the way to the fields or local market. For men, on the other hand, besides their chats in the fields, most contacts take place in the local coffee shops (*lapo*), where they meet on Sundays and after work on weekdays to drink *tuak* (local sugar-palm wine) and play cards.[17] Issues of public interest are discussed and it is the venue for meetings concerning village affairs. Each coffee shop has its own clientele. For example, in Simatupang, one coffee shop at the T-junction is mainly frequented by the village elders; and the postman usually stops for a chat when he passes by. In addition, the *voorganger* (lay preacher) and retired schoolteachers, as well as some ordinary elderly men, can be found there.[18] For me these visitors proved a valuable source of information on village life and *adat* matters. Younger men tend to visit other coffee shops, where playing dice is the favourite pastime. No women are found in these places, the only exception being the female co-owner of the coffee shop. Conversely, stores belong to the women's domain. Besides that, Simatupang women can attend a small morning market where local women sell surpluses (of rice, fish, and vegetables) and some snacks. Another meeting place is the lake or the stream while doing the laundry or collecting water for cooking. Women also see each other when paying visits to kin or neighbours. For marriage and death ceremonies, female kin assemble before daybreak to prepare food for the guests.

Men are not only seen as heads of household (as discussed in Chapter IV), they also hold positions of authority in the church as deacons, *voorganger*, or minister. For men, the church provides one important avenue for positions of leadership. The big men, in other words, are often also church leaders. Ironically, it is the women who attend church in great numbers,

---

[17] It is easy to fall into stereotypes of lazy and spendthrift men who squander the family income on drinking and gambling while their wives drudge in the fields. This is the popular picture in urban newspapers and part of it may be correct. But we should also keep in mind that a cup of coffee costs only Rp 100, and one can sit in the coffee shop with one cup for several hours. In the meantime children's education may be discussed, the last harvest, or even politics. Often, the newspaper in the coffee shop is the only one available in the village.
[18] Interestingly, the favourite pub of the village head is another coffee shop.

sitting together with their small children in the middle pews, increasingly outnumbering the men. Every self-respecting woman sings in the *koor ina* (women's church choir), which practices once a week.

Local representatives of organizations that extend beyond the village level are also heavily dominated by males: the nationally organized Koperasi Unit Desa (KUD or village cooperative),[19] the agricultural extension service, the schools, and, as just mentioned, the churches. While women's conversation and main interests are largely restricted to local activities and individuals, men's conversation may touch on topics that extend beyond the village, such as regional events. These discussions, it should be noted, almost invariably end with a shrug of the shoulders and 'Aha ma bahenon?' (What can we do?). The villagers are interested in the outside world, but regard it with resignation and fatalism. They have little control over extra-household political and economic decisions like government policy on farm prices, taxes, or social security.

The dichotomy between the genders is evident not only in everyday conversation, but especially in the rhetoric of male oratory at family or village meetings. Oratory is seen as a male skill and a male domain – women talk only in the margins of public meetings. This marginality applies both to discourse and to space – while men cluster in the centre, women sit in the back rows. Likewise, in gatherings of the extended family or other mixed groups, there is little interchange between men and women. Each prefers, and feels more comfortable in, the company of his or her own gender mates. Women, however, often play a powerful role in influencing men's opinions. A strikingly similar situation was described by Tanner for the Minangkabau:

> 'Decisions concerning ceremonies (a wedding, for example) or matters involving the lineage as a whole are made in the context of formal consultations in the lineage house. [The lineage males] sit on the floor and discuss the matter in a relatively formal manner. One of the young women usually serves the men coffee and a snack; the senior woman or women generally sit informally on the floor a bit apart from the men, perhaps leaning against a wall near the door to the kitchen. She listens to the discussion; if it does not go as she wishes she interjects her opinion. When she feels the need to comment, she does not stand on formality [...]. In addition to the respect the men have for her views, she also controls the rice necessary for any ceremony.' (Tanner 1974:144.)

In other words, there is an opposition between male authority and prestige, supported by national law and cultural tradition, on the one hand, and

---

[19] Several forms of village cooperation which existed before 1965 have disappeared and have merged into one central authority: the Koperasi Unit Desa. In contrast to what the name suggests, the KUD serves several *desa* and has little to do with village initiatives (Hüsken 1988:256). The same has happened with women's and youth organizations.

female power, springing from more covert traditions and interpersonal relations, on the other.

In terms of economic life, it is usually maintained that Toba Batak women are full partners in nearly the entire scope of the family's activities and its relations with others (Nasoetion 1943:97; Sherman 1990:297). While I do agree that men and women play complementary roles, I would like to stress that the pattern is often unequal in the sense that women's range of options is narrower than men's and their obligations are usually more time-consuming. As girls they help clean the house, wash, and cook with their mothers, collect firewood, and participate in all stages of farming. As wives they cultivate their husbands' fields. Financially, however, far from being under their husbands' supervision they are, in fact, the prime handlers of the family's economic resources. In marketing, decisions about price and quantity are made by women, as are household decisions involving purchases of food or clothing. Many women are involved in market activities; some sell only at the tiny village markets, while others participate in the weekly regional markets. The latter travel considerable distances by bus to these markets, where they sell rice, peanuts, and onions for other villagers.

Women of all ages perform labour nearly constantly throughout the day, while men have considerable leisure time to spend in the coffee shop or to attend *adat* ceremonies. Many commanding *raja* (hamlet heads) are supported by hard-working farm wives. As I will argue in the next chapter, this competence of working women as wives and mothers is one of the reasons why, historically, Toba Batak men have had the opportunity to leave their home villages.

Simarmata women doing the laundry in Lake Toba

CHAPTER III

Men and women in the migration process

In North Tapanuli today, a relatively large number of individuals are involved in migration. In the early part of this century, population movement was largely rural – rural, as men moved to work on rubber plantations, either seasonally or for more prolonged periods, but there was some urbanward movement as well. Broadly speaking, men who moved to the towns were either literate and went to work in the lower echelons of the colonial bureaucracy or as teachers, or they were illiterate, in which case they provided unskilled labour for the colonial government. In this chapter I will discuss some of the structural forces that formed the context of male-dominated migration as it evolved from the late nineteenth century, through the colonial era, to the present day.

The nature of gender relations among pre-colonial Toba Batak

Until the establishment of Dutch colonial rule, Toba Batak society was 'stateless' and the political map consisted of numerous small territories, each occupied by one ruling *marga*, or clan (Castles 1972). The first migratory movements were the result of the splitting up of clans, whereby new settlements were founded elsewhere. This kind of division was generally motivated by land shortages[1] or disputes among the land-owning clan, and was carried out under the leadership of a lineage or sublineage head (Cunningham 1958:18). It seems that the expansion of the Toba Batak was very energetic, and by the nineteenth century most of the highlands was inhabited, although sparsely. This does not mean, however, that no frontier was left. In the 1920s large areas of the highlands with only *ri* (*alang-alang*, or tough grasses) were observed (Janssen 1924:359; Joustra 1910:73). The most populous areas were (and still are) situated on the shores of Lake Toba.

The English Baptist missionaries Burton and Ward are reported to be among the first Europeans to have visited the Batak highlands in 1824

---

[1] The scarcity of arable land was not absolute, but must be related to the technology employed at the time and the availability of other land easier to cultivate.

(Keuning 1948:9). One of the observations made by them, and later by other travellers as well (for instance Van Asselt [1906]:69, 85, 91), was the prevalence of women working in the fields. Though the connection between this observation and male mobility was not always made, the phenomenon was clearly considered unusual enough to comment upon. The following excerpts are characteristic of a wealth of similar remarks made about the economic roles of women in the Batak highlands.

> 'The condition of the women appears to be no other than that of slaves [...]. They alone, besides the domestic duties, work in the rice plantation. The men, when not engaged in war, their favourite occupation, commonly lead an idle, inactive life, passing the day in playing on a kind of flute.' (Marsden 1811:382.)

> 'With so few luxuries or refinements, and with so much assistance from the opposite sex [...], it will be readily inferred that the men lead a life of extreme inactivity. It seemed to us, indeed, a matter of some astonishment, that such an appearance of civil order should be maintained, with so much leisure for the operation of the evil propensities of human nature.' (Burton and Ward 1827:512.)

Sherman (1990:29) wonders whether such travellers' accounts were not biased by the unusual visit of the explorers – 'whether their very presence brought about the effects they observed by drawing crowds of men to their retinues, while modesty, which remains a social imperative for women, kept the latter busy at their work'. I think, however, that there is little reason to trivialize the above quotations as mere bias. The remarks point to a gender division of labour that has evolved in North Tapanuli and which can still be observed today.

There are good reasons to believe that in times past Toba Batak women had to handle agricultural production almost entirely on their own. All farm tasks, except felling the virgin jungle or ploughing wet-rice fields, could be carried out by women. It was the men who had effective political power and who were responsible for settling disputes and maintaining order (Krause 1981:63). In the ritual sphere, too, men held the key positions. They were the important orators at public meetings on community affairs. Virtually every married man regularly spent whole days attending and discussing trials for various offences. The wealth of complex *adat* (customary) rules, related expressions, and proverbs are a vivid illustration of male preoccupation with legal matters. Occasionally, unsettled conflicts resulted in wars which could bring men far from their *huta* (Van Asselt [1906]:181). These were often wars of attrition, which produced few casualties but preoccupied the men constantly. Within the family as well, men were the representatives on public occasions like betrothals, marriages, births, and burials. These involved extensive ceremonies and required comprehensive knowledge of *adat* rules. Men controlled the major resources, which were land and livestock. Men could pioneer new land as well. Women only had use rights to land through either fathers or husbands, even though these use rights were well protected by custom.

Despite their restricted rights to land, women were largely autonomous farmers, growing rice and sweet potatoes, weaving cloth and mats, and making pots. Men were occupied with tree felling in remote forests for house construction, and some were skilled in woodcarving and metalworking. Local markets were the scene of a lively barter, in which both men and women participated. Women exchanged food crops, fish, and handicrafts, while men sold cattle,[2] meat, and some imported articles. Men also controlled trade with other regions outside the Batak areas (Burton and Ward 1827:275). Toba Batak merchants travelled to the port towns for cotton, dried fish, and manufactured goods, in exchange for horses, slaves,[3] forest products, and benzoin, and sometimes rice from the interior (Van Asselt [1906]:84, 99, 145). Special merchants carried loads of sea salt from the salt beds of coastal Sibolga through Sipirok north into Toba. The men followed narrow footpaths, crossing dense forests and open plains. The inhabitants of Samosir Island had even more difficulty travelling: they first had to cross Lake Toba in canoes (*solu*) made from hollowed logs, some of which could be powered by fifty or more paddlers. On the whole, pre-colonial trade involved long and often dangerous journeys, from which women were practically excluded.

Throughout the nineteenth century, male mobility was more than an economic and political necessity. Migration was also associated with a person's life cycle, and was identified with a boy's entry into full adult life. At this stage a young man apparently acquired an independence from responsibilities in the village that allowed or actively encouraged migration. Most adolescent Toba Batak males (*doli-doli*) left their homes and undertook a long journey called *mangaranto* to gain experience worthy of an adult male. In some instances a son might contribute some of his earnings from migration to the bride-price his parents had to pay for his future wife.

The Toba Batak are not the only people who have a tradition of what

---

[2] Cattle were exclusively men's property since they were used in bride-price transfers.
[3] The missionary Van Asselt ([1906]:35) recounts how he once met several merchants who had bought a slave boy in Bakara on the shore of Lake Toba. Estimates of the proportion of slaves in the population have been as high as 30 percent (Castles 1972:20), but when the Dutch took a count in 1909 they found only three percent (Middendorp 1913:12). In the early nineteenth century about 300 slaves per year were exported to the Straits Settlements. They were sold to the slave depots of Penang and the tin mines of Perak and Selangor in the 1860s. The majority of these slaves were reported to be women, the trade being 'of immense advantage in procuring a female population for Pinang' (J. Anderson 1826:298). After the establishment of the Netherlands Indies government in the area in the early twentieth century, slavery was forbidden. In the early 1930s Vergouwen (1964:327) mentions that 'all traces of [peonage] have now been expunged, except in South Tapanuli [...]'.

Couillard (1982:7) terms 'men's journey'. The Iban call it *bejalai* (Freeman 1970:222), the Dayak of Borneo *sanorui* (Hudson 1967:173), the Acehnese *rantau* (Siegel 1969:54), and the Minangkabau *merantau* (Naim 1985:111). The island of Bawean in East Java is even known as *pulau wanita* (island of women), because of its great preponderance of females due to male out-migration (Vredenbregt 1964:113; Subarkah, Marsidi and Fadjari 1986). The numerous terms for travelling, journeying, and wandering in the Malay language seem to point to the importance it has in society. These journeys are undertaken for material gain and social prestige. Likewise, in Sumatra's interior it seems that short trips, directed inland in search of jungle produce for sale and lasting from a few months to a year, have been prevalent. Every young man, soon after reaching puberty, must have wished to undertake such trips.

In short, the gender division of labour was such that women performed the majority of the work in the area of reproduction (water carrying, fuel provision, food processing) and agriculture, as well as being engaged in local trade in foodstuffs. Men raised cattle, conducted long-distance trade, and acted as part-time political specialists.

The colonial period: increased male mobility

According to Pelzer (1961), Christian missionaries were the first contact that the Batak people had with Western culture. Around 1860 the Rheinische Mission entered the area to establish their stations and to try to win the souls of the Toba Batak, thereby competing with Muslims from the south and the north. It was only towards the end of the nineteenth century, between 1878 and 1907, that the Netherlands Indies government gained a foothold in the Batak highlands – or North Tapanuli, as it soon became known. Both the missionaries and the colonial government wanted to change Toba Batak social institutions that organized economic, political, legal, and religious life. After some initial difficulties, the missionaries succeeded in converting numerous Toba Batak to Christianity. Members of each parish were recruited from the local patrilineage, and lineage representatives (all men) were given key positions in the new church as pastors and deacons (Bruner 1961:510).

The establishment of the Netherlands Indies government in the Batak highlands was extremely late, compared to other areas of Indonesia where the VOC had earlier gained considerable influence. North Tapanuli had remained outside the VOC's field of interest because it produced little of value except the forest products benzoin and camphor. The Dutch had induced the Batak to bring these products to the port of Barus on the west coast without having to dominate them politically. The colonial government was not very eager to set foot in the mountainous interior. The Toba Batak had a reputation for being unfriendly and they were feared as cannibals (Van Asselt [1906]:61). Only when internal warfare and widespread possession of firearms were frequently reported by German missionaries did Dutch soldiers and government officials try to 'pacify' the area. It was, then, the political turmoil in the area in the 1860s and 1870s – partly a result of the arrival of the Mission – which finally induced the colonial power to intervene. Gradually, the different parts of the Toba Batak homeland were brought under control (Schadee 1920). Several military campaigns were necessary to bring the Toba Batak priest-king Singamangaraja XII and his dwindling armies to their knees. He was captured and killed in 1907. From then on, the Batak converted en masse to Christianity. They saw advantages in church affiliation, especially in the form of educational opportunities outside the village. Dutch colonial servants were stationed in a few larger villages, which quickly developed into small towns like Tarutung, Balige, Laguboti, and Siborong-borong.

The colonial era set in train events which had and continue to have significant effects on gender in North Tapanuli. Colonial policies (taxation, wage labour, recruitment for plantations) considered the adult male as the head of household, which resulted in a 'patri-orientation' cited in much of the literature on peasant societies.[4] As Harris points out:

> 'Many aspects of male power over other household members may be seen to derive from the nature of the state [...]. In most state formations, household heads are made responsible for paying taxes and other dues to the state and are answerable in law for other household members.' (Harris 1981:59.)

Government officials in Tapanuli were charged not only with collecting taxes, but also with halting fighting and hearing disputes, changes that impinged directly on men. And it was also men who were more likely than women to be called on to work in state projects, such as road construction, plantation labour, and land colonization. The occupational and social roles of women underwent few changes. Toba Batak women continued to be the producers and the sustainers:

> 'the woman is an important worker, firstly in housekeeping, but also in work on the field and in keeping small livestock and poultry. In most cases a married man's livelihood is guaranteed – through his wife. This explains a decrease of activity and zest for work among many men after they have married.' (Joustra 1912:15.)[5]

---

[4]   Etienne and Leacock 1980; Bossen 1975; Goldschmidt and Kunkel 1971; Harris 1981.
[5]   '[...] is de vrouw een belangrijke werkkracht, allereerst in de huishouding, maar ook niet weinig bij den veldarbeid en bij de verzorging van klein- en pluimvee. In de meeste gevallen is een getrouwd man verzekerd – door zijn vrouw – van zijn levensonderhoud. Vandaar bij velen een vermindering van activiteit en van werklust na hun trouwen.'

In other words, women's work enabled the state to extract labour power (from men) without weakening the basis of subsistence.

One of the first transformations introduced by the colonial government was in the administrative field. Pre-colonial hamlets were part of larger territorial arrangements called *bius*. Each *bius* was occupied by related clans, headed by a *raja doli*, a hereditary position in the male line. His main functions were to organize inhabitants for communal activities, like the construction of waterworks, and to settle disputes within his own *bius* and between *bius* organizations (Ypes 1932:161). A *bius* was not only a constitutional community, but also had a sacrificial character. However, the position of the spiritual dignitary (*parbaringin*) was undermined when Dutch colonial administrators prohibited sacrificial ceremonies. This heralded the end of the *bius*, not only as a ritual organization but also as a territorial arrangement. Dutch colonial administrators considered the tiny *huta* inefficient and therefore reorganized them into larger units called *kampung* (the Malay word for 'village'). No longer were the *huta* organized on the basis of close kinship relationships, but on the basis of physical proximity and number of people. This made them easier for government officials to survey (Vergouwen 1964:127). The basic territorial and administrative unit became the *negeri*, a confederation of *kampung*, headed by a *kepala negeri* who represented the Dutch government. The *raja doli* was replaced by a small hierarchy of salaried officials. Personal ability and political connections replaced kinship as the basis of leadership (Castles 1972). To outlaw internal warfare, the Dutch established formal courts where disputes could be settled. Jurisprudence was thus concentrated in a handful of formal administrators. It is conceivable that village men who had previously spent much time on warfare and legal matters now started to look for new opportunities. Or, in the words of a Dutch missionary:

> 'Former conditions provided men ample opportunity to sharpen their minds (intelligence); the vast majority of physical labour was done by women. Men's strength of mind, formerly mainly concentrated on legal matters, warfare, etc., has presently become available, due to the peaceful conditions brought about by the government, and is searching for other avenues. Partly it has found its way in the direction of education, government positions, etc., but there is not enough room for all.' (Joustra 1912:68.)[6]

---

[6] 'De vroegere toestanden gaven den mannen gelegenheid te over hun geest (verstand) te scherpen; het overgroote deel van lichamelijken arbeid kwam voor rekening der vrouw. De geestkracht der mannen, vroeger vooral geconcentreerd op rechtzaken, oorlogvoeren e.d., is thans, onder de vreedzame toestanden, door het gouvernement gebracht, vrijgekomen en zoekt andere wegen. Ten deele heeft zij haar weg gevonden in de richting van onderwijs, gouvernementsbetrekkingen e.d., maar hier is geen plaats voor allen.'

Schooling, introduced by German missionaries but taken over by the colonial government, also sharpened gender inequality, as boys were encouraged to attend school while girls' education was perceived as unimportant. Formal education prepared village boys for the colonial civil service and thus was an important means of social mobility, a topic further dealt with in Chapter VI. Not only had rural women to endure inferior social status because of their limited schooling, but, partly as a result of this, they also faced restricted opportunities in urban labour markets.

Another change effected by the colonial government was the introduction of taxes and compulsory labour. For male heads of household corvee labour became the predominant means of paying government taxes. Elderly men told me they had been forced to construct roads, often far from home. A maximum of 36 days a year could be claimed by the colonial government from each adult male for the construction of roads or waterworks. Later on, by collecting taxes in cash, the Dutch, like colonial administrators elsewhere, were probably trying to induce their subjects to seek wage labour on plantations or to grow cash crops, with the deliberate aim of encouraging transition from a pure subsistence to a cash economy (Scott 1976:97-8; Van der Meulen 1977:51-2). Thus, the Toba Batak villages gradually became incorporated into the national economy.

Dutch-imposed peace made it possible to travel in relative safety over large areas where previously most people would have been loathe to venture. Or, as one missionary put it, 'No more struggle but peace. Today the women and girls can travel for hours on end unaccompanied' (Van Asselt [1906]:68). As a result of corvee labour, roads were constructed and North Tapanuli was opened up at a rapid rate, which increased overall mobility. Improved infrastructure not only benefited Western plantations by enabling them to import rice from the Toba area, at the same time it enhanced the mobility of Batak men and women. Until the 1930s most markets were one to three days' travel from upland communities, and traders had to stay overnight in distant towns, a serious matter for women responsible for child care. Villagers insist that it was this that prevented women from playing more than a minor role in long-distance trade. The opening up of the highlands enabled women to extend their market activities. One source reports Samosir women selling hundreds of *pandanus* mats (*lage*) a week to East Sumatra (Siregar 1939:142).

But no doubt the processes of political and economic change particularly extended male mobility. Some men in Simarmata told me that in the 1920s they crossed Lake Toba by canoe and then walked all the way to Simalungun to work as farm labourers. Another villager reported having been recruited for a Simalungun tea plantation in the 1930s. Likewise, men from Simatupang regularly left the village to harvest in other areas where rice ripened earlier or later. Others travelled to Angkola in the south as lumbermen. Having bought their tools jointly, they remained in the forests for a couple of months at a time to saw trees (Eggink 1923). There were also migrants who put to use locally developed specialties or skills. For example, in the area of Sipahutar, I came across a village where for decades men had been leaving to construct false teeth, a craft passed down from father to son. They had found it profitable and started a tradition of periodic migration to sell their skills as *pande ngingi* (dental technicians) at urban markets.

Plantations

At the start of the twentieth century the core of Dutch colonial economic interest had shifted away from Java to the Outer Islands, particularly to Sumatra's East Coast, where European plantations were established. Almost the entire lowland region of North Sumatra was eventually cleared and transformed into a vast estate area in which tobacco, rubber, palm oil, coconut, and other agricultural products were cultivated. According to Castles (1972:129-37), European companies were also interested in exploiting the Batak homeland. However, local leaders emphasized the collective land ownership of Toba Batak clans as an argument against expropriation. As a result, no plantations were established in Tapanuli and the land remained under the control of village and kinship groups.

Compared to other ethnic groups, the Batak population was not actively recruited for estate work on Sumatra's East Coast. Most of them preferred working their own plot of land, be it tiny, to being cheap labour for capitalist enterprises. So, rather than enlist labour locally, plantation agents in Singapore, Hong Kong, and Java brought in Chinese and Javanese workers (Bruner 1970:125; Geertz 1963:110). Likewise, Vergouwen estimated that the flow of cash into the Toba Batak area prior to 1930 'in the form of the wages earned on Sumatra's East Coast by labourers engaged in temporary work, especially during the dry monsoon, [...] amounts to only a few thousand guilders' (Vergouwen 1964:295).

It is impossible to estimate the number of Toba Batak leaving for the estates, since temporary movements were not (and are not) registered. However, I found evidence of temporary moves (and the resulting cash earnings) in statements on several redemptions of corvee labour (as stipulated in some end-of-term reports, for instance Verhoef 1934:148; Welter 1935:63). Tichelman (1936:402) notes that because those working as plantation coolies were exempted from corvee labour, thereby dismissing them from redemption, corvee budgets suffered in less affluent Tapanuli. Facing an expanding population and rising consumption and tax requirements, a considerable number of Toba Batak men, especially from relatively depressed areas, took advantage of the improved economic opportunities on

East Coast estates.[7] The plantations were only a day's journey away, which enabled them to return home at planting and harvesting times. In the 1930s the number of Toba Batak working on estates diminished rapidly. The Depression heavily reduced the income of the tobacco and rubber plantations of the East Coast, and the need for wage labourers declined.

As far as I could gather, although wage labour on plantations was not the exclusive domain of men, women's participation in this sector seems to have been limited. Women are mainly mentioned as wives of wage labourers, constituting a possible labour reserve.[8] Tichelman (1936:403) notes that married *koelies* (wage labourers) earned more than bachelors, a measure intended to stimulate the formation of nuclear families, the ultimate aim of which was to obtain a steady supply of labour. Another source discussing Toba Batak migration mentions female workers on tea plantations, and adds that their wages were lower than those of men (Anonymous 1935a). Some women in Simarmata, Samosir, told me that during a severe drought in the 1950s they had moved in small groups to Simalungun tea estates to work as tea pickers side by side with Javanese coolies. But on the whole, female migration in search of wage labour outside the villages was limited.

The effect of this whole process was to involve men more and more in the cash economy while keeping women in the non-monetized subsistence-farming role. An unforeseen side effect was the spread of venereal diseases in North Tapanuli, 'which must be mainly attributed to the men who work on the East Coast estates and to the cloth and vegetable traders. It is notable that the villagers call these diseases *sakit kebon* (estate disease)' (Oerlemans 1937:32).

Land colonization

By the 1920s, apart from drifting to the plantations, a new type of migration attracted many land-hungry Toba Batak households: northeast to Simalungun and Asahan, northwest to Dairi and Alas, and south to Angkola and

---

7   'De landbouw is op het eiland [Samosir] in hoofdzaak rijstladangbouw. [...] De opbrengst is niet voldoende om de bevolking te voeden. Door veeteelt en door te gaan werken op landbouwondernemingen of aan de wegen ter Oostkust van Sumatra is zij in staat het jaarlijksch tekort aan rijst uit Toba te halen.' (The island's [Samosir] agriculture is mainly rice farming on dry plots. [...] The yield is not enough to feed the population. By keeping livestock and by working on agricultural estates or on the roads on Sumatra's East Coast the annual rice deficit can be imported from Toba) (*Handschriften 806*, 1920). See also Oerlemans 1937:19; Ruychaver 1936:182; Tideman 1934:16; L.R. van Bemmelen 1931:13.
8   'De Bataksche vrouwen worden in de gelegenheid gesteld om betaalden arbeid te verrichten en zij maken daarvan een geregeld gebruik. Ook op den arbeid van deze aan werken gewende vrouwen kan de werkgever staat maken.' (The Batak women are given the opportunity to perform paid labour, an opportunity which they often take. The labour of these women who are used to hard work can be relied upon by the employer) (Tichelman 1936:403).

Mandailing (Castles 1972:72; Reid 1979:50). Cunningham (1958) mentions a *huta* in the Meat valley in the Balige area, where almost half the families migrated between 1920 and 1940. They left their home village to open up new rice fields (*manombang*) in the northeast, initially by travelling back and forth, later by settling permanently.

It was not only land hunger, but also prestige, that prompted Toba Batak to migrate from their homeland. In the pioneer areas in Simalungun and Dairi, one who opened up land could claim the status of *raja* (local chief) as soon as he had attracted fifty followers (Tideman 1922:188; see Lineton 1975:194 for a similar phenomenon among the Buginese from Sulawesi).

One of the most popular destinations was Simalungun, which at the start of the twentieth century was still sparsely populated. While the land was well suited for the development of wet-rice cultivation, it did not yet have much economic value. The area was attractive for Batak in search of land, most of whom arrived penniless. Settlers lived in makeshift huts made from tough grasses (*ri*) and leaves, but after the first harvest better dwellings could be constructed, gradually expanding into permanent settlements. Despite some cholera epidemics which inflicted severe losses on the population, immigration into Simalungun steadily increased. Between 1907 and 1920 the number of Toba Batak in Simalungun grew from less than 300 to over 21,000 (Tichelman 1936; Tideman 1922:187). In the same period the land area under *sawah* (irrigated) cultivation increased tenfold (Liddle 1967:84). As a result of this steady infiltration, Toba Batak already numbered about 30,000 by 1930 (Pelzer 1958:iii). Likewise, Clauss (1982:2) observed that a large part of the population of the Simalungun village he studied in the 1970s consisted of immigrants from Samosir Island.

The Toba Batak were not just 'pushed' out of their overpopulated villages; Dutch colonial rulers recruited Toba Batak rice cultivators to the sparsely populated northeastern territory. By providing free farmland to immigrants, they encouraged them to construct irrigation systems in order to guarantee a steady food supply for the estates.[9] The indigenous Simalungun Batak were mostly swidden cultivators, and lacked the requisite skills (Lando 1979:193).

Apart from government incentives, the missionaries also encouraged converted Toba Batak to migrate to Simalungun to spread the virtues of Christianity among the pagan Simalungun Batak.[10] Other sources, however,

---

[9] On the East Coast, land colonization by individual pioneers was restricted to leave the way clear for plantation expansion. It seems that only Toba Batak from the Silindung and Balige areas, as renowned rice cultivators, were allowed to settle on the East Coast. They were granted newly created wet-rice lands (served by a Dutch-financed irrigation system) to provide a local source of rice for the plantations.
[10] The large-scale occupation of agricultural lands by Toba Batak was far from smooth and

assert that most missionaries valued the isolation of the Batak highlands and were generally opposed to emigration to the modernized coastal regions (Wertheim 1969:186; Kraemer 1958:67). The Toba Batak themselves, however, did not bother much about the missionaries' concerns, and they continued to migrate in large numbers. Some even named their new settlements after their original hamlet, so that even today we find several Toba *huta* in Simalungun.

> 'Within the irrigation districts of Tanah Djawa and Sidamanik, the Toba people, with Netherlands East Indies assistance, developed their own villages in the seas of irrigated rice, re-creating as best they could, the social atmosphere of Tapanuli' (Cunningham 1958:86).

Simultaneous to the migration to Simalungun, another group migrated northwest into Dairi. By the mid-1930s, the total of immigrant Toba Batak amounted to some 23,000 there (Castles 1972:191-2).

While the Toba Batak population increased (more than doubling during the eighty years of Dutch rule), they migrated in all directions, not only to other Batak areas but also establishing large communities in Deli, Aceh, and Java. After the independence struggle thousands of Toba Batak began pouring from the highlands into the coastal plains and lowlands of East Sumatra, where most of them settled as squatters on estate lands (Pelzer 1982:48).

In the 1930 census the Tapanuli Batak[11] are depicted as Indonesia's most mobile population group, with 17.8 percent residing outside their native area (compared to 5.5 percent of the Minangkabau). Male dominance is reflected in the fact that there were 117 male migrants recorded per 100 females among the Tapanuli Batak (Kato 1982:125-9). Special mention is made of a relative surplus of women among those who stayed behind in the subdistricts (*onderafdelingen*) of Hoogvlakte van Toba (92 men per 100 females), and rural Silindoeng (95 per 100).[12] 'It is likely that in many of these regions the surplus of women can be partly attributed to emigration in which more men than women participated' (*Volkstelling 1930*, IV:8).

From the start, migration (especially permanent moves) was not only selective by gender but also by class. Although some sources (for example

---

often raised antagonism among the original inhabitants, the Simalungun Batak. Some missionaries therefore criticized the encouragement to migrate (Joustra 1918:314; Vuurmans 1941:39). For more details on internal relations between the two groups, see Cunningham 1958:86-8; Liddle 1967:84; Van Langenberg 1977:101-2.
[11] Kato (1982:124) explains that unfortunately it is not possible to concentrate exclusively on the Toba Batak because the Batak were not subdivided into separate subgroups in the census enumeration outside the residencies of Tapanuli and Sumatra's East Coast.
[12] Sex ratios for some other subdistricts are: Toba: 96 men per 100 women, Samosir: 98, Baroes: 101, and Dairi: 103.

Haibach 1927:14) claim that those who left Samosir Island were usually *parripe* (immigrants), who were often landless, it is doubtful whether the poorest could emigrate. Permanent out-migration was limited by the need for identity papers, which could be obtained only by paying a tax of ten guilders (*wang pindah*) (*Handschriften 806*, 1920:365; Oerlemans 1937:50; Tichelman 1936:400). This was the equivalent of the annual tax on a rich household, so it may have inhibited emigration of poor people. Nor did all migrants leave out of sheer necessity, but rather because they chose not to remain farmers (Bruner 1972:210). The growing availability of employment, particularly white-collar jobs in the colonial administration, together with the limited investment opportunities in North Tapanuli, encouraged the Toba Batak to educate their children in urban areas.

During the first half of this century, those with some schooling developed new aspirations and values, their slogan being *hamajuon*, or progress. They felt an urgent need to 'catch up' with the Javanese by means of education and prestigious government jobs. This resulted in an image of the Toba Batak as an aggressive and ambitious people, but as such they were popular among Europeans, who employed them in the lower ranks of Western businesses and the colonial government (Bruner 1972). Slowly, a white-collar emigration of mission-educated Toba males began, as more and more literate and semi-literate personnel were needed to fill low-level administrative positions on the plantations and in the cities. They started working as clerks, surveyors, craftsmen, and mechanics, in commerce, and in the service of the Deli Spoorweg Maatschappij (Deli Railroad Company). Contact with other ethnic groups reinforced the Batak's self-esteem. Meeting the Javanese contract coolies on Sumatra's East Coast – exploited, subordinated, uneducated – further confirmed their feelings of superiority. Prosperous families of the village elite succeeded in securing for their children salaried city jobs, as civil servants, teachers, army men, lawyers, and so on. These migrants became models, success stories for the young to emulate.

The history of North Tapanuli indicates that the wish to migrate is not just dictated by present economic problems, but also by a migration tradition which gradually evolved during the pre-colonial and colonial periods. In the early twentieth century the first migration wave was a direct response to the demand for labour on Sumatra's East Coast. This was followed by agricultural pioneering from densely populated areas to East Sumatra. Improvements in communication and transportation whetted the desire of many Toba Batak to move. The biggest upsurge in the number of migrants, however, began in the mid-1950s. Today, the reasons to migrate may still be very much the same, but a different pattern has developed. Present migrants consist mainly of individual merchants, students, and government officials who have left their home villages. And migration is no longer reserved exclusively for men.

Changing patterns of migration

> 'Where once migration had been undertaken to perpetuate the peasant community, it was now becoming an end in itself: an opportunity to break with the community, its ways, its heavy pressures, to free oneself from the charges and restrictions of the family, and also from the slavery of agricultural labor' (Weber 1976:285).

The main factors leading to postwar migration from North Tapanuli have been land scarcity and lack of alternative employment opportunities (see Cunningham 1958). However, these factors alone are not sufficient to understand why Toba Batak opted for emigrating to cope with economic stagnation. To explain Toba Batak mobility, a comparison with other wandering groups may be worthwhile. In an interesting article, Lineton (1975) discusses the differences between the Bugis of Sulawesi and the Javanese. She argues that in West Java during the fifties people suffered from widespread land scarcity and overall poverty, but instead of emigrating the Javanese responded to the economic hardship by moving temporarily to nearby towns (see also McNicoll 1968:44-5). Although we would expect many Javanese to leave the island in search of land and other economic opportunities, few people have voluntarily participated in government-subsidized transmigration programmes. The Javanese explain their disinclination to migrate by saying: 'It does not matter whether we are able to eat or not so long as all of us [Javanese] can be together' (Penny and Singarimbun 1973:66). Such strong sentiments towards the home area are found neither among the Bugis nor among the Toba Batak. Apart from a response to economic necessity, emigration is seen by the Toba Batak as a way to achieve upward social mobility. In other words, the Toba Batak have an 'ideology of migration' – or, as one end-of-term report states, 'a natural inclination' – which is comprised of propositions and shared understandings about the promise of migration for social mobility and improved living conditions. The most common topic in village coffee shops is travel – the coming and going of someone in the community, or personal migration experiences. Wanderlust is expressed in songs and folklore that provide models of social roles, and in jokes about young men who are afraid to leave.

The differences between Bugis and Toba Batak on the one hand and Javanese on the other are probably related to their different environments and histories. Lineton states that the Javanese are simply not used to long-distance travelling, but she does not go into the underlying reasons. I would hypothesize that because of the relative abundance of economic opportunities on their densely populated island (partly as a result of early colonialism), the Javanese did not need to travel far in search of jobs. The Bugis and the Toba Batak, however, were initially forced out of their homelands because of a scarcity of employment opportunities, thus fostering a migration tradition and creating a tight network between the migrants and those who stayed behind. Batak newcomers are usually welcomed by their fellow-migrant clanmates, who offer financial and moral support. For the Toba Batak emigration is seen as a means – for many the only means – to achieve wealth and a higher social status. Consequently, in the village of Simarmata, in 61 percent of the households at least one member was absent, either a male 'head of household' or an unmarried son or daughter. In Simatupang 53 percent of the households were directly affected by the migration of at least one of their members.

Despite its overall scope and pattern, Toba Batak migration has manifested itself in a variety of ways in North Tapanuli. In the early twentieth century, although the conditions on Samosir Island were pressing, few inhabitants emigrated permanently. Having no tradition as *sawah* cultivators, they were not eager to become wet-rice farmers in a new environment. Rather, they left as casual labourers or pedlars, and returned to their homestead after the work was finished. Moreover, it is said that they were too attached to Lake Toba to leave their homeland forever. In contrast, the area south of the lake had a long tradition of *sawah* cultivation but was too densely populated to provide everyone with sufficient land. It is from this region, especially from Balige and Muara, that the largest number of permanent migrants left to develop new rice-farming areas elsewhere (Tideman 1922:191).

These different patterns have left their traces. Today, migration from Simatupang, Muara, is unquestionably of the type Gonzales (1961:1277) has termed 'permanent removal', although I would say that for most villagers migration is more a matter of not returning than of leaving in the first place. The only circular migrants presently found in Simatupang are a handful of agricultural wage labourers. In Simarmata, Samosir, on the other hand, apart from permanent moves, circular migration is still quite common. Those who engage in this type of migration are mainly pedlars, working in regions elsewhere in Sumatra or sometimes as far away as Java.

In everyday village conversation, no different term is attached to the two types of mobility. Both are referred to as *mangaranto* (or *merantau* in Bahasa Indonesia), which literally means 'to leave one's home area'. While the word *pindah* is used exclusively in the context of definite moves, *mangaranto* includes both. The term *marjaja*, which is frequently heard on Samosir, is not related to a time period either, but refers to a specific occupation in the migration area, namely itinerant peddling. Nevertheless, at the analytical level a distinction between circular and permanent migration is useful because, as will be elaborated in the following chapters, the two types of mobility attract different household members and have different repercussions for those who stay behind.

Circular or temporary migration mainly involves husbands of village women, while permanent migration is generally undertaken by adolescent children (both sons and daughters) or siblings of village women, or by complete households. Few wives are involved in circular migration. It is clear that once women are married, their mobility is restricted. A woman cannot leave her children, house, and fields in the care of her husband for longer than a few days, and then only if there is a daughter or other female member of the household to take over her duties. It is, then, not just the structure of the labour market which limits employment opportunities for married women, as is often stated. Socio-cultural notions of the organization of the rural household seem far more important in restricting the labour participation of a married woman (Radcliffe 1986:41). In short, circular migration is usually undertaken by husbands. Their main purpose is to make sufficient money to invest in their children's education, or to ensure comfortable retirement. As a consequence, circular migration (together with remittances sent home during the migrant's absence) does little to boost local agricultural production.

While the departure of husbands is said to be inspired by their responsibility for supporting their families, migration of young people is based mainly on more individual motives, such as looking for experience or attending university. Nowadays it is considered 'normal' to leave the village after completing junior or senior high school. Migrant husbands and fathers, on the other hand, are likely to return, because there are strong family ties or because of their stake either in property or political life in the village. In other words, they are still considered to be part of the household and there is no short-term prospect of staying away forever. Under normal circumstances, as long as the wife and children remain in the village, the circular migrants will return regularly. Therefore, in this study, the distinction between circular and permanent migration is based on qualitative criteria (relational ties), rather than on more conventional criteria, such as time spent away (Hugo 1978; Mantra 1981; Maude 1979) or migrants' residential intentions (Naim 1985; Zelinsky 1971). First, there are considerable variations in the time period involved: one spouse may come home monthly, while the other returns only once a year. Second, a circular migrant may have the intention of sending for his family to join him and of settling permanently in the *pangarantoan* (migration area), but due to economic insecurity this plan may never be realized.

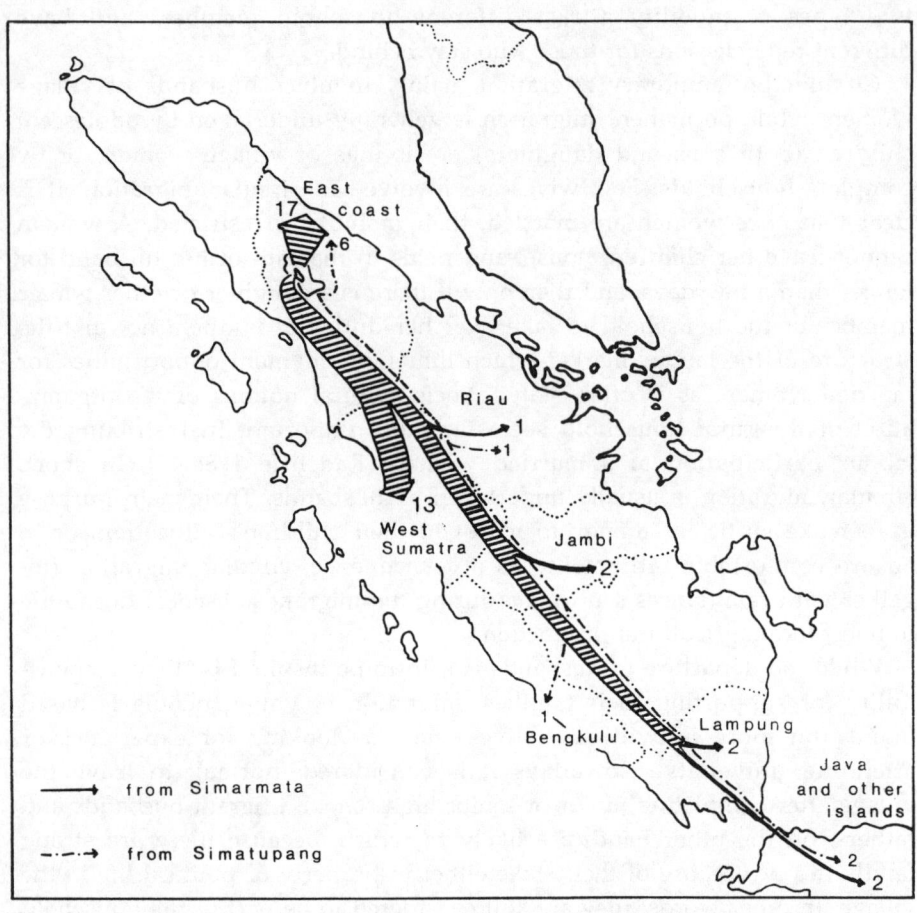

Map 4. Destinations of migrant husbands from Simatupang and Simarmata, with absolute numbers indicated

Migration of husbands

When asked about the migration experiences of their household, dozens of adult women in Simatupang (Muara) told me that when their husbands were younger they regularly left the village to look for employment elsewhere (*mangaranto*). Many moved to East Sumatra or Simalungun to work as farm labourers. The migration was usually for a few months, during the slackest period in agriculture at home. Bringing their own hoes and cooking utensils, they would live in the field huts or houses of their employers. They were paid in both food and cash. In the sixties tractors started to replace these labourers. In the Simalungun village where Clauss (1982) conducted his research, the last Toba Batak migrant workers came in 1973. Other Simatupang women told me their husbands had been offshore fishermen or had worked for oil companies in the south (Palembang). Several others had opened additional rice fields outside Muara, for instance in the swampy coastal area of *kabupaten* Labuhan Batu. The husbands, sometimes accompanied by their wives, went down from the highlands twice a year for planting and harvesting. For some seasonal migrants this was a transitional status only; sooner or later they would take their families and become permanent settlers in the new environment. Those who were less lucky, however, were forced to abandon their land and return to Simatupang due to frequent illnesses, flooding of the fields, or plagues of insects.

Once double-cropping was introduced in Muara during the seventies, seasonal migration of husbands waned. Due to more intensive cultivation, demand for labour grew and those with some land saw their rice yields increase. Consequently, at the time of my study in 1988, only in 13 households (6 percent of the total) were husbands reported to have been away for part of the previous year. During the off-season, six of them worked as harvesters in other rice areas, mainly in East Sumatra where wages are twice as high, or in the neighbouring area of Balige.[13] Their absence rarely exceeded a month and, in general, the men quickly returned to the village for the next season when the rice started to yellow again. The other husbands stayed away for longer periods (three merchants, a taxi driver, and an offshore fisherman) or came home regularly (two civil servants) (see Map 4). Long-term and long-distance migration of married men was rare, and was found in only four (of these thirteen) households. My impression (supported by comments from others) was that in the later cases the reasons for separation were mainly personal, such as the couple's disharmonious relationship. Women from Simatupang frequently expressed the view that a married couple should live together, since this is 'natural'.

---

[13] They were accompanied by two unmarried men from Simatupang.

In the Simarmata region, on the other hand, the temporary absence of husbands was generally accepted as 'a fact of life'. Thirty-nine households, or 12 percent of the total, were de facto headed by women because the husbands were circular migrants for most of the year. With few exceptions, these men were engaged in commerce, selling cloth or kitchenware in other parts of Sumatra.[14] Folk tradition holds that Samosir Batak are traders, and that trade is a rational response to the unfavourable agricultural situation.

> Nai Jusun (55) was one of the first village women whose husband (Ama Jusun, now 58) migrated to Aceh in the early fifties, working as a hawker on the rubber estates. Nai Jusun stayed behind with one child. After a few years, her husband moved to Kisaran (East Coast) because of anti-Batak hostility among Acehnese Muslims. In Kisaran he bought some land to build himself a house. Finally, in the seventies, he tried his luck in Tanjung Karang (Lampung), some 1,000 kilometres away. Although he earned more money, he saw his family only once every two years. By the time I came to know Nai and Ama Jusun, Ama had retired to Simarmata, and seemed content living in the village. Their two sons have received higher education and now hold steady jobs in the urban police force.

When they first arrive in town, most traders stay with friends or relatives (Hugo 1975:461; Mantra 1981:159). Urban kin usually provide shelter and funds during the initial period, when the new migrant is still struggling to find his way and set up his enterprise. Living with co-villagers also gives the men the opportunity to send home messages or money when one of them returns to the village. For a wife, this network is also important in another way since, to a certain extent, it means social control over her husband's activities. Although the kin network is no guarantee, a wife will probably soon find out should her husband have an affair. One woman from Simarmata told me that when her husband proposed to move to Peninsular Malaysia where earnings were much higher, she rejected the plan since she did not know anyone there.

The importance of a network of trading acquaintances is also apparent from the husbands' destinations in Map 4. The majority remain within the province of North Sumatra, mainly in the plantation areas on the East Coast or in the vicinity of Medan. The second most popular destination is West Sumatra (Padang and Bukittinggi), 650 kilometres away. The remaining husbands work in the provinces of Riau, Jambi, and Lampung, and some had even moved to other islands.

---

[14] Toba Batak women can also be temporarily absent to engage in trading activities. The *Ina Batak* in Jakarta are a well-known example. It seems that many of these women are single (often widows) or have grown-up children that permit them maximum mobility. In his study in neighbouring Pangururan, Wolfs (1988:75) found four female circular migrants. In Simarmata, however, I met only one female circular migrant, a widow who engaged in *mardua huta*, cultivating land in both Simarmata and Tebing Tinggi, while her schoolgoing daughter remained at home on her own.

Apart from three men – two of whom worked for oil companies, and one as a guard – all migrant husbands from Simarmata were reported to be traders. Most of them bought goods in town and sold them in remote villages, or they travelled to the plantations when labourers had just received their monthly wages. They generally purchased on credit and also allowed customers to buy on credit (*parkredit*).

Although the wives claimed their migrant husbands were all *parjaja* (hawkers or pedlars), or *dagang* (traders), the men had a wide range of incomes and living standards. Most were just petty traders who barely subsisted from the profits of their business. They usually had limited stock and income, and very few could make the transition to entrepreneur. Most were confined to their present small-scale trading by lack of capital, connections, experience, and ambition. They revisited the same neighbourhoods every few weeks, collecting a few coins from each debtor and leaving new articles with some. Over a six-month period, with accrued interest, they supposedly made a profit of 100 percent. Indeed, some of the hawkers said that they made good money and could earn some Rp 250,000 to 500,000 (US$ 125–250) a month. They are, however, in a vulnerable position, since the relationship between buyer and seller is mainly based on mutual trust. If several clients do not pay their debts, a hawker may easily go bankrupt.

Hawkers generally earn the respect of villagers for their perseverance and for their knowledge of the world, which enables them to sell their goods. They are distinguished in social rank by what they sell, their capital expenditure and turnover, and their living standards. Cloth (*abit*) requires greater capital than kitchen utensils (*alat dapur*), the two main articles sold, and for that reason cloth hawkers hold higher rank in their home village. From the Simarmata region there were 22 husbands who sold cloth and 12 who sold kitchenware. Instead of selling articles, some used their savings to engage in money lending, a profitable business since high interest rates can normally be charged if one has the spare cash, as well as the strong arm required to collect. Only four husbands could afford to engage in this kind of business.[15]

Not only may the migrants change their merchandise, the example of Ama Jusun above shows that some of them also regularly change location, seeking more profitable markets. Eleven men were said to have moved several times before settling in their present location.[16] The relative success

---

[15] The villagers said that Christian Toba Batak have an advantage as money lenders in Muslim areas because Muslims themselves are not allowed to lend money. Some of them engaged in a combination of money lending and selling cloth. Therefore, when added up, the total number of hawkers exceeds that of 36.

[16] This is in contrast with the situation in neighbouring Pangururan, described by Wolfs (1988:77), where all circular migrants were reported to stick to their original destination.

of the hawkers can also be measured by their property: 16 had been able to buy a motorbike for their trading trips, and nine had their own house in the *pangarantoan*. But on the whole, the life of hawkers is hard and full of risk, and while the majority of them never progress beyond petty trade, it is the socially mobile traders whom people have in mind when comparing the advantages of migration with residence in the village. Half of all migrant husbands have been away from their family for five to fifteen years; the other half have been absent for fifteen years or more. Even the migration of the latter is still considered temporary, in the sense that they regularly visit their wife and children in Simarmata. Some of them, particularly those who travel long distances, see their family just now and then, for instance once every year or two, but others come home more often: quarterly or every six months. They return to the village for religious holidays (especially at Christmas), or when an emergency arises.[17]

Why do these husbands leave on their own? Some women say that having 'one foot in town and one in the village' is a necessity for many Batak families that do not have enough resources to survive in either place.[18] Moreover, villagers who have barely enough land to live on face the serious problem of financing their children's schooling. The income from farming is seldom sufficient to pay for secondary, let alone tertiary, education. Since local income-generating opportunities are scarce, many couples see no other option than splitting up the household. The cultural expectation is that the man will fill the main breadwinning role and earn a cash income.

Another reason women stay behind is because men do not want to sever ties with their home area, but prefer to leave their wives to guard their property (*manjaga arta*). Indeed, 24 of the 39 migrant husbands had inherited some land in the village. Wives not only helped accumulate the starting capital or sold their own possessions to help finance the migration, but also cared for the children and tended the crops during the husband's absence. A final reason some women gave for not accompanying their husbands into town is that men alone have easier access to work, especially as hawkers. The women did not see any productive role for themselves in the urban environment and they said they would miss the independence a farm gave them.

[17] In contrast to the situation in Simatupang, where irrigated rice farming has definite peak labour demands which require a husband's return, agricultural activities in Simarmata are more evenly spread over the year.
[18] Interestingly, one migrant husband who had previously lived in Padang with his family claimed that life had become more expensive since his wife and four children had returned to Simarmata due to an illness in the family. His wife no longer being around, he now has to pay for his food and his laundry. Moreover, he said, giving me a wink, 'single men are more inclined to spend money on drinks and other forms of entertainment'.

The decision for the husband to go on his own was usually taken jointly. In some cases, after hearing of the successful experiences of others, the wife actually suggested and encouraged her spouse to migrate.

> Nai Yanti (42) recounts how her husband finally decided to try his luck in the *pangarantoan*. They got married in 1968. He was born in Simarmata and she came from a neighbouring village. Their family soon began to grow until they had eight children. 'The children went to school with only one cup of tea and a handful of cassava for the whole day.' In order to augment the family income, Ama Yanti had left for the East Coast six years before to hawk kitchen utensils. According to his wife, after two months he felt desperately homesick for his young children and returned home. At Nai Yanti's instigation, he tried his luck again in 1988, this time in Berebes, Central Java. Nai Yanti shows a letter he recently sent by express delivery – with an excess of stamps – to his wife, a clear sign he still feels homesick. In her view, he should try a little longer since peddling in Java can be very successful.

All couples agreed that circular migrants should return to the village at the end of their working lives when they became unfit to travel. It is clear that for the majority, emotional ties and to some extent their economic security (in the sense of land and kinship ties) remain in the village.[19] They know that there is a limit to their occupational mobility in the *pangarantoan*. Absence of adequate state welfare means that migrants afflicted by old age, illness, or misfortune (*ndang marnasib*) have to return to the care of their rural relatives for want of alternatives. Ideally, migrants' earnings are sufficient to educate their children so that they can expect some support from the children in their old age, a topic explored in Chapter VI. Some of the returned hawkers occupied special positions, for example the village head in Simarmata. Experiences in the *pangarantoan* can give returned circular migrants a greater ability to act in local economic and political systems. They have acquired a 'cosmopolitan education', knowledge and links produced by outside work (Connell et al. 1976:131).

Finally, husband migration can also be the first step towards 'familial migration'. The longer a man stays in one location, the more he feels the need for company, not only to run the household but also to satisfy his emotional needs. Of course, the wife may also miss her husband and urge him to let his family join him if his enterprise turns out to be relatively successful. In fact, nowadays a family's reunion in the *pangarantoan* is an important sign of a migrant's success (he is *tolap*, or financially capable) (see

---

[19] In contrast, *pangaranto naung pegawai* (migrated civil servants) rarely return. Their guaranteed salary and old-age pension give them more security in the urban environment (Bruner 1961). This applies not only to the Toba Batak, but also, for instance, to the Minangkabau (Naim 1985:117). Evidence from other studies (Hugo 1975; Mantra 1981), however, indicates that in West and Central Java even migrants with permanent positions prefer to retire in their home villages.

also Kato 1982:152). Sometimes, the wife starts trading as well when she arrives in the city. Unfortunately, the nature of my village-based investigations does not allow me to give a more comprehensive picture of family migration. It seems, however, that for many Toba Batak migrant households the assumption of dual interests (in village and town) is no longer valid today. The rapid expansion of urban areas and the attraction of large markets have motivated many hawkers to settle permanently in the *pangarantoan*. Split households with husband and wife living in different places no longer fit in with the national ideology of the *keluarga sejahtera* (the safe and prosperous family). Moreover, now that women are catching up with men in terms of education, they feel more confident in an urban environment. This goes along with my earlier statement that present population movements are dominated by emigration rather than circulation.[20]

Migration of children

While a considerable number of village women have to manage without their husbands for extended periods, many more are confronted with the out-migration of at least one of their children. In the past, temporary residence outside the home village constituted a critical rite of passage to male adulthood, with young men spending time alone in other areas, either for work or education, before returning to settle down and marry in the village. What we see today, however, is that few of these young men come back. And it is no longer only young men who go to urban areas: for an increasing number of young women as well, rural life has little to offer. Most children, who see all wealth coming from outside, quickly perceive the importance of migration. After finishing their education, male and female youth alike leave for the cities in large numbers. Still single, they are relatively free to migrate. To search for work, higher education, and profitable activity – when home offers none of these – are socially acceptable explanations for motives more difficult to express. Of course higher pay can be earned in town. But apart from economic opportunities, young people stress that the city provides better educational and recreational facilities. It is also an escape from the conditions of rural life. Life in town looks easier and more pleasant. In the village, 'amusements are few and obligations numerous'. Moreover, parents are proud to see their children well dressed and having a salaried position in town. And as more and more people leave, the

---

[20] In both villages there were also households which, having migrated permanently for some reason or other, had to return to their home village. I found 20 returned households in Simatupang and nine in Simarmata.

self-esteem of those who stay behind drops still further. Villagers repeatedly reminded me of the fact that young men who remained in the *huta* were those who were unable or too 'lazy' to migrate. A low opinion of farming is widespread, especially among young people. This situation is not unique for North Tapanuli. Vredenbregt, who did research on the island of Bawean (East Java) in the late fifties, notes:

> 'The contrast between the life of peasant and fisherman on Bawean and the opportunities in Singapore, which were brought to the attention of the stay-at-homes, also led to *merantau* and thus to migration. This undermined a sense of the inevitability of living on Bawean, and brought about a feeling of unease, which is such an important psychological condition for emigrating.' (Vredenbregt 1964:117.)

The reasons for migration given by migrants' mothers are all very similar: their children moved away in order to make money and to settle permanently elsewhere. To most women, it was in the natural course of things that their children left after finishing school: '*Merantau lebih hormat*', or 'Migration has more status'. Whenever I asked male adolescents why they did not move to town, they replied that they did not have enough education or skills, so they were forced (*tarpaksa*) to stay in the village. Likewise, these young men working in agriculture were generally pitied by age-mates who had migrated.

Today, daughters migrate almost as often as sons. My census data show that daughters constituted 48 and 42 percent of all permanent migrants in *desa* Simatupang and Simarmata, respectively, either having left on their own or together with their husbands. This is a fairly recent phenomenon, however. According to elderly villagers, daughters moved away in the past either to be with their families or to marry. They were not encouraged to leave their homes for other reasons, because their contribution to household and agricultural work was essential. Moreover, Toba Batak parents thought that if girls were to move elsewhere without supervision, they would go astray and would consequently be at a disadvantage when they entered the marriage market (Siahaan 1983). Also, during the colonial period there were no respectable jobs in the urban areas for any but the most highly educated young single women (S. van Bemmelen 1992). Nevertheless, one older village woman told me that when she was in her late teens she had gone to town with a female friend without their parents' approval to experience life there and look for work.

During recent decades girls have clearly developed higher aspirations due to better education and expansion of low-paying jobs in government and industry. In North Tapanuli these aspirations directly lead to migration, and actually the daughters' only alternative is marriage in the region. In recent decades nearly all women who remained within the subdistrict have done so because of their marriage to a local man. Those who left for education rarely returned, since they either found employment or a husband in the towns and cities where they had attended school.

When I asked women why their daughters had migrated, I noticed that the migration of lowly educated daughters was often described as *ikut suami* (following one's husband), even in cases where the daughter had left on her own prior to marriage. My interviews suggest that there is a need to examine this 'associational migration' more closely. I found that the female role in many of these movements (which in the past were presumed to be initiated wholly by husbands and fathers) was often far from that of a passive follower.[21] Talking about her daughter's departure to Palembang, a woman sighed: 'She does not want to marry. She just behaves like a man.' There is still cultural pressure for daughters to remain under the surveillance and protection of their family. Sons have more freedom to move than daughters and are better equipped in terms of education, training, and access to work.

While in other parts of Indonesia female migration is often attributed to increasing proletarianization of the agricultural workforce (Hugo 1985; Collier et al. 1974), this is not the case for the Toba Batak. As we shall see in Chapter V, no major agrarian transformations have taken place in North Tapanuli. Rather, the recent influx of young, unmarried females into the cities is related to the wider social and economic changes Indonesia has experienced in the last quarter century. These changes have reshaped the roles of women and increased their propensity to migrate. These include higher levels and changing patterns of education, increased mass media exposure, and the 'transportation revolution'. As a result, more young women, usually unaccompanied, leave the village in pursuit of work or higher education. They want to improve their standard of living and, in many cases, to achieve individual freedom, a response to shifting norms in society (Ariffin 1978; Rodenburg 1993). They migrate to an urban setting in order to escape drudgery in the fields and subordinate positions in the village economy.

In sum, in more ways than I expected, Toba Batak daughters are like sons: they migrate in their late teens or early twenties, they are usually single, and education is the most significant motivating factor. Individual women travel with female friends and relatives or look for work on their own. They

---

[21] There may also be associational migration of men. During my stay in Simarmata, a 21-year-old man was married to a Toba Batak tradeswoman living in Padang. She was five years his senior, which is rather exceptional among Toba Batak, but her business was said to be thriving. Village gossip had it that this was how she had 'arranged' her husband, for she was squint-eyed and thought to be unattractive, while he was handsome, albeit the son of a landless widow. He had never migrated before, but went to Padang straight after the marriage.

feel that they have the right to do this and they are aware of the employment opportunities because of other villagers' experiences. In the words of a Simarmata woman, aged 22:

> 'For me, the reason to go to town was to gain experience. When we stay in the village we don't gain experience, we just live in the mud. I wanted to be independent. Moreover, all my friends had left. Some went for education, some were asked to come and stay with a brother or sister, some already have a nice job. When you stay in the village, there are no friends left.'

But there are also differences. Compared to the migration of sons, the economic motives of daughters are mixed with social and family factors that additionally constrain or facilitate a daughter's mobility. As one girl (a nineteen-year-old factory worker in Medan) put it:

> 'To be honest, I do not dislike farming, but the problem is that you are never self-reliant (*mandiri*). We women are still dominated by *adat* rules. We just help our parents – that's what they call "working together". After harvest we only get a pittance; the whole earnings are controlled by our parents. If we need something we have to ask for it. If boys help their parents, you could say that at least they are investing in their own future land. But for girls it is different because they do not inherit. Sometimes, parents will allow a daughter to cultivate a field on her own, and have her own harvest – only then do you feel autonomous (*berdikari*).'

Occupations and destinations of children who migrated

In line with the fact that more boys than girls attend secondary and tertiary education (see Chapter VI), Table 4 indicates that more sons than daughters have found employment in the public sector (white-collar workers and teachers). This is evident in both villages, but the differences are more outspoken in Simarmata. It is probably the better economic situation in Simatupang which enables more parents to provide both their sons and daughters with education and to secure them white-collar jobs. The relatively large number of migrant students from Simarmata can be explained by the absence of a senior high school within commuting distance, which means that children who want secondary education must move to Pangururan or Pematang Siantar.

Few women reported that their children work as wage labourers in the private sector. By and large, Toba Batak frown on the idea of a blue-collar job. They express a preference for independent work. Young men with little education often find work on buses and lorries, the main form of transport in Sumatra. Usually a bus or lorry crew works as a team and team members are often connected by kinship ties.

In both Simatupang and Simarmata, many daughters were said to be occupied in agriculture elsewhere. The large percentage when compared to migrant sons is striking. Most of these daughters appear to have moved

Table 4. Occupations of children age 15 and over who migrated

	Simatupang				Simarmata			
	sons		daughters		sons		daughters	
Farmer	28	12%	56	25%	10	6%	27	21%
Blue-collar	26	11%	20	9%	14	8%	6	5%
White-collar	68	28%	21	9%	18	10%	3	2%
Teacher	36	15%	37	16%	7	4%	11	8%
Student	44	18%	37	16%	50	28%	20	15%
Trader	17	7%	14	7%	67	37%	40	30%
Housewife	0	0%	30	13%	0	0%	8	6%
Other	22	9%	11	5%	13	7%	17	13%
Total	241	49%	226	44%	179	64%	132	46%

Notes: Percentages in bottom row express the proportion of children migrants to total children (migrants and stayers) of that sex. Percentages in the other rows give the proportion of that occupation to total children migrants of that sex.

away because of marriage with a farmer from elsewhere, or they had left with their husbands for one of the land colonization areas. For Simarmata daughters, to engage in trade was the most popular option and they did so almost as often as Simarmata sons (30 compared to 37 percent).

Interestingly, in both villages, few daughters were said to work as domestics or in factories (for example in a biscuit or cigarette factory), occupations rather popular in other parts of Indonesia and in peninsular Malaysia (Heyzer 1982; Jones 1984; Mather 1985; D. Wolf 1990).[22] Many Batak families, characterizing factory work as sexually or morally loose, refuse to allow their daughters to seek such employment. This can be demonstrated by the fact that, despite the general lack of employment opportunities in North Tapanuli, a textile factory in nearby Balige faced a serious labour shortage (*Analisa* 1987).

While in Medan, I met several Toba Batak girls who worked in factories. At the most they earned some Rp 100,000 (US$ 50) a month – not a small wage, but they had to work from seven in the morning until seven in the evening. The majority of them had completed senior high school; they said that their parents could not pay for further education (*ndang tolap*). Their main motive for doing this kind of work was not to have to depend on their parents in the village and 'to gain experience':

---

[22] It appeared that for some girls lending a hand in a relative's household was an important means of adaptation to urban life and the urban labour market. It is thus possible, for example, that the actual number of student migrants is smaller, while the actual number of migrants working as domestic servants (or working in any other low-valued occupation) is larger.

'In fact, I never planned to migrate and work in a factory, but when I saw my friends on their visits home I also wanted to go to Medan. They had nice clothes, went shopping in the big *plaza*, and gained a lot of experience. I thought, if I stay in Simatupang my future will be worse than if I go to the city. So I took courage to leave the village, but until now the rewards are disappointing.'

Destinations

According to the 1930 census, during the first decades of this century Simalungun and Asahan to the northeast were the most common destinations for Toba Batak migrants. These destinations were directly related to the migrants' occupations, most of whom were engaged in farming. A large number of villagers in Simatupang and Simarmata reported that their children remained within the province of North Sumatra, but a substantial number also appeared to live in other parts of Sumatra and in Java. This is summarized in Maps 5, 6, 7, and 8.

Table 5 shows that Toba Batak sons and daughters have not only moved further away, they have also turned away from agriculture, increasingly opting for office work in urban areas. However, faced with the scarcity of white-collar jobs within North Sumatra, educated people nowadays sometimes have to travel to other Outer Islands to take advantage of their relatively high level of schooling when compared to the level of the indigenous population. As discussed in Chapter VI, there is an almost excessive preoccupation with getting a position in government service, not because of the salary involved – which is low – but because of prestige, old-age pensions, and other 'fringe benefits'.

While for many years rural-to-rural migration was possible because of the existence of an agricultural 'frontier' where lands on the periphery were available for colonization, this frontier has now virtually disappeared. Likewise, the once flourishing plantations of the former East Coast have largely ceased to attract new migrants. Instead, the urban centres of Medan, Tebing Tinggi, and Pematang Siantar, and last but not least Jakarta, have gained in popularity.[23] In 1930 Toba Batak comprised just under 2 percent of the Indonesian population in Medan (almost half of Medan's residents were non-Indonesians). We have no information on ethnic composition since 1930, because ethnic affiliation has not been elicited in government surveys after that time. But Pelly (1983) estimated the Toba Batak population in Medan in 1981 at 14 percent, making them the most populous ethnic group after the Javanese, who accounted for 29 percent of the population. In

---

[23] The popularity of urban over rural destinations is also reflected in the national situation: between 1950 and 1975 the population of urban centres increased three times more rapidly than that of the countryside.

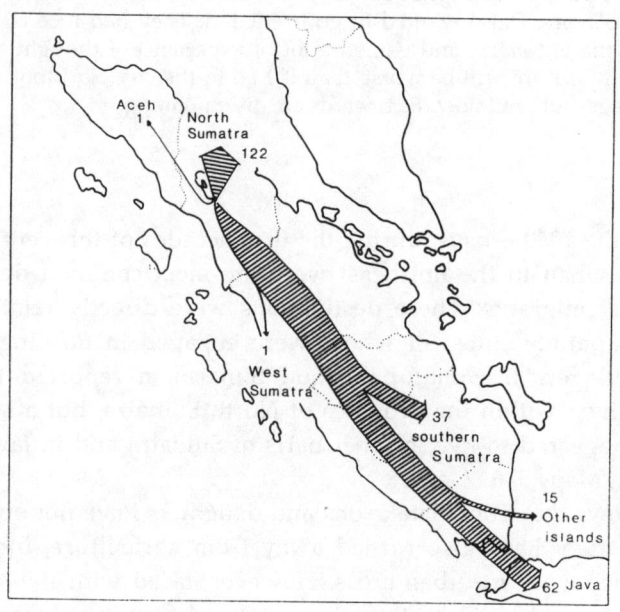

Map 5. Regional destinations of Simatupang sons

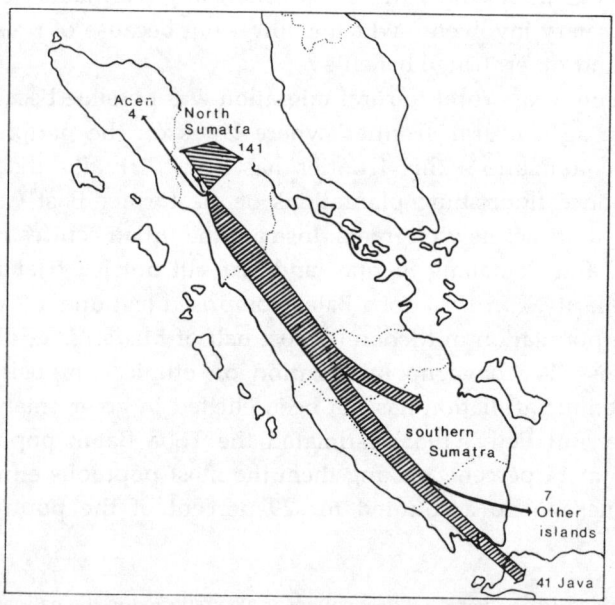

Map 6. Regional destinations of Simatupang daughters

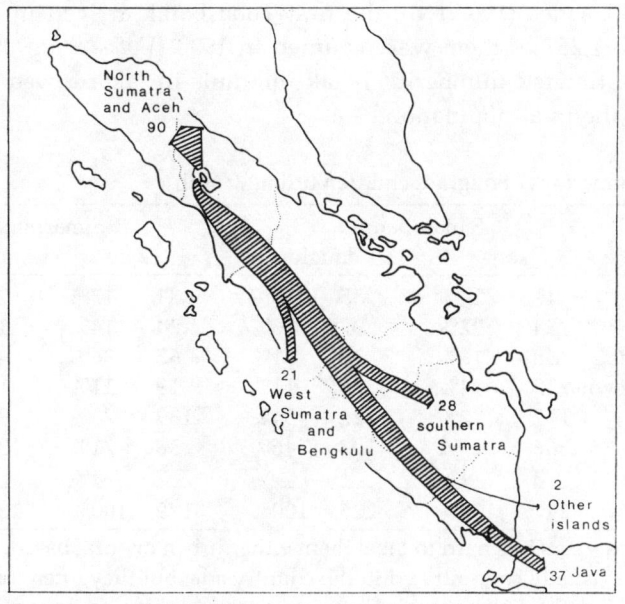

Map 7. Regional destinations of Simarmata sons

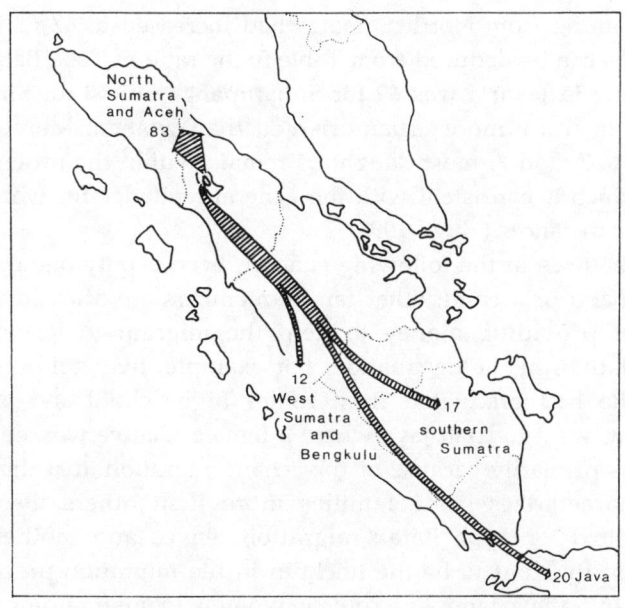

Map 8. Regional destinations of Simarmata daughters

Jakarta as well, the proportion of Toba Batak has increased rapidly. According to Castles (1967:168), the first Toba Batak arrived in the capital in 1907, while 1,267 of them were counted in 1930 (*Volkstelling 1930*, I:149). In 1961, the estimated number of Batak migrants in Jakarta was 20,700, or 1.6 percent of the total population.

Table 5. Destinations of migrant children (urban/rural)

	Simatupang				Simarmata			
	sons		daughters		sons		daughters	
Medan	47	20%	35	16%	31	17%	25	19%
Jakarta	54	22%	37	16%	24	14%	12	9%
other cities	38	16%	25	11%	65	36%	43	33%
regional towns	33	14%	25	11%	19	11%	16	12%
Urban	172	72%	122	54%	139	78%	96	73%
Rural	66	27%	103	46%	38	21%	36	27%
Unknown	3	1%	1	0%	2	1%	0	0%
Total	241	100%	226	100%	179	100%	132	100%

Notes: For hawkers it is hard to label them either urban or rural based. Their hawking activities are usually concentrated in the countryside, but they often live in or near an urban area. For the latter reason I have categorized them as 'urban'. 'Cities' means provincial capitals.

While in 1930 the ratio of women to men among the Batak in Jakarta was only 48 to 100 (856 men and 411 women, *Volkstelling 1930*, I:149), the ratio for those coming from North Sumatra had increased to 67 in 1961 (Castles 1967:190). As can be deduced from Table 5, the ratio of Toba Batak daughters to sons living in Jakarta was 69 for Simatupang, and 50 for Simarmata. On the whole, men are more urban-oriented than women. Moreover, as seen in Maps 5, 6, 7, and 8, most daughters remain within the province of North Sumatra, which is consistent with the general tendency for women to travel over shorter distances (Hugo 1993).

As we shall see in the following chapter, even if only one person moves, be it a husband or a child, other family members are often involved, either in terms of providing money to help the migrant to leave, or hosting migrant relatives at the destination. For example, five children from Simatupang, who had graduated from senior high school and were seeking employment, went to Irian Jaya where a female relative worked as a schoolteacher. It is primarily because of this 'chain migration' that the tendency to migrate characterizes some families more than others. Because of the 'family context' of Toba Batak migration, wives and mothers who stay behind often turn out to be the linchpin in the migration process. In order to understand the prominent role of women in maintaining the kinship network, the next chapter will start with a discussion of Toba Batak family organization, rules of marriage, and residence and inheritance practices. It is necessary to take into account women's place in the kinship system and the household, which on the one hand gives them ample room for manoeuvre within the realms under their control, but on the other hand severely restricts their social and economic freedom in the wider society.

CHAPTER IV

The moral economy of kinship

Migration provides freedom. Even then, however, influence from and obligations to kin continue to persist across considerable distances. In Toba Batak society, kinship is very important, for men as well as for women. Marriage rules, in particular, have enormous significance for women: where they live, with whom they ally, whether they can leave, and on what terms. Kinship also determines access to economic resources, including ancestral land. In this chapter, I shall highlight the crucial role the kinship system plays in determining the extent to which women may gain or lose control over their lives because of migration of close relatives.

Stationary men and women sojourners

> 'When the daughter is still with her parents, her right with respect to her parents is to aid. After she goes to live in her husband's village, her right to aid is with respect to her husband. Then, if she becomes a widow, her right to aid is directed towards her son. Why? Because as long as there has been adat, the person who receives aid may not inherit possessions or heirlooms. Such is the right of a mother or daughter. From her birth until she becomes a widow and then dies, her only right is to aid.' (Tampubolon 1964:314-5, translation in Niessen 1985:77.)

Whether a Toba Batak child is male or female is decisive for its future rights in the kinship system. A newborn male child is hailed as 'guardian of the house, someone to repair the earthen walls [of the villages], an addition to the [marga] population' (Niessen 1985:76). He can claim membership of a clan, irrespective of whether he is married or not, and, consequently, is a permanent inhabitant of a village and owner of a house. As in other societies based on patrilineal descent, sons are valued among traditional Toba Batak as a source of security for parents' declining years.

Daughters are also automatically members of their father's clan, with residential rights in their *huta* and farming rights on the land. However, within their natal clan they are always seen as 'transient' because they will eventually marry and leave. Consequently, daughters do not count as inheritors, because upon marriage they cast their lot with their husband and his *marga*. When a woman dies, she is buried in the grave of her husband's lineage, and not in that of her natal lineage. What happens upon marriage is that women move while men remain stationary. Patrilocal residence (meaning the couple after marriage lives with the husband's father) and the necessity for women to migrate from their previous home can be seen as weakening women's social and economic position in the household and the community.

Although Toba Batak adhere to patrilocal residence there is some room for flexibility, and a man who is unable to bring to a marriage his proper portion of the establishment fund (costs of setting up the household; see Fegan 1983:32) might go to live with his wife's lineage. A newly-wed couple may decide to live near those parents who can make the best offer. My census data on Simatupang show that in 17 instances (8 percent) the wife was born in the village of the couple's residence while the husband was from another village. In Simarmata I counted 24 cases (21 percent) of such matrilocally married couples (*sonduk hela*).[1] While women who stay in their natal village may be socially supported in their own family, the general practice of patrilocality scatters women among different families while clustering related men in neighbouring ones.[2] In this respect, some authors discussing patrilineal descent groups even refer to women's essential 'rootlessness' (Bisilliat 1983), or depict women as 'peripheral sojourners' (Josephides 1985).

A Toba Batak woman finds herself in a similarly ambiguous position. As Niessen (1985:75) aptly puts it, a Batak woman is placed between her father's clan (*hula-hula*), who gives her as wife to her husband's clan, and the clan of her husband's father, who accepts her as daughter-in-law (*boru*).[3] In a traditionally patriarchal community such as the Toba Batak, membership and position of a woman are subject to change according to periods and

---

[1] In the neighbouring area of Limbong, Sherman (1990:191) found 8 percent matrilocally residing couples. The fact that matrilocality in Simarmata is more widespread than in Simatupang seems paradoxical because in several respects Simarmata is more traditional than Simatupang. As will be discussed in this and the following chapters, the difference is probably due to the relatively low economic value of the land and the frequency of husband migration in Simarmata.

[2] Since several clans can be found in one village, clan exogamy does not necessarily force a woman to leave her village. But marriage usually implies at least a move to another hamlet. The situation within the Simatupang clan is different from the general rule since the Togatorop, Sianturi, and Siburian subclans are allowed to intermarry. As a result, in 1988 in 23 percent of all marital relations both husband and wife belonged to the Simatupang *marga*. While there is no objection in the ancestral homeland (*bona ni pasogit*) to Simatupang intramarriage, in urban areas where people have a wider choice, such relationships are preferably avoided.

[3] The Toba Batak have an intricate kinship system which is the model for their social organization. It connects every one of them in a network of classificatorily extended relations by marriage and by birth. The offspring of the woman are called (*anak*) *boru* by her father and his immediate relatives. The latter are the *hula-hula* or family-in-law of the *boru* and are also regarded as such by the woman after marriage. Together with one's own patrilineal clan (*dongan sabutuha*), the wife receivers (*boru*) and the wife givers (*hula-hula*) are conceived as a unity, referred to as *dalihan na tolu* (Vergouwen 1964:45).

phases in her life, such as the change in her status when she gets married or when she proves her ability to give birth to children and raise them (Simbolon 1994). The fact that women change their group membership at least once in their lives puts them at a disadvantage.

Apart from stressing their relative marginality, it should be noted that women may also make use of their dual position between two *marga* by acting as intermediaries, as we shall see below.

Women in between

> 'The lot of a Batak woman is a peculiar one. One moment she is the most abused, the next the most protected; now she is bent under the hard yoke of the adat and then, again, she becomes arbiter in the circle of her house companions and nearest relations. On the one hand she is treated as a commodity for sale, on the other she not infrequently stands forth, adorned and jewelled.' (Neumann 1887:250; translation in Loeb 1933:48)

As in many other peasant societies, Toba Batak marriages were organized from the standpoint of family solidarity rather than personal choice (Michaelson and Goldschmidt 1971:335). Some kind of systematic exchange of women between clans was favoured for forging new links between clans, or for strengthening already existing ties. Broadly speaking, there are two types of marriage strategies. The first is marrying into a local group, which strengthens the relationships with close kin, for example between father's sister's son and mother's brother's daughter. It was not necessary that men actually exchanged their true sisters, but simply that reciprocal alliances between two clans were maintained. Cross-cousin marriages are said to ensure harmonious relations in the household, keep landed property within the family, reinforce existing kin ties, and be easier to arrange (Vergouwen 1964:45).

The second strategy is marrying out. In this case the interests go beyond the mere retention of property and may have a more political character. Through marriage, connections are established with higher-status or wealthier groups (S. van Bemmelen 1992; see also Wolters 1991:169-70). In the past, marriages were sometimes arranged to obtain vital resources like land or labour. A landed household without sons, for example, could further its interests by marrying a daughter to a young man whose family had too many sons and not enough land. This groom would be willing to live and work on the fields of his wife giver (Vergouwen 1964).[4] In the same

---

[4] In the past every major *marga* had its own tribal territory. In most villages, however, there were a number of minor clans that did not own land. In order to gain access to land they could marry daughters from the land-owning clan, since these daughters sometimes received a piece of land as a wedding gift. We will come back to this in the next chapter.

way, a trader could urge his daughter to marry a potential partner – to ensure mutual trust and avoid being cheated. Or a man who was indebted could offer his daughter as a bride to his creditor, exchanging his debt for the bride-price which he would otherwise have received. The marriage was usually arranged by the kin group, who also determined the amount of bride-price (*sinamot*) to be paid, and it was not uncommon that the young couple knew each other only by sight.

Traditional analysis of kinship systems in anthropology largely ignored women as independent social actors or initiators. The implicit assumption was that women operated within the domestic sphere, while men utilized their links with other men to operate in the public/political domain where alliances between families were created and maintained (Moore 1988:60-1). Women were considered merely one of the mechanisms for establishing those links (Moore 1988:132). Some authors have even viewed marriage as the exchange of women by groups of men, just like any goods can be exchanged (see for instance Lévi-Strauss 1969). Yet, Toba Batak men and women themselves feel that their practices are an essential part of tradition, that kin ought to be compensated for losing a woman's labour and reproductive powers, and that the removal of such customs would mean the collapse of inter-clan exchanges. As demonstrated by S. van Bemmelen (1986: 56), Vergouwen was one of the first Westerners who convincingly refuted the idea of Toba Batak women being 'bought'. I would add that, although women are exchanged *for* goods (money, cattle, etc), they are not exchanged *like* goods. Women still influence the direction of the exchange, and may leave their 'possessors' in case of conflict (Josephides 1985:65).

Through her marriage, a Toba Batak woman contributes to the formation of alliances between two patriclans. She is in a strategic position to learn intimately the characteristics of two households and patriclans. She is not only an intermediary in a symbolic sense, she can also be an effective mediator for promoting cooperation and extending favours between two kin groups (Niessen 1985:84; S. van Bemmelen 1992). Her husband and her father and brothers may find it useful to cooperate in the fields, in building a house, in lending draft animals, or in land transactions. It is the woman's relationship with each of them that guarantees trust. With regard to disputes between agnates, the obvious peacemakers are the affines. As a rule, they are the most suitable intermediaries between parties who stand in equal relationship to them. This is expressed in the following maxim, cited by Vergouwen (1964:65):

> 'The grass is mown and goes into the horse's fodder bag.
> If the daughters, the *boru*, quarrel, their father settles the dispute.
> If the fathers quarrel the *boru* settles the dispute.'

The *boru*'s position as a possible arbitrator may be one of the reasons why parents, in the past, preferred to have one married daughter and her husband and offspring in the paternal house. Conflicts between sons or between a son and his father frequently arise. Because the *hula-hula* (wife givers) are highly esteemed by the *boru* (wife receivers), the mere presence of the *boru* reduces such conflicts (Tobing 1956:138-9).

Furthermore, through their extensive, regular contact with female relatives and friends, Toba Batak women maintain the social relationships between domestic groups that hold the kinship network together. Women stay in constant contact with other relatives, circulating information through the network and mobilizing support during life crises.

Although women 'marry out' and do not receive title to land from their patrilineal kin, they remain members of their natal kin group. They are known all their lives by their patrilineal surname, for they do not change it upon marriage. A woman of the clan Sianturi, for example, will always be known as *boru* Sianturi, a Sianturi daughter. Although after marriage a woman enters into a new family, the relationship between her and her natal family remains close (Nasoetion 1943:36) and her children, particularly her male offspring, will be permanently connected to her lineage (by a son marrying his mother's brother's daughter, as discussed below). The relative density of settlement may facilitate this, as, until recently, most women did not move more than a short journey from their natal lineage areas, and it is quite easy for them to maintain relations with their brothers and fathers. Frequent contact between a woman's natal family and her in-laws is also facilitated by the ideal pattern of matrilateral cross-cousin marriage. The bond of a married woman with her natal family, especially her ties with her brothers (*tulang*), is confirmed in all life-cycle ceremonies: 'The *tulang* is constantly by his sister's side and assists in the upbringing of her children, of whom the eldest son will ideally be his future son-in-law. He treats his sister's daughters as his own and they will be as sisters to his sons.' (Vergouwen 1964:196.) In marital quarrels, separation, or widowhood, a woman can return to her parents' or brother's house, where she is entitled to protection, shelter, and maintenance. Apart from providing economic and social security, a brother is expected to play a ritual role in her children's weddings. As will be argued in Chapter VII, however, material support from brothers is not always forthcoming or necessarily significant, especially if they have migrated.

The ideology of motherhood

Besides establishing alliances between families, another major purpose of marriage for the Toba Batak is continuation of the family line.[5] As I was twenty-eight and childless at the time of my research, many women asked me when I would start having children. They warned me against economic insecurity and loneliness if I grew old without offspring, while pointing out some elderly village women who suffered the plight of childlessness.

On marriage, a Toba Batak woman experiences not merely a change in residence from her natal place to her husband's hamlet but also a change in personal identity. Once she bears a child she is no longer known by the personal name of her childhood; instead, she is given a new name, such as '*Nai* Pasulan', the mother of Pasulan. Although her husband may also call himself *Ama* Pasulan (the father of Pasulan), he can also be referred to by his *marga* name, by his function (for instance, *sintua* = church elder, *pandita* = evangelist, *guru* = teacher, *kepala kampung* = village head) or by his *adat* title (for example, *raja huta*). But a woman's source of social status within the family and in the community is usually the bearing of a child. From a minor household member, she becomes a person who can make demands, first on her husband on behalf of her children, and later on the children themselves. When asked about the ideal number of children women would like to have, most women said they wanted at least five (some of whom could be expected to die at an early age).[6]

It seems that the desire for large families will not change dramatically in the near future. A survey I held among third-year students of the senior high school in Muara indicated that most girls hoped for four children. Interestingly, only six girls (6 percent) agreed with the national slogan '*Dua cukup*' (two children is enough), while 36 percent wanted to have more sons than daughters.[7] Most adult women in Simatupang and Simarmata have heard of modern methods of birth control, but still tend to raise large

---

[5] Many of the decorative features of an *adat* house are concrete prayers for fertility. A carved decoration hanging from the tall peak of the roof is often obviously phallic, expressing a hope for many sons. Carved wooden breasts placed on either side of the main entrance express a hope for many daughters (Lando 1979:57).

[6] I counted the average number of living children for mothers of 45 years and older (i.e. those beyond reproductive age). In both villages the average was 6, which is considerably higher than the fertility rate in the province of North Sumatra (4.17 in 1985), or in Indonesia as a whole (3.26 in 1985) (SUPAS 1987). At the same time, infant and child mortality was high: in Simatupang it was 202 per 1000 live births, while in Simarmata it was 272. Unfortunately, mothers were only asked about their deceased children under four, without any distinction between infants (below age one) and older children. Infant mortality rates for North Sumatra and Indonesia in 1985 were 58 and 71 respectively (SUPAS 1987).

[7] The survey among male students revealed the following figures: the majority desired five children and 63 percent preferred to have more sons than daughters; only three male students intended to follow the government's advice of having only two children.

families. '*Adat* demands we have many children,' they say, 'and moreover, who will take care of us when we are old?' They usually assume that some of their children will leave the village. One woman warned against having too few children, saying: 'If you have only one or two children, they might go away, leaving you alone. But with more children, one will stay behind'. Even one couple in Simatupang, who in their jobs as health-care workers are supposed to promote family planning, have seven children.

Though one might expect women with migrant husbands to have fewer children than those whose husbands are present (Connell 1984; Findley and Williams 1991:53), this does not correspond with my findings. It appears that when return visits occur relatively frequently or, if on an annual basis, for a period of several weeks, the absence of husbands has no effect on the number of children. Or, in the words of one villager, 'When the husbands return to the *pangarantoan*, several wives have become pregnant. If possible, the husband's next visit is then timed with the moment of giving birth'. For young wives left behind by husbands for long periods of time, children are a source of security. The presence of children satisfies partially, if not wholly, their emotional needs. As children become older, they become a source of support to their mothers in the day-to-day running of the household.

On the whole, a fair number of women show a keen interest in birth control if they are still of childbearing age. Over the years it seems that the birth rate has declined somewhat: the 0–4 and 5–9 age groups are smaller than the 10–14 group (see Figure 1), partly a result of the later age at marriage[8] and the family planning activities of the Indonesian government. Despite the active birth control programme, rural women still have limited access to information and methods of family planning that they themselves can control. The government offers free sterilization, but few men give permission and women fear the operation. 'That is only for rich people who do not need to work,' they say.[9]

Having older children gives women a great deal of confidence and support, especially when their husbands are absent. With the help of their children they can fulfil several of their responsibilities independently of other relatives. The less they have to depend on these relatives, the more independent they feel. Moreover, motherhood grants women rights over

---

[8] A check of the records of the Catholic and Protestant churches in Simatupang revealed that the average age at marriage for women was 22 in 1974 and 25 in 1988.
[9] Several women expressed a need for suitable contraception, and they complained that none of the existing methods from the regional health centre were convenient. The most common contraceptive offered, the pill, was said by the women to go badly with hard physical work of the sort women do in the fields. So did the IUD, which only a handful of women have accepted in any case.

the labour of daughters and daughters-in-law. It carries with it control over children's reproduction, such as arranging their marriages. Under patrilineal, patrilocal rule the only way a woman can gain access to productive resources and gain emotional support, security, and some public influence is through her sons. A widowed woman with male offspring, for example, can control the family farm even if legal ownership rights have been transferred to her sons. Women's access to land will be dealt with in more detail in the next chapter. Having a son is also important because it is his responsibility, and that of his wife, to support his parents in their old age.[10] Once daughters have married, they are not expected to carry out this task.

Besides provision for old age, Toba Batak have another reason for desiring sons. The main aim of marriage is to provide offspring for the husband's lineage, and it is only by bearing male children that a woman may guarantee the continued existence of her husband's lineage and also strengthen her own position within his lineage (Bovill 1987:211). Traditionally, it was believed that in the absence of a son, the deceased parents' souls would wander restlessly because there was no one to worship them:

> 'There has to be a son. Sons are simply what a Batak father expects of life. This is the law of the Elders, the law of self-preservation in the face of life and death, the only path that can lead to ultimate peace in a country from where no one returns.' (Renes-Boldingh 1942:6.)

Adoption of a son is rare among Toba Batak. It is not easy to find a boy to foster, for no parent readily parts with a son, whether they have many or few, since sons are the promise of extensive offspring. If parents do so, it is because they want to help a relative. Vergouwen (1964:230) notes that in the past, when there were many uprooted people and slaves, adoption was easier.

Even the fact that a sonless couple has a host of daughters is barely a consolation to them. Daughters cannot bring their parents the necessary offerings to secure them a position in the ranks of souls. However, despite its undeniable patriarchal ideology, Christianity brought Toba Batak women some relief. With the church repudiating ancestor worship, a woman no longer needed to feel guilty about endangering the souls of her husband and herself if there were no male children (Sarumpaet-Hutabarat 1954:8). It is, however, questionable whether this new perspective has been fully accepted by the Batak themselves.

To a woman in particular, sons are crucial as insurance that her husband

---

[10] An adult customarily changes his or her name upon the birth of the first child, thereafter calling him/herself 'father of ...' or 'mother of ...'. Further evidence of the importance of sons is that, if the first child is a girl, some parents prefer to call themselves after a subsequent male child.

will not divorce her or take a second wife for lack of descendants. If no male offspring are produced, blame will usually fall on the woman, as the following quotation illustrates:

> 'Hard and much to be pitied is the fate of a man to whom only daughters are born. And shame be upon the housewife who will not bear him sons.' (Renes-Boldingh 1942:15.)

If her husband has extra-marital affairs, a sonless wife finds herself in a weak bargaining position (Krause 1981:65). I knew one woman with nine daughters and no sons whose husband had a relationship with a young widow from the same village. Even on the eve of the birth of the tenth child (which, thank God, was a boy!), he had to be fetched from his mistress's house. A sonless woman beyond reproductive age is even more at her husband's mercy, as in the following example.

> Nai Ester (about 55) lives in Simarmata and has two daughters of 15 and 11 years old. She rents 2 *rante* (0.08 ha) of land. Her husband has been a migrant for more than ten years, hawking cloth in East Sumatra. After a brief return to the village, he recently left without notice. Only later, Nai Ester learned that her husband had taken a second wife (a younger widow). According to Nai Ester, he had only done so at his family's instigation. He is the sole heir and needs sons to continue the family line. Nai Ester has already reached menopause and it is clear that she will never bear her husband a son. Because her husband did not divorce her but just left, she is entitled to keep the daughters. Fortunately, upon her marriage she had remained in her natal hamlet, which ensures her of a support network of kin. Her younger brother, who lives next door, helps with small amounts of food and cash when necessary.

I was told that in the past, a woman who could bear no children would sometimes urge her husband to take a second wife, preferring to share her husband with another woman rather than be divorced. There were sufficient women in the Batak area to permit at least the chiefs to have several wives, for many of the men were sold into slavery and others migrated to East Sumatra or Malaysia (see also Loeb 1933:40).

Among Toba Batak couples, separation seldom results in official divorce, and accordingly the number of divorced women is, and historically has been, fairly small. In the 1930 census, 1.6 percent of the adult women in Tapanuli were registered as divorcees (*Volkstelling 1930*, IV:54). This low number compared to other ethnic groups is related to the prevailing marriage system, which makes legal divorce virtually impossible. By paying a bride-price to the bride's kin at marriage, rights to the woman's reproductive potential (that is, to any children she may bear) are transferred from her kin group to that of her husband. In contrast, in Indonesian bilateral societies, marital breakdown is fairly frequent. When a bride-price has been paid by the husband's family, it is generally returned if the wife is blamed for the breakdown and not returned if the husband is found guilty. In matrilineal communities, like the Minangkabau, marriages take place without a bride-price and divorce is no exception, being obtainable on either the wife's or the husband's initiative.

One of the consequences of divorce among the patrilineal Toba Batak, then, would be that a woman is not allowed to keep the children because they belong to her husband's *marga*. By having to part with her children, and her sons in particular, she also loses the economic security they might have provided in the future. Moreover, upon divorce, women are not entitled to share in jointly acquired property. It is therefore not surprising that, although I found a fair number of marital separations due to migration of the husband (as discussed in Chapter VII), none of the women desired a legal divorce. Because of the husband's departure, these households do not correspond to the nuclear family promoted by the Indonesian state on billboards and in women's magazines. In the following section I will discuss the main characteristics of the Toba Batak household.

The domestic group

Although households are part of Toba Batak lineages, in 'earning a living' each household operates as a relatively autonomous enterprise. In North Tapanuli over the past 70 to 80 years, there has been a transition from multi-household to single-family dwelling.[11] Elderly people still remember that sometimes as many as six related households shared one large *adat* house. The interior was divided into separate 'rooms', demarcated at night by walls of unrolled mats. Rice stores were kept in separate bins, shawls and other valuables in separate caches. Every domestic group (*ripe*) had its own fireplace in the centre of the house.

Today, despite what postcards and paintings suggest, the traditional image of a large adat house occupied by a patrilineal family no longer corresponds to reality. Instead of extended families, most couples today try to establish a home of their own soon after marriage. The nuclear family has become the basic social and economic group which – ideally – works, sleeps, and eats together.

Traditionally, a young Batak woman married in her mid-teens and joined the household of her parents-in-law. She was viewed as a replacement for daughters given away to other families in marriage, but she lived

---

[11] Although the concepts 'household' and 'family' are often used interchangeably, I define a household as a number of individuals who live together and provide the basic needs for themselves, their children, and relevant others (those who live under one roof and share a common pot). A family, on the other hand, is defined as those who are related by blood or marriage, though not necessarily living together.

without the same emotional security. During the early months of her marriage, the young wife had to work under the authority of her mother-in-law who controlled the household management and budget, while her husband worked under the authority of his father on whom he depended for access to land.

It is not possible to say precisely when the newly-wed couple would set up their own household (*manjae*). If the mother-in-law and the daughter-in-law got on well together, then the live-in arrangement could continue for a while; otherwise the *manjae* took place after only a few months (Tobing 1956:141). In most cases the new couple aspired to have their own household before the birth of their first child. The young wife then received a bag of hulled rice and some kitchen utensils from her mother-in-law, with which she could start her duties as a housewife on her own. The husband received a *hauma panjaean* (rice field as settling-in gift) from his father and perhaps a plot of garden land (*pargadongan*) as well. The young couple then constituted an independent family: they could cook their own food and they were financially independent (Vergouwen 1964:218). Establishing a separate household and receiving land and kitchen utensils thus had special economic significance for each sex with respect to their ability to direct their own labour and receive its rewards. Parents had the moral obligation to provide each of their sons at marriage with the means to set up an independent household. In this context, Fegan (1983:31) introduces the term 'establishment fund', meaning 'the cost of setting up a household with access to a means of living adequate to support the culturally given lifestyle of the last generation'.

The youngest son, the *siampudan*, who would care for his parents once they entered old age, was usually not given a *panjaean* (settling-in gift) because he would continue to live in the parental home after his marriage. So, for an ageing mother the wife of her youngest son was particularly important when she was not able to work herself anymore. Here we see the importance of sons again: without them a woman would have no access to the labour of another younger woman. This was even more crucial if she had no daughters of her own or after her daughters had already married out.

To summarize, the basic pattern of a woman's life in Toba Batak society based on patrilineal descent entailed serial membership in three distinct households. First, she was daughter and sister in her parents' household, but this relationship became weaker after she married out. In the new household of her parents-in-law she would assume the roles of wife and daughter-in-law, both of which had relatively low status. Finally, the couple would become economically independent and set up their own nuclear household. To each of these three households, in succession, a woman contributed all her labour, in productive or reproductive tasks or both, and her

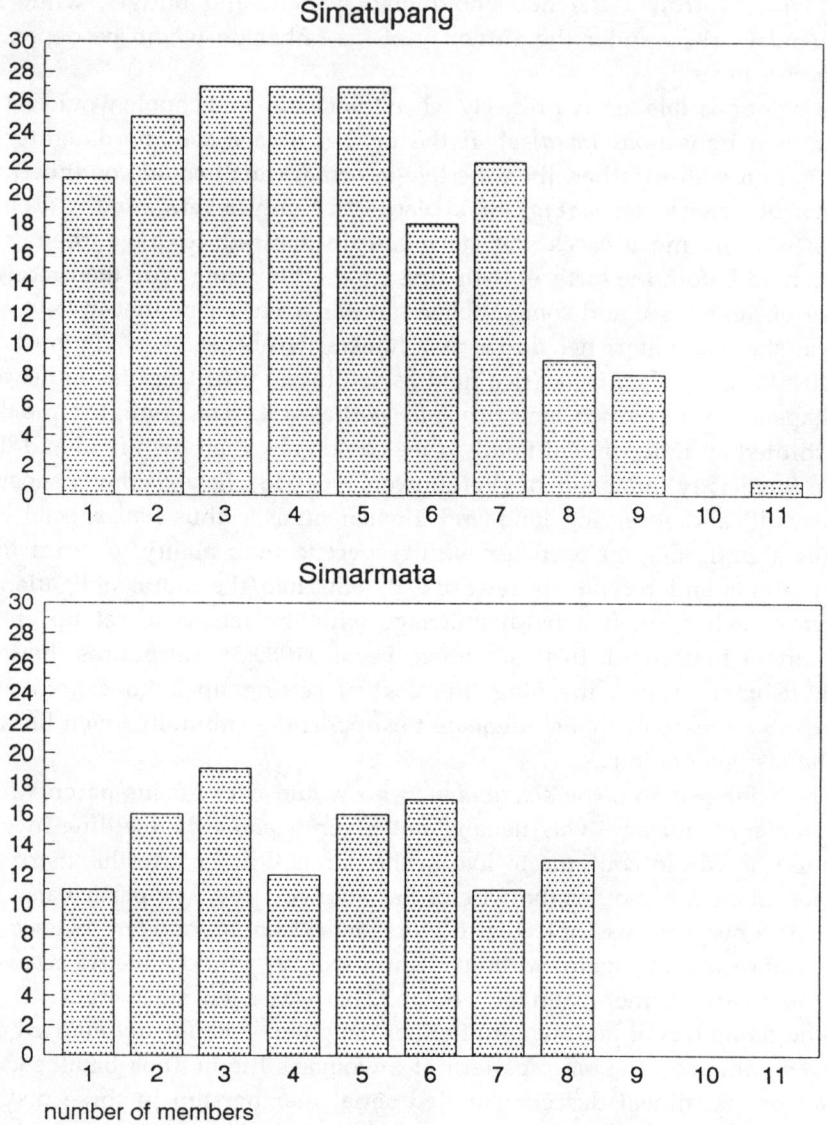

Figure 2. Distribution of households according to size

emotional commitment. From each in turn she derived her sole source of material support as well as her sole sense of identity, meaning, and belonging. In relation to her husband she always had an inferior position, but in due course she would become more powerful if she became a mother, and later a mother-in-law (see also Michaelson and Goldschmidt 1971:338).

Despite the fact that the man is the official household head, husband and wife have their own responsibility and authority. Many Toba Batak women have complete economic responsibility, because the men have either migrated or are unable (because of age or infirmity) to earn a livelihood.

Household composition

When I started my research, Simatupang and Simarmata had 206 and 115 de facto households, respectively. As we can see in Figure 2, they varied considerably in size: while the smallest units were those consisting of one person, the largest units had 11 members. In Simatupang the average number of members per household was slightly higher (4.9) than in Simarmata (4.4). Both were below the average for *kabupaten* North Tapanuli as a whole, which was 5.6 in 1986 (*Kecamatan Muara dalam angka* 1986).[12] It is likely that the relatively small household size can be attributed to out-migration. (As discussed in Chapter II, growth figures for Muara and Simanindo subdistricts were also below the average for North Tapanuli.)

In relation to migration, the term 'household' merits a brief explanation, since most families (62 percent in Simarmata and 54 percent in Simatupang) have at least one member living elsewhere who does not share residence and daily consumption activities, the two characteristics most often attributed to a household. With all the coming and going it was sometimes unclear who to include in the domestic unit. Another problem was that some relatives, though living and working elsewhere, contributed so much to the upkeep of the household (like some migrant husbands) that their presence was felt to the extent that they seemed to be part of the household, even though they did not live there. I will therefore distinguish between de facto household members – those present at the time of enumeration – and de jure household members – those present plus possible absentees. In the villagers' definition, the de facto household is the unit of co-residence and consumption, although this unit is not necessarily self-sufficient since it may partly depend on the earnings of absent migrants. The de jure household is defined as a set of shared relationships among people that entail obligations and revolve around the pooling of common resources (Friedman 1984; D. Wolf 1986). We should be aware that, given the large number

---

[12] According to the 1990 population census, average household size for the whole of Indonesia was 4.5 (*Penduduk Indonesia* 1990).

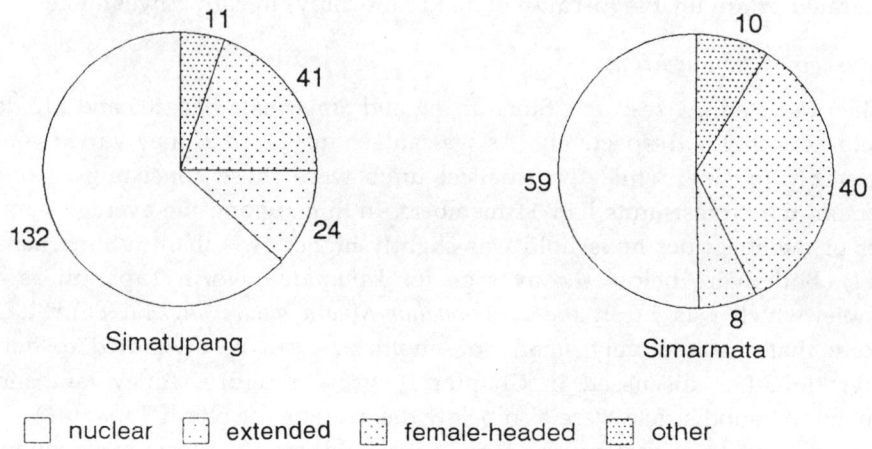

Figure 3. Household types in Simatupang and Simarmata

Notes: Numbers around the circle are absolute numbers of households. In each of the villages, two of the households can be defined as both female-headed and extended family.

of student migrants, a household is not just formed around income pooling, but also around income distribution.

While an independent household is the preferred arrangement, this does not mean that everyone lives in nuclear families (*keluarga*) of husband, wife, and children. The more varied range of household types shown in Figure 3 reflects the fact that, while the nuclear family remains the central unit in most households (64 and 51 percent respectively), its composition varies with the life cycle of its members and the needs of close kin. Many households temporarily accommodate relatives unable to constitute a household of their own.

Figure 3 shows that roughly one-fifth to one-third of all households are headed by females: wives, widows, and unmarried women of various ages. Extended families consist of a nuclear family with one or two elderly parents. In these households, either a parent lives with one of his/her children, or one of the married children together with his/her family resides with the parents. Composition changes not only with the life cycle of the domestic group (as children are born, grow up, and leave to marry or bring in their spouses and begin to have children themselves, as old people and parents grow old and die) but also in response to other social and political factors.

The fact that so many women manage their own household after their husband's death or after separation (while men seldom do so) is an indication of their social and economic independence in the village community. From the 1930 census it appears that 15.7 percent of the adult women in Tapanuli were widows; a corresponding figure for widowers is not given, probably because it was negligible (*Volkstelling 1930*, IV:54-5).[13] While men and women are obviously interdependent, women seem to support themselves alone more successfully than men. The remarriage rate for widows is far lower than that for widowers. For example, in Simatupang I counted 43 widows and only 5 widowers. While this is partly linked to age differences at marriage, what is of interest here are contrasting attitudes towards living without a spouse on the part of men and women. It is widely understood that while a woman is able to manage on her own, no man can live by himself without a wife or daughter to cook, clean, and take care of household finances. 'He cannot even bring a contribution of rice to a feast; his daughter must carry it for him' (Sherman 1990:191).

Although in both villages the majority of female-headed households are headed by widows, about 14 percent, or 40 households, in the Simarmata

---

[13] This percentage is still relatively low because levirate marriages were still common at the time. Only in Aceh is a higher percentage of widows found (19.1 percent), while the percentages in the rest of Sumatra were much lower. In total there were 13,147 female heads of household, of which 121 were unmarried, 1,796 were married, 10,848 were widows, and 347 were divorcees (*Volkstelling 1930*, IV:194).

region[14] were de facto headed by a female as a result of the husband's circular migration. In Simatupang such households accounted for only three percent (6 cases). Within the formal politico-legal system, women who manage farm and household on their own cannot be recognized as de jure heads, but for all practical purposes they serve as the heads of households.

It seems that during recent decades more elderly people live alone in the village because all their children have migrated (some 10 percent of all households in both Simatupang and Simarmata).[15] Some of them are kept company by a grandchild whose parents have migrated (these households form the greatest part of the category 'other' in Figure 4).[16] The children can assist their grandparents in daily tasks like fetching water and firewood, thereby substituting for the labour of their absent parents. Moreover, with their parents having migrated to the city, it is not only said to be healthier for children to live in the Batak highlands, it is also cheaper to raise them in a village than in a city. In fact, fostering children in rural areas provides a means for strengthening links between migrant Toba Batak and those at home. Migrants supplement their parents' income from rice and cassava with cash remittances, and receive rice and other produce from the village, a situation also described in other studies (Izzard 1985; Stivens 1981; Trager 1984). In these cases migration does not simply lead to the loss of household members. Rather, migration may add to the considerable flexibility in domestic arrangements that has always existed among rural Toba Batak, leading to situations in which family members are physically absent and yet remain integral to the support of their rural relatives. Having indicated how the composition of households is affected by migration, we shall now discuss which members of a family are the most likely to migrate.

Family relations and migration

Family and household relations influence who within a family will migrate. Within the family and household, different roles are assigned to its members, based on gender, birth order, and marital status. We have seen that, strictly speaking, Toba Batak women have always been mobile, although mainly over short distances, because due to patrilineal exogamous marriage rules they were expected to marry out and live in their husband's

---

[14] The 'Simarmata region' as used here comprises the three adjacent villages, while 'Simarmata' in Figure 4.2 covers only one village where a survey was carried out (see section on research methods and site selection in Chapter II).
[15] A similar pattern was found by Chan (1983:10) in Malaysia, where in depressed states like Kelantan 'age selective out-migration leads to the neglect of elderly persons who, for various reasons, are much less mobile and have consequently been left behind'.
[16] As can be expected in a society based on patrilineal descent, the majority of the children lived with their paternal grandparents.

village. While female mobility at marriage was thus virtually a requirement of the patrilineal social structure, what is the relationship between Toba Batak kinship rules and male migration?

In general, in societies in which impartible inheritance is the rule, a father will bequeath all the land to one son and the others must either accept subordinate positions or seek their fortune elsewhere. As a result, the population is divided into heirs or potential stayers, and non-heirs or potential migrants (Brandes 1975; Iszaevich 1974; E. Wolf 1966). In these cases migration has become an institutionalized 'safety valve' that inhibits still further fragmentation of the land.

Among the Toba Batak, on the other hand, partible inheritance prevails, resulting in a division of property among all male descendants. Over the centuries the custom of splitting up the family land among all the sons has led to fragmentation and depletion of the soil. North Tapanuli is a poor area which offers little more than farming. Rather than cultivating a tiny plot, many sons choose to migrate. Besides economic considerations, there is another reason men may desire to leave. Despite observing strong feelings of lineage unity and solidarity, Bruner also noticed an overt sibling rivalry, 'a tremendous striving to better one's position in society relative to others in the peer group' (Bruner 1959:58). Indeed, I observed that apart from clan rituals, brothers seldom mix. Commonly, this is attributed to quarrels over inheritance of land or houses. Hirschfeld (1979:143) adds that another conflict might have been the succession of a *raja* (hamlet head), a position which usually passed to the most capable of the *raja*'s sons. In short, blood ties and joint property rights tend to bring together male siblings, while at the same they may be divided by conflicts over land, housing, or title.

Although partible inheritance is the rule, the eldest son (*siahaan*), who replaces his deceased father in the management of the estate, and the youngest son (*siampudan*) occupy special positions in relation to the middle sons (*silitonga*). The youngest son gets the ancestral house because it is his duty to look after his elderly parents and to tend their graves after their death. The first-born has a right to extra privileges or gifts, either better-quality land or a larger part than his brothers (Vergouwen 1964:280-4). The custom in Simarmata (Samosir) appeared to be slightly deviant, as it is the eldest son who both inherits the parental house and has a larger claim on the land (Tobing 1956:142). In general, given the special positions of the eldest and youngest sons, we would expect them to be less migratory than middle sons. As can be seen in Figure 4, I found some evidence for this in Simarmata.

More than half of the Simarmata men were first-born sons and another 17 percent did not have male siblings. The majority of them had inherited

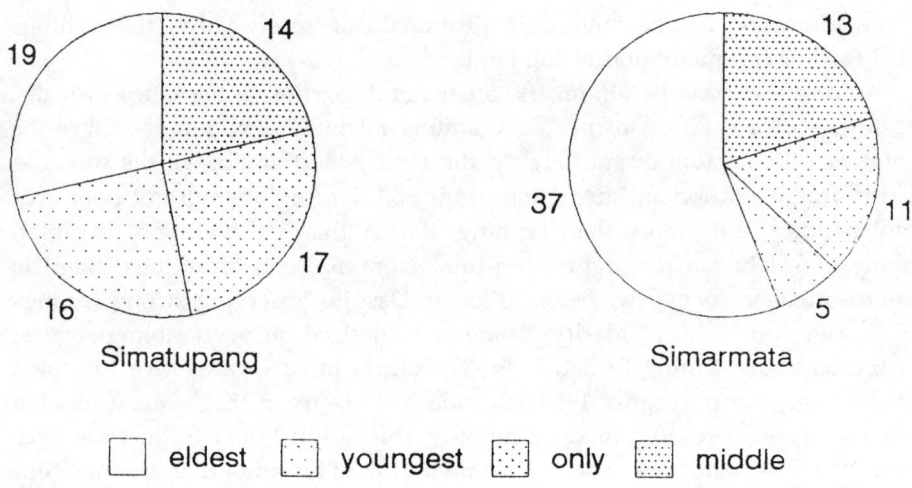

Figure 4. Resident sons without brothers in the village (in absolute figures)

land. It seems that their position as heir has been an incentive to keeping a stake in the village, as exemplified by the case of Ama Anwar below.

> Ama Anwar (70) is a hamlet head (*tunggane ni huta*) in one of the more remote hamlets on the slope in Simarmata. As far as I could gather, he owns more than 30 ha. Most of this property, however, is unproductive land, either fallow or planted with pine trees, the rest being rented or lent to co-villagers. He has two younger brothers, one of whom is a farmer on Sumatra's East Coast, the other one a trader in Lampung. Ama Anwar himself has been a temporary migrant for years, hawking cloth in East Sumatra. His wife (and seven children) managed the farm in the meantime. Although he earned good money, he never dreamt of leaving the village permanently. His only son followed his father's footsteps and engaged in trade. He seems to be less attached to the ancestral land, however, and took his family to settle in Lampung. Although Ama Anwar says he regrets his son's absence, he realizes that trade is economically more viable than working the upland fields. Three of Ama Anwar's daughters remained in Simarmata after marriage and are allowed to use their father's land.

In contrast to Simarmata, in Simatupang dutiful sons like Ama Anwar were the exception, not the rule. Clearly, eldest and youngest sons could not be kept in the village by the sheer prospect of inheriting land or the family house.[17] Instead, it appeared that the least educated usually stayed at home, a tendency I also found in Simarmata among the younger generation.

> Ama Jujur (40) is the youngest son of a family of six. Scarcely educated, he is the only one of his family who stayed in Simarmata. When he married his two older brothers had already migrated and had become traders in Jakarta and Kisaran. They felt it was important that one of them remained in Simarmata to look after their mother and the land, so they pressed Ama Jujur to stay on in the *huta*. Together with his wife he cultivates about 3 *rante* of onions (which yield some 100 kg a year), some dry rice, and ten clove trees; a large part of the property lies idle. His brothers support Ama Jujur by regularly sending money. In addition, three of his twelve children live with his brothers while attending secondary school and one daughter stays with his sister in Jambi.

In this case, the brothers' permanent absence appears to be conditional upon Ama Jujur's willingness to stay in the village. The brothers who migrated seem to be paying off their traditional responsibilities by means of financial support of their rural relatives.

While the above examples show that permanent migrants may have a brother as caretaker of the land, as a rule it is their wives that temporary migrants depend on to carry out the essential tasks connected with the maintenance of the family farm. The minimal differentiation of agricultural tasks by sex within families no doubt facilitates a husband's migration (Connell et al. 1976:47), as discussed in the next chapter. It can be argued that the practice of patrilocal residence has contributed to the circular character of male

---

[17] See Cho (1984:203) for a similar situation in the Republic of Korea.

migration because Toba Batak men have a fixed village in which they enjoy continuing rights to land.[18] Not only can they leave the village because their land rights are guaranteed, but also because they have wives who keep the farm running.

Whereas young, single Toba Batak women are increasingly migratory, for most women marriage marks a break. Their activities become closely linked to the rural household and few are attracted by wage opportunities outside the village. Cultural expectations and practices strongly identify married women with the village home. They are supposed to remain in the community and care for the day-to-day management of the household economy and children. As the tasks for which they are responsible are numerous and varied, women's continuous presence is necessary. Their activities include field work (planting, weeding), processing and storage of crops, child care and socialization, budgeting and commerce (selling and buying).

Besides her economic role, a migrant's wife may also use her intermediary position between wife givers and wife receivers to act as a broker in migration situations. In some instances she mediates between her male relatives in the city and her migrant husband. While not all temporary migrants had close kin who could help them in setting up a livelihood in the *pangarantoan*, several of them had received help from a wife's relative (a brother-in-law or father-in-law) who had migrated earlier, as the following example illustrates.

> Although her husband had never migrated before, one year ago Nai Tiurma (30) 'sent' him to Padang. While his family has no trading tradition, several of her relatives are hawkers in West Sumatra who were willing to initiate Ama Tiurma in the art of trading. He therefore went to live with his wife's brother, who hawks cloth. He did not feel like going, though. His wife recounts how he wept for two weeks prior to his departure. He is the youngest son and occupies his parents' house in Simarmata. Nai Tiurma cultivates 4 *rante* (0.16 ha) of *ladang* and takes care of the three children and her mother-in-law. Her widowed mother and a younger sister live in the same village and occasionally share in child care and farm activities.

Not only can women like Nai Tiurma provide trade connections, they also act as intermediaries by representing their migrant husbands in the village. In the absence of their husbands, the wives do most of the kin visiting and they engage in mutual help. They do not act as 'gatekeepers' or 'brokers', but rather as social 'nodes' (Strauch 1984), as the following case illustrates.

> Nai Bonggas (48) was born in Pangururan subdistrict. At age 18 she married her present husband from Simarmata. Her parents liked him because he was her *anak namboru* (matrilateral cross-cousin) and the eldest son. 'I married him because they urged me, but it was no great love.' His parents had already died, and marrying

---

[18] Interestingly, migration of Minangkabau males is generally attributed to their lack of land rights (Naim 1971; Kato 1982).

Ama Bonggas implied becoming the wife of a hamlet head (*tunggane ni huta*, which is a hereditary function). After ten years of marriage, Ama Bonggas started hawking in Kisaran and since then comes home only once a year. Apart from her two youngest daughters, all nine children have migrated. If necessary, Nai Bonggas replaces her husband and acts as hamlet head in *adat* rituals or village meetings.

For Ama Bonggas it was in the natural course of things to keep a stake in his natal *huta* through his wife's presence there. In some other instances, however, permanent migration of a male heir may induce his sisters to reside matrilocally after marriage in order to have access to their father's land, as in the example of Ama Anwar above. For mothers, the proximity of the married daughter clearly helps to compensate for the lack of a resident daughter-in-law, both in household assistance and in companionship.[19] Among the migrant households in the Simarmata region, 30 percent (10 households) lived matrilocally.[20] This is seen as more practical than living with the husband's family (see also Colson 1970; Van den Muijzenberg 1973:309-12). If serious conflicts with her husband arise, a woman will be more easily backed by her natal family, and in case of marital separation, the husband is the one to leave.

The moral economy of kinship

As the core of each Toba Batak village is a localized patrilineage, and as membership in the lineage is determined by descent rather than by residence, Bruner (1961:516) observes that the Batak who have migrated never lose their lineage and village affiliation. This 'primordial attachment' (Geertz 1973) creates the expectation that relatives will assist each other preferentially over those with whom no kinship bond can be established. It is generally believed that only relatives can be relied upon; they are *sejiwa* (lit. 'one spirit'), they have the same views on life (Lineton 1975). Should land become available, for example, it is more likely to be rented to a kinsman than to an 'outsider'. Should there be shortage of labour during the harvesting period, one should accept an offer made by kin rather than by another villager. Such rights to goods and services are thought to be defined by social obligations rather than by calculations of return. This 'moral eco-

---

[19] One of these women whom I knew quite well acknowledged that it was unusual for her to live near her own mother rather than with her absent husband's family in a village some 20 kilometres distant, but she maintained that all women in her husband's village were active in weaving traditional cloth, a craft which she did not master, so she would feel embarrassed – a euphemism that tactfully avoided mention of the familiar problems all too often inherent in relations with in-laws.

[20] Most couples decided to live in the wife's *huta* right after marriage and not necessarily upon the husband's migration. Nevertheless, I find it plausible that the decision to live near the wife's parents is related to the relative frequency of husband migration.

nomy' is based on continuing descent ties, and the concept has been used in studies of Southeast Asian peasants to explain income-sharing practices (Scott 1976). From the perspective of moral economy, families are considered as harmonious groups based on sharing, rather than on economic calculation that is typical in more distant relationships.

For the Toba Batak, assisting one's kin certainly has advantages. For one thing, it ensures that relatives can be called upon in future to return the favour. A person who is generous and quick to fulfil the obligations of kinship gains considerable status and 'respect' in the community. Merely acquiring wealth and property is not enough to assure one's status; one must also use one's wealth and property to assist the 'family'.

Even when they have migrated permanently, Toba Batak operate in a cultural context where strong obligations to one's (rural) relatives are expected and internalized. As Bruner (1981) convincingly demonstrates, Toba Batak communities in village and city are part of a single social and ceremonial system. They are linked through a complex communication network in which modern goods and ideas flow from *pangarantoan* (migration area) to *bona ni pasogit* (ancestral homeland), while the flow of people and of the moral support and vitality of *adat* is in the other direction. There are other reciprocities. Political influence and money generated in the city flow back to the Tapanuli villages. Those staying in the village are caretakers of lineage land, property, and ancestral graves and tombs. It is through the kinship network that people move into the city, living in the same households or in clusters of kin, and supporting each other. Urban Toba Batak help their relatives by employing them in low-ranking positions in business, by letting them farm part of their inherited land in the village, and by financing education. Usually these services are geared towards siblings and their children, though sometimes more distant relatives also take advantage of their urban connections (Bruner 1961:515; see also Stivens 1991:86). Studies in other Indonesian areas, such as West Sumatra and Sulawesi, confirm that migration and increasing integration into a market economy do not inevitably spell decline in family unity (Kato 1982; Lineton 1975). Maintaining a kin network is important because Indonesia 'lacks a strong central government, political stability, a rapidly developing economy, and a wide extension of welfare services' (Bruner 1970:130). Kinship groups may perform tasks that in more developed countries have been taken over by the state or other organizations. Stivens (1991:86) even asserts that rural–urban migration in Peninsular Malaysia encourages the 'welfare role' of kinship.

Villagers assume that migrants have easier access to money and other resources than non-migrants, and therefore have an obligation to share these resources with less fortunate relatives remaining behind in Tapanuli. Especially those who have been upwardly mobile into the new, fast-growing

Indonesian middle class are supposed to help kin. They attend the necessary rituals, contribute towards the cost of a relative's ceremonies and, in most situations, conform to the requirements of their kinship role. But they also guard their capital against excessive demands from rural relatives. Those who cut themselves off from their relatives are considered mean, stingy, and selfish.

Clearly, the existence of values regarding reciprocity and close family relations does not mean that everyone behaves in accordance with those values. In some areas, like West Sumatra or Central Java, the results of migration are easily observed from the number of new brick houses and even schools or mosques built with money sent from migrants (Hetler 1989; Kato 1982; Subarkah et al. 1986; *Tempo* 1984). This contrasts sharply with the situation in Simatupang and Simarmata, and in North Tapanuli in general. Many houses have fallen into decay and contain only a minimum of furniture. Villagers readily acknowledge that although 'family' should help each other, they do not always do so. A kinship relationship gives one a claim, but does not guarantee that it will be fulfilled. Where the moral economy model presumes the existence of consensus and cooperation, from the perspective of a political economy dissension and division are to be expected (Popkin 1979). The direct contribution to relatives who stay behind in the village or to the village economy as a whole appeared to be minimal. I was told several stories of villagers who had migrated and cut off ties with home completely. Several migrants 'ran away' both from village and family obligations without a trace. I heard of a young man who had stolen his mother's gold chain and gone off to Palembang four years ago. He has not been in touch since. Another man went to Singapore eleven years ago to become a sailor. He never returned, nor did he send word.

These examples raise doubts about the strength of 'loyalty' to the family as a social and economic unit. Loyalty is sometimes overtly displayed at times of major family events, like marriages, deaths, and religious holidays. Towards the end of the year, the village population swells as dozens of migrants return to visit their family, participate in the celebration of Christmas, and have their children baptized in the *bona ni pasogit* (ancestral homeland). When a parent dies suddenly, migrants leave their jobs at an hour's notice in order to travel home. But other occasions for visiting kin seem rare. Trying to make ends meet in the cash-dependent urban environment, many migrants of necessity neglect some family obligations, thereby becoming more selfish in the eyes of their rural relatives.

Striking evidence of migrants' funds are the cement monuments or *tugu* dedicated to clan ancestors. While *tugu* have always been built by the Toba Batak, a resurgence began in the sixties and has continued to the present. The evidence, in the form of clan tombs, is everywhere and has literally

Tomb at Tuk-Tuk

changed the rural landscape. According to Bruner (1987:137), it was only from the 1960s on that the economic benefits of independence enabled the Toba to have the wealth and resources to care for their ancestral graves. It is not uncommon for a childless woman to bring an offering to the monument of her *marga* ancestor asking his help in securing children. Stories abound in which the illness and misfortune of migrants is attributed to the neglect of one or another moral obligation towards the ancestors. These stories indicate the migrants' need to invest in ancestor worship.

With the erection of each *tugu* there is a three- to five-day ceremony attended by clan members in the home area, as well as those from the *pangarantoan*. The *tugu* are expensive investments in custom which involve the transfer of resources on a massive scale from urban areas to rural areas.[21] The more excessive the economic expenditure, the more successful the *tugu* is socially, a token of the solidarity of the *marga* to which the migrant belongs (Bruner 1981; see also Krause 1981:58; Schefold 1988; E. Wolf 1966:7). The recently built Sianturi *tugu* in Simatupang cost Rp 7 million (US$ 3500). The migrants seem to be paying off their traditional moral responsibilities to their rural family simply by means of building *tugu* (Bruner 1987).

In the Netherlands there is a proverb 'A near neighbour is better than a distant cousin', indicating the importance of a support network nearby. My observations among the Toba Batak, however, suggest that village households which are not related seldom forge networks for loyalty or mutual aid. Some people even distrust their neighbours ('They stole our goldfish from the *sawah*'). Villagers admit that although a household organizing a wedding feast or a funeral would certainly rally contributions from migrant members, neighbouring households are loathe to cooperate in constructing a water pump or carrying out other community works. When asking about the extent to which neighbouring households organized themselves around common needs, people just smiled and commented that everyone tried to better him or herself. Such comments were based on their experiences in the past, for example the supposed corruption around the communally-owned diesel engine in Simatupang.

Throughout this chapter I have tried to elucidate the central role of kinship in the process of out-migration. Kinship is also crucial in regulating access to land. This is most notable with respect to inheritance and usufruct patterns. In the next chapter we shall see that the possibility of owning land is by definition related to clan ancestry and gender. While it has generally been assumed that it is especially those without land rights who migrate, I will argue that for successful out-migration from North Tapanuli land ownership can be an important precondition.

---

[21] See Murray 1979 for a similar situation in Lesotho.

Tugu, Simarmata

CHAPTER V

The value of land

'A shortage in the family property makes emigration necessary, but the family property also makes it possible. The paradox is resolved when it is understood that shortage encourages the emigration of [poor people] but the second case is a matter of [rich people].' (Chadwick 1991:64.)

Access to land according to clan

Legend has it that the Toba Batak descended from the Pusuk Buhit volcano on Samosir Island. From there they migrated outward until the whole territory now known as Tano Batak was populated. From the beginning there have been two moieties, one of Raja (king) Lontung, the other of Raja Sumba (Vergouwen 1964:5).

The early settlement of Muara, as reported by Ypes (1932:367) and affirmed by the former *kepala negeri* (chief) in *desa* Simatupang, took place some ten generations ago. The three youngest sons of Si Raja Lontung, named Simatupang, Aritonang, and Siregar, were forced out of their home area in Sabulan, Samosir, and crossed Lake Toba in search of new territory. They entered the heartland of the valley of Muara. While Siregar, after committing adultery with Simatupang's wife, fled to the Toba plateau, Simatupang and Aritonang divided the Muara area into two parts. Later on, Aritonang sent for Siregar, who was allowed to live in the Aritonang area. From here, other parts of Muara were colonized.

Most of Simatupang's land was divided among his three sons, Togatorop, Sianturi, and Siburian, whose descendants became the three subclans presently residing in the village. The distribution of land and the arrangement of houses according to clan is still discernible in the village. The *raja adat* (village elders) related that the three clans each received a more or less equal share of the irrigable and nonirrigable acreage. This careful distribution of land indicates an acute sense of the balance of power between the three groups. *Marga* Sianturi took the land to the west and the Togatorop subclan the land to the east. The fields in between were occupied by *marga* Siburian.

The dominant clans in the area of Simarmata are *marga* Simarmata and Simanihuruk, both descendants of Si Raja Sumba. They have usufruct rights to most of the land. Other clans that have been living in the area for centuries include Sihaloho, Sinaga, Situngkir, Nainggolan, and Sipayung. As far as I know, Simarmata has no clear settlement history comparable to the one for Simatupang, but that may be just my ignorance (for more information see Ypes 1932:40).

In the traditional system, relations to land can be roughly divided into two main categories: land inherited through the patriliny and land obtained from wife givers.

Patrilineal land

In principle, land rights in a village belong to the descendants of the founding lineage or lineages (*marga raja*), whose early ancestor is said to have established that village. Only sons are eligible to inherit exclusive rights to land, whether they reside in the village or not. In the patriarchal Toba Batak society, it is sons who continue the family line. They have to care for the family's possessions, especially land, and pass them on to their sons. Their sisters are expected to follow their husbands and live off their husbands' land which, in turn, has to be maintained for their sons.

The formal division of land usually does not take place until both parents have died and all sons have married or completed their education (Vergouwen 1964:283). But before the final division, resident sons usually receive land from their fathers as *panjaean* to establish an independent household, as discussed in the last chapter. In addition, informal arrangements are often made, such as a son using his father's land during his lifetime. As the parents grow older and their ability to cultivate their fields lessens, the sons gradually take over the operation of the land and reserve part of the crops to support their parents.

Land for wife receivers and other in-dwelling clans

In the past, when the Toba Batak area was still scarcely populated, it was possible for outsiders who were not descendants of the ruling clan to gain access to land. They were given usufruct rights as long as they or their descendants stayed in the village. Such immigrants are called *parripe*. In some areas, such as Silindung, many of the residents are members of in-dwelling clans. In other regions, like Samosir Island and the Toba area (including Muara), the number of people who belong to in-dwelling *marga* is much smaller (Vergouwen 1964:51).

Another way for landless men to acquire land rights is to marry a daughter from a *marga raja*. The wife receiver can request a field as a 'path of life' or a 'blessing-shawl field' (*juma parulos*). Descendants from these in-marrying men are called *pargellengan*. Finally, newcomers can also acquire access to land through the dowry of their wives, an arrangement discussed below. Although formally women do not share in their fathers' inheritance, in some cases land can be transferred to daughters.

Women's access to land

Land as a gift

Although according to Toba Batak *adat* women cannot inherit land because they leave their natal homes to live with the husband's family, a woman can be given a plot of land by her father or her brothers out of generosity. In other words, while sons have 'a right to inherit', daughters have 'a right to ask'. A woman and her husband could 'beg' for a piece of land and bring a meal to make her father (or, if he is dead, her brothers) willing to give. Batak males are expected to be compassionate and to treat their female kin well, or at least that was the case in the early thirties when Vergouwen (1964:286-7) wrote: 'it is not consistent with the *hula-hula–boru* relationship that brothers withhold part of their estate from their sisters, and they hardly ever do so'. There are different types of land gifts depending on when or why they are given to the daughter; for example, to enhance her chance of marriage, at marriage itself (as a dowry or *pauseang*), upon the birth of a child, or after her father's death (Vergouwen 1964:285-9).

Dowry has long been interpreted as the transmission of inheritance before one dies (Goody and Tambiah 1973). However, to consider dowry as a kind of inheritance would, in the case of the Toba Batak, blur an important distinction between the inheritable legal rights enjoyed by men and the privilege of women receiving dowry if their fathers or brothers are kind enough to grant it to them. Moreover, a crucial question is how much real control women have over this property.

It is not entirely clear to what extent a land gift is a woman's individual property or a couple's joint property (see for instance *Handschriften 806*, 1920). For the neighbouring area of Balige, Cunningham (1958:21) notes: 'If a daughter does receive land, this land enters the marga of her husband and is under its authority so long as there is a male descendant of that daughter to make a claim'. In any case, it seems that women do not have control over this land to the same extent that men do over the fields that are allocated to them. A woman is not allowed to transfer the ownership of the land to somebody else outside her father's family. In fact, the land is not given to her personally; it belongs to her children or future children.[1] In most cases it

---

[1] The idea of ownership among Toba Batak, as in other kin-based societies, is highly complex. The simplest way of understanding some of the major problems is to separate property rights into two: use rights and rights to alienate. While in non-kin-based societies, ownership is regarded as consisting of both classes of rights, in North Tapanuli ownership tends to mean use rights for the individual, as the community is the legal land-owning entity.

is given as security for a woman after marriage and as a symbol of her kinsmen's expectation of her reproductive capacities. This is illustrated by the fact that the land is sometimes transferred only after a child has been born, an indication that the woman is fertile and can bear sons. In exceptional cases a piece of land can be given to a childless woman to 'stimulate' the predisposition of her soul to give birth. Land given as *pauseang* can later be used as dowry for a daughter or as *panjaean* for a son when they set up their own households (Nasoetion 1943:105). The transfer of *pauseang* also symbolizes the wish that men from the next generation of the *marga boru* (land-/wife-receiving clan) will keep taking daughters from the *marga raja* (land-giving clan) as their wives to maintain the marital relationship between the two clans and to keep the land in the family.

It is hard to verify how widespread *pauseang*[2] was in the past because it has never been systematically registered. Because Toba Batak themselves mention differences among regions, I assume that the custom of *pauseang* was more common in the Toba area (especially Balige) than in other regions. This is affirmed by Simandjuntak (1983:36), who notes this as the reason men from Sipahutar were eager to marry women from Toba. The transfer of land to women may be related to the fact that divorce was relatively widespread in the Toba area (Simbolon, personal communication). As discussed in Chapter IV, it is divorce and widowhood that threaten women's economic position, and for precisely this reason parents in the Toba area considered it important to give their daughters some land.[3] In any case, the custom of giving *pauseang* seems to have been more common among the more privileged, such as *raja* (local chiefs), than among ordinary people (De Boer 1921:81; *Handschriften 806*, 1920:366). In Simatupang thirty women (14 percent of the total) told me they had received land in *pauseang*.

It seems that giving *pauseang* was more common in the past. One probable cause of so few women enjoying *pauseang* today is the severe land shortage. Few farms are so large that they can support a household head and his married sons' families, as well as afford the 'luxury' of letting a married daughter have a part of the land. A second important limiting factor is the distance between a woman's hamlet of origin and her husband's hamlet where she lives as a married woman. In an area where people most commonly travel by foot, distance can be an important limitation to a woman's ability to exercise any land rights her father may be inclined to give her. In

---

Permanent usufruct rights are passed down the generations through inheritance. Rights to alienate property rest with the kin group as a legal body, that is, to alienate (sell) such property is a matter for group rather than individual decision.

[2] In everyday speech, all land gifts to women are generally referred to as *pauseang*.

[3] See also Stivens (1985:35-6) on how women's perceived vulnerability in divorce in Negeri Sembilan, Malaysia, is used to explain the transfer of land to women.

Simatupang, however, distance may not be a serious obstacle because more than half of the married women live in their natal village or originate from a directly adjoining village.[4]

Few Toba Batak women are aware of the national land law which stipulates that sons and daughters have equal inheritance rights and that they are equally entitled to parental land.[5] Consequently, I did not come across any cases in which women had claimed a rightful share of their father's inheritance. The villagers all agreed that a woman should never exercise her formal rights, by taking the matter to court for example. She would then be severely criticized by relatives and associates because this act is regarded as threatening to the traditional kinship system (Krause 1981:66; Nasution 1987). Especially when she has a husband to look after her or has already received *pauseang* or other gifts, her request would be turned down because she would be demanding more than she is entitled to.

> 'The right of ownership [...] is a social phenomenon consisting of the fact that vast numbers of people accept a given owner's use of a given property as he/she sees fit, given certain socially defined limitations. An individual woman confronts patriarchy in the fact that other men and women accept a man's right to make some decision for her. She may or may not do as she is told, but in order not to, she must overcome a social environment that accepts that man's right to make that decision.' (Curtis 1986, in Riley and Gardner 1993:200-1.)

In this example, the dominant patriarchal system of norms is stronger than women's formal possibilities for action. Toba Batak women act against their own interests because of their ties to the dominant norms. As we have seen in Chapter IV, according to Batak kinship ideology a sister should be concerned with the prosperity of her brother's household for which she personally takes responsibility. For a woman to claim her legal share of her father's estate is believed to destroy the intimate relationship between a brother and a sister. A woman who has claimed land can no longer expect to rely on her brother in clan rituals, or in case of an economic or social emergency. There

---

[4] The practice of transferring land to daughters is more widespread among the Acehnese in Sumatra, who adhere to matrilocality. If the parents can afford it each daughter receives a rice field, in addition to a house (Siegel 1969:52; see also Swift 1965:36.) But among the patrilocal Karo Batak, women are also said to receive land from their parents' legacy (Portier and Slaats 1987:306).

[5] The Basic Agrarian Law (UUPA) stipulates that 'every citizen of Indonesia, man or woman, has the same opportunity and rights to acquire a plot of land and to use the acquired plot, for his/her own benefit as well as for his/her family's benefit' (number 5 1960 Chapter 9 article 2). However, it has never been the government's intention to strictly observe this law. It is true that women were given a right to inherit land, but the right was not clearly specified. In 1963 the Indonesian Supreme Court stated that the civil code (including the bilateral inheritance law) 'henceforth [would] be regarded only as a guide to the "adat" law of those to whom the code had formerly applied', that is, it was not to conflict with the *adat* law of the different ethnic groups (Lev 1972:313; see also Myers 1984:52).

are also practical reasons why village women seldom demand their rights to land by going to court. They may feel unfamiliar with it, find it strange, or do not trust the court's ability to solve their problems.

Access to land through husbands

According to most villagers (male and female), there is no need for women to inherit because *adat* guarantees the right of women to cultivate and harvest produce from the land of their husbands. While married, a woman's access to land is more or less secure: she can work in the fields inherited by her husband and she is responsible for their maintenance. Women's rights to land are contingent upon her marriage, however, and can be revoked when the marriage relationship ends. As argued in the previous chapter, in-marrying women are regarded as 'sojourners', for the group that determines access to land is the male core group which does not admit wives as full members with rights in perpetuity.

In Toba Batak tradition women's rights to land are heavily dependent on their ability to give birth to sons. If a woman has male children, after her husband's death she will retain control over the land by virtue of being the heirs' mother (Nasoetion 1943:104-5). When her eldest son reaches adulthood, the mother and her son will control the property together.

The access to land of a widow without a son is seriously at risk. Her right to cultivate her deceased husband's land has usually been conditional on her not remarrying outside the family. If a woman is still of child-bearing age, she may marry a younger brother-in-law – as did a 24-year-old widow in Simatupang – or someone else from her husband's immediate family, in order to secure access to the land. It seems that women seldom oppose this custom, because it guarantees their access to economic resources.

If the widow does not marry one of her husband's relatives, all her husband's fields and houses are taken over by the closest brother (Vergouwen 1964:271; Ypes 1932:374). In such a case a widow is sometimes left with a bare minimum to keep herself (and her daughters) alive. Stories abound about the pitiful situation of sonless or childless widows. As a rule, widows who already have a son are not very eager to contract a second marriage.

To summarize, in North Tapanuli, direct allocation of land rights to women as individuals is rare. This means that they have access to land only through their relation with their husband or other male relatives; they do not have independent access. Their position is therefore precarious: the temporary nature of women's rights of land use may become only too obvious when a connection through which they are derived is severed by disagreement, divorce, or death.

During and after the colonial period women's access to land improved somewhat. The impetus for change was brought about by conversion to

Christianity, the spread of education, and the state's imposition of non-discriminatory law. For example, it has become more accepted that women without sons are given the right to their husband's land (Simbolon 1992), which can later be designated as the *pauseang* of her daughters (Nasoetion 1943:104-5; Ypes 1932:417). It should be noted, however, that in most of the cases cited as verifying the existence of female inheritance, women are residual heirs. That is, a daughter inherits failing a son. Although missionaries tried to advocate legal inheritance rights for Toba Batak daughters, this idea only reached the Christian upper-class, which already had more land to distribute. The practice was more often adopted when land outside Tapanuli had to be divided, since this was non-ancestral land. Finally, another development in women's access to land is the possibility to cultivate the land of a relative who has migrated, and keep the produce. We shall elaborate on this phenomenon in the last section of this chapter.

Tenurial arrangements

With the exception of traditional areas of pasture on the higher hillsides, the land in both Simatupang and Simarmata has been brought entirely under cultivation. Despite the migration of excess population, both now and in the past, land is scarce and highly fragmented.

For most villagers the overriding concern is to have enough land to farm: land from inherited and pawned holdings, land gifts from wife-giving affines, and sharecropped fields. Land ownership in both villages is fairly evenly distributed.[6] Most smallholders are able to obtain sufficient rice and other food crops for their own needs if the harvest is good, but rarely have a surplus large enough to tide them over a bad year. If the harvest fails for one season, they may be forced to eat their seed-rice (saved from the previous harvest), which makes their position even more vulnerable the following year. At the same time, quite a few households own more land than they can cultivate, or have moved away altogether. As can be seen in Figure 5, most households own at least part of the land they cultivate, while a minority have access to land only through tenancy and sharecropping.

Population pressure on the land is reflected in tiny landholdings. According to my census, in Simatupang the average farm size per household is 9.5 *rante* (0.38 ha),[7] with 68 percent cultivating even less than this. Although

---

[6] By national standards, the land in North Tapanuli is fairly evenly distributed, with 77 percent of the farmers operating less than 1 ha and only 6 percent operating more than 2 ha. Figures for North Sumatra as a whole are 70 percent and 9 percent, respectively (Van der Mijl 1988:40).
[7] 1 *rante* = 0.04 ha. For an average family on Java 0.25–0.5 ha of *sawah* is considered to be sufficient. Mean farm size in North Tapanuli was 0.82 ha in 1983 (Van der Mijl 1988:39).

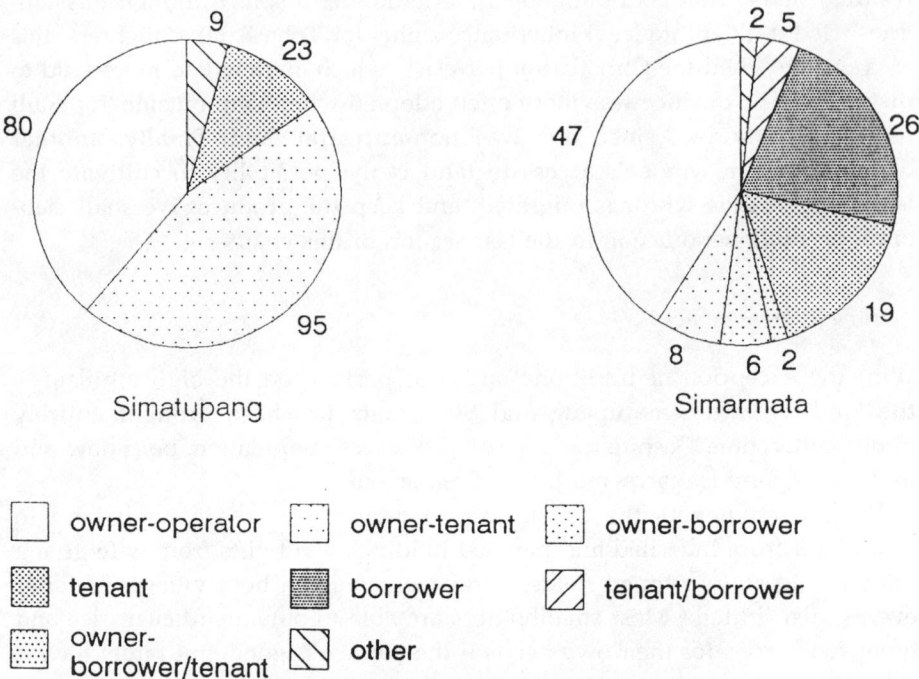

Figure 5. Land tenure of Simatupang and Simarmata households

Notes: Following local usage, having acquired land through pawning is also referred to as 'owning' land. The low number of owners in Simarmata is related to the absence of pawning practices in that village. 'Tenant' also includes sharecropping arrangements. Figures indicate number of households.

average farm size is rather small, Simatupang can be considered a relatively well-off village, since in Muara subdistrict as a whole, 80 percent of agricultural households operate less than 0.25 ha (Van der Mijl 1988:39).[8] In Simarmata, on the other hand, most of the land consists of tiny and infertile parcels, and this resembles the situation on Samosir as a whole, where more than half of the farms are smaller than 0.25 ha (Van der Mijl 1988:39). Below I will discuss the main tenure arrangements in more detail.

Sharecropping and renting land

For those who do not have enough land of their own, there is the possibility of cultivating someone else's field in return for a share of the crop. This practice is referred to as 'splitting betel nut' (*mamola pinang*). In general, such sharecropping arrangements are a means of access to *sawah*, while dry fields are rented for a fixed amount of rice (*sewa*). In Simarmata most immigrant clans (*parripe*) have to rent or borrow, and can remain landless for many generations unless they receive usufruct rights upon marriage with a *boru* (daughter) from the land-owning clan.

In Simatupang the tiller hands over one-quarter to one-third of the harvest to the owner. The tiller usually provides seeds, fertilizer, and labour. Sharecropping means that the work needs minimal supervision and that the risks are shared; it is therefore considered an easy and comfortable arrangement by most landowners, especially for those living elsewhere, as the following example illustrates.

> One Sunday morning in July, a car drove into Simatupang and an elderly widow, supported by her son, groaningly got down. The woman appeared to be my landlady, whose house I had been offered by one of her village relatives. Her children all having migrated, she was spending her old age with one of them, a lawyer in Medan. As a rule, after the rice harvest she returns to the village to collect her *eme* (rice) rents and to catch up with her old village friends. She has sharecropping arrangements with at least four households, while two other households had pawned a plot from her. After a stay of two weeks, she left again for Medan with her sacks of milled rice, not to return before the next harvest.

Pawning land

While land is not considered a commodity and therefore cannot be sold, there is a system of pawning or mortgaging land (*dondon*) which can last for several years (Simandjuntak 1983:48; Simbolon 1994; Vergouwen 1964:339).[9]

---

[8] Land scarcity in North Tapanuli is even more significant when compared with a village in Central Java where in the late 1970s only 18 percent of the households owned less than 0.25 ha (Hüsken 1988:128).
[9] Irrevocable selling of land is called *gadis pate*. It is seldom undertaken since, strictly speaking, the land belongs to the entire family (see note 1). Consequently, it can only take place when all members agree. For the owner, pawning (*dondon*) has the advantage over

In everyday speech, pawning is often referred to as 'selling', and taking in pawn as 'buying'. No wonder, then, that a person refers to a pawned land parcel as 'mine', despite the fact that he does not officially own it. Aside from rights to sale, he does have true control over it. What is crucial, however, is that the land can be bought back (*tebus*) by the original owner after a specified time. In fact, *dondon* is a way of borrowing money with the land as security, that is, mortgaging the land. The money is paid at once and is covered by a written, notarized contract in most cases. Similar arrangements have been observed in other parts of Southeast Asia (for example Kahn 1980; Scott 1985; Van den Muijzenberg 1973). Whereas in former times new land could be acquired by means of clearing the forest, today one of the few opportunities for obtaining a plot of land is pawning. Because of the relative abundance of land and its low quality, fields in Simarmata are seldom pawned but rather lent or rented out. This explains the smaller number of land 'owners' in Simarmata (55 percent) compared to Simatupang (85 percent), as depicted in Figure 5. In Simarmata three-quarters of the landowners belong to the ruling clan.

In Simatupang the most frequent pawning arrangements are between relatives. When forced to mortgage a field, the owner is expected to try to keep the land within a restricted circle. But it is evident that fields are also pawned to non-kin. In these instances 'pawning provides a way of denying access to land to close kin if they are unwilling to provide commensurate favors' (Sherman 1990:362). Fields may be pawned for a year or longer, up to several decades. During this time the buyer has the right to operate the land and to harvest the crop.

The price is settled by both parties and depends on several factors, such as kinship ties, quality and location of the land, and time period. Or, in short, as some villagers assert, on *rap olo* (mutual wanting). In Simatupang the price of pawned land appeared to be relatively high. One *rante* (0.04 ha) of sawah land could cost as much as Rp 500,000 or Rp 600,000. This is almost twice the price of the less fertile land on the adjacent Humbang plateau. The exact amount of money, however, is difficult to assess as the period may be extended, and the price consequently increased, several times. A relatively low price means that the pledger prefers not to borrow more on his land than he has need of, since he might have difficulty in redeeming it (Vergouwen 1964:339). Conversely, a high price may indicate that the pledger has no intention of redeeming the land, for instance because he is leaving the village permanently.

Why would people want to pawn their land? Motives for pawning fields

---

gadis pate that official ownership of the land is retained even though use rights may be transferred for many years.

include financing children's education, a trading or pioneer-agricultural enterprise, medicine, and *adat* ceremonies. Simbolon (1994:14) cites the example of a sonless widow in Porsea subdistrict who pawned her husband's rice field. She has no ownership rights to the land, but by mortgaging it she can finance the schooling of her three daughters. Should her husband's family claim the land, she will let them redeem it and repossess it. In the early 1930s, Vergouwen (1964:294) stated that the mortgaging of land by those moving out was a recent phenomenon. An earlier source, however, suggests a system which resembles *dondon* (*Handschriften 806*, 1920). When members of the *marga raja* (ruling clan) migrated from the village, they were not allowed to sell their *sawah* land but were instead supposed to transfer it to the direct heirs, who paid a certain amount of money as compensation in exchange.[10] Upon his return to the village the *sawah* could always be reclaimed by the original owner. Given the large local vocabulary on pawning, there is ample reason to assume that pre-colonial and colonial emigration and trading ventures were, to a certain extent, financed by pawning land (Sherman 1990:261), as they are today.

Borrowing land

In certain situations fields may be lent to others. This may happen when the supply of land is relatively abundant compared to demand and, as a result, its economic value is relatively low. In Simatupang borrowing rarely occurs, which is an indication of the land scarcity in this village. In Simarmata, on the other hand, borrowing (*maminjam* or *manompang*) appears to be more common than renting or sharecropping (see Figure 5). The owner and the borrower usually have a close relationship, such as parent–child or siblings. Loaning a field is not necessarily one-sided generosity, but can also be advantageous to the owner, as illustrated in the following example.

> Nai Ridawati (55) is the widow of a former *tungga ni huta* (hamlet head) and lives in one of the upland hamlets in Simarmata. After her husband's death, she was left with several hectares of land, which normally would have been divided among her male children. Since only one of the six sons (the least educated!) has remained in Simarmata, Nai Ridawati lends land to at least five landless households in the hamlet. Rather than lying fallow, the land remains in a workable state and will not become overgrown with weeds.

---

[10] When assessing the consequences of migration on land tenure, it is important to distinguish between those who belong to the *marga raja* (ruling clan) and those from the *parripe* (immigrants who have 'married in'). In the past, when a member of the *marga raja* moved, he retained his land rights, his house, and his plantings. On the other hand the *parripe*, who did not belong to the ruling clan, did not have land rights (Ypes 1932:204). It is they who constituted the majority of the emigrants (Tichelman 1936:400).

Rural differentiation

Land ownership in North Tapanuli has historically been vested in small peasant proprietors. Or, as a Dutch administrator wrote upon leaving Samosir, 'Almost everyone has his own parcel of land so as to provide for his livelihood' (Welter 1935:26). In the past, each Toba Batak *raja* (local chief) ruled over his own small territory, and there is no evidence that any *raja* ever controlled a large area (Cunningham 1958:35). Only certain descendants of the former chiefs have greater resources than ordinary villagers, and, at least in Simarmata, these are typically the ones who lend some plots to co-villagers. One of the reasons for the general fragmentation of their holdings is the practice of polygamy among former *raja* and the resulting number of sons who each had to inherit a plot of land (Cunningham 1958:153).

Sharecropping and renting have long been considered characteristic of feudal-type social systems in which landlords and tenants had opposing interests. However, Bray and Robertson (1980:211), who studied tenure relations in Kelantan, peninsular Malaysia, assert that the interests of sharecropper and landowner are often complementary. Moreover, it seems that whether one is an owner or a tenant is closely related to the development cycle of the household, and is thus a temporary affair. In North Tapanuli we also see that both size of area operated and total production vary with changes in the composition of the household. Each household passes through its own development cycle of expansion, the ageing of children and adults, marriage of children, and finally, segmentation. Labour availability depends on the stage of development of a household, as well as the health status of its members. At some stage, a household might have to contract some of its land out to sharecroppers. At other times it might take land in. In my view, one should not dwell too long on differences in tenure status or in the size of landholdings in an attempt to characterize class relations in Simatupang and Simarmata.

Land is far more equitably distributed in Toba Batak villages than, for example, in Central Java (Hüsken 1988). I assume that this is related to Toba Batak settlement history, whereby land rights were granted to all male descendants of a particular village founder. Relatively large landowners usually belong to the *marga raja* (ruling clan). Their households may either rent out some plots or they may use all the land and hire additional labour to work it. Having enough land also ensures a steady food supply, which allows them to experiment with new cash crops like cloves. Access to more working capital enables them to raise livestock such as buffaloes or pigs – a source of quick cash and of meat for life-cycle rituals. If necessary, both land and livestock can be used to finance trading activities or children's migration. Middle peasant households tend to follow production strategies similar to those of rich peasants. Some will hire labourers during labour peaks. Poor peasant households, finally, usually have to rent all or part of their land. They are far more restricted in engaging in profitable ventures since for them risk avoidance must take priority. Not being able to produce enough food to ensure the reproduction of the household, the members must buy rice and a few other bare necessities. Some of them have to seek wage labour to supplement their income. Wages are spent on subsistence and cannot be used to purchase inputs to improve the productivity of the land.

On the whole, few households in Simatupang and Simarmata try to enrich themselves by buying additional land. Under present circumstances there are few incentives for investment in agriculture or expansion of agricultural production, and social differentiation along these lines is insignificant. Within the village there also appears to be a considerable degree of social pressure on people who attempt to strike it rich. Anyone who accumulates a surplus is constantly 'threatened' by relatives wanting to borrow money. At the same time, the stability of subsistence production has so far prevented the impoverishment of economically weak households. As argued by others (Hefner 1990:117), landholding provides an incomplete measure of class. It is incomplete not just because the quality of land varies, but also because non-agricultural activities (sometimes as part of migration) may yield substantial income. As we shall see later in this chapter, internal economic disparities between village households, though moderate, have consequences for the migration opportunities of their members. In other words, socio-economic differentiation takes place outside the village.

Farming practices and farm labour

In both Simatupang and Simarmata agriculture is primarily a household affair. Farm labour involves little large-scale mobilization, at least as long as the bulk of production is consumed by the producing household. The traditional subsistence crops of rice and cassava can, in theory, be well cared for by household labour, supplemented only occasionally by a few relatives or neighbours.

Geertz's (1963) concept of agricultural involution, the process whereby economic activities become more and more labour-intensive and complex as high rates of population growth and changing agricultural systems lead to increasing pressure on scarce land resources, seems to be much more a feature of the Javanese setting than of other parts of Indonesia or Asia (but for critical reviews, see Alexander and Alexander 1979; Van Schaik 1986; White 1983). Instead of leading to involution, in North Tapanuli land shortage due to population increase has been accompanied by a rapid growth in out-migration, especially since the substantial improvement of transport networks in recent years.

Under the New Order government, improving the productivity of agricultural land became a major national goal. The main efforts were directed towards boosting production through cultivation of more land, enhancing the quality and extent of irrigation, and seeing that high-yielding, hybrid seeds were used along with chemical fertilizers and pesticides. In much of North Tapanuli, however, the hilly terrain has prevented agricultural intensification and mechanization, forcing villagers to retain most of their traditional technology. In Simatupang, there was little additional land that could be brought under cultivation, but rice production could be increased by using improved varieties (*padi unggul*), which allow the cultivation of two crops a year. In Simarmata, on the other hand, where rice is only grown on dry fields, no major agricultural improvements have taken place in the last few decades.

What did bring immediate benefits to the farmers were road improvements, lowering transport costs. The availability of inexpensive transport also gave farmers the options of selling crops themselves in other villages, thereby avoiding middlemen and securing a larger share of the profits. If one can speak, then, of a green revolution in North Tapanuli, it involved not just the introduction of new farm inputs, but also changes in transportation and marketing.

In 1986 an ambitious programme, Opsusdu Maduma, was launched to enhance the economic position of the rural population in North Sumatra. It was aimed at five 'poorer' districts, namely North, Central, and South Tapanuli, Dairi, and Nias. North Tapanuli got special attention because the average per capita income in 1985 was Rp 240,000, compared to Rp 370,000 for the whole of North Sumatra. The target of the programme was to increase per capita income to Rp 600,000. This was to be achieved by intensification of production in all rural sectors. Despite numerous speeches and promises, the Maduma fever has gradually abated without leaving any tangible results in Simatupang or Simarmata.[11]

Sawah cultivation

Unlike the area east of Lake Toba, which was already a rice-exporting area during the colonial period, in Muara most rice is consumed by the producing households. Notwithstanding its subsistence orientation, early in

---

[11] In October 1990 the Governor of North Sumatra changed his tack by launching a new integrated village development programme called 'Martabe'. Interestingly, this operation calls on North Sumatran emigrants, and particularly on the migrants from Tapanuli, to pay attention to their home villages by raising funds for community development for instance (Pelly 1992; *Suara Pembaruan* 13-10-1990).

this century it was noted that 'the Toba Batak are very skilled in the construction of water works and only a very small part of the present *sawah* in this subdistrict is wholly dependent on rain' (Adamse 1913:11). Most rice fields in Simatupang are situated in the valley south of the village, just across the river (see Map 2). There are no big technical water works; water from several streams and wells originating on the plateau or in the crater wall is led to the fields through small weirs.[12] The irrigated area is subdivided into blocks that are interdependent for their water supply, and each block has its own 'water master' (*raja bondar*). The water master is chosen from among all landowners within a particular block and is therefore, by definition, male. While in the past the members of a *bondar* cooperated in the cleaning of the canals and weirs, today this job is usually carried out by wage labourers, who are paid by the annual subscription of members (*boni*), which amounts to one percent of the rice harvest. The irrigation units were traditionally maintained by patrilineal descent groups, but partly as a result of out-migration they are now formed on the basis of new non-kin-based alliances (Lando 1979).

At the beginning of this century agricultural modernization began with experiments with new rice varieties, accompanied by the introduction of fertilizers in the early 1930s (Auer 1933:61). A few years later, transplanting rice instead of broadcasting was introduced. But it was only in 1977 that modern rice varieties were extensively used in Muara and double-cropping became possible. By 1988 the combination of a second crop, fertilizers, and new seeds had pushed production in Simatupang to about 5600 kg/ha of husked rice per harvest, which is above average for North Tapanuli. Without the introduction of chemical manure and pesticides, the far more intensive utilization of land would not have been possible. The use of chemical fertilizer, available through the village cooperative (KUD) or at the weekly market, is extensive (Bosch 1990:12).[13] Agricultural extension services are virtually absent.

Labour division by gender in sawah cultivation

Although there is no evidence that agricultural intensification has led to a sharper differentiation in social classes – as has been reported for parts of Java – from the villagers' accounts I noticed some changes along gender

---

[12] Frequent fires on the steep slope and resulting erosion probably have negative effects on the available water supply. These fires are usually due to carelessness on the part of farmers, but sometimes they are started wilfully as a protest against government afforestation on *adat* land.

[13] For 1987 the KUD provided chemical fertilizer on credit at one percent interest a year. While it is easily available to the villagers, it is more expensive than the fertilizer at the local market. According to my census, almost half the Simatupang households spread KUD fertilizer.

Women from an up-hill hamlet, Simarmata

Harvesting rice with a sickle, Simatupang

lines. Given the gender division of labour in wet-rice agriculture, double-cropping meant a considerable extension of women's work in transplanting rice. But because land preparation continues to be done by hand, men's workload has also increased. Only in one flat area southwest of Simatupang, encompassing 6.2 ha (or 17 percent of all *sawah* land), was a hand tractor occasionally used for ploughing. Because in most other parts terraces are steep and narrow, it is difficult even to use a plough. It is mainly men who are seen hoeing these fields with a *cangkul*. Women predominate in the subsequent pulling and planting of seedlings (*marsuan eme*), back-breaking or at least back-aching work. Although Cunningham (1958) casually notes that 'the women join to help in the remaining duties, from planting to harvesting', women are, in fact, responsible for a large part of rice cultivation. Transplanting is a time of intense activity as it must be accomplished quickly so that the crop matures evenly and the seedling rice does not remain in the nursery bed too long. Groups of women usually work in each other's fields either on a cooperative basis (*marsiadapari*) or for wages.

It is common to find men minding the children while their wives are transplanting. Women carry out their work in an autonomous fashion. It is often they, for instance, who estimate how much help they will need and whom to approach among their kin and neighbours to join in a labour-exchange group. Such groups are the outcome of personal negotiation by the senior female member, a situation similar to that described by Freeman (1970:234) for the Iban in Sarawak. Cooperative work starts early in the morning and continues until sunset, with a pause in between for lunch. The women know each other well and the work atmosphere is usually pleasant. They take ample time for lunch, which is provided by the household whose lands are being worked that day, and jokes are made. About one month after transplanting, the first weeding (*marbabo*) is done. This, like transplanting, is traditionally women's work. If necessary, the men and teenage boys repair the bunds between the fields and cut grass.

Once the weeding has been completed, the period of intense labour on *sawah* fields is through until the harvest begins. Meanwhile the dry fields get more attention. During this period women also mend the *pandanus*-leaf mats that are used for threshing rice, and together with their children gather, split, and store enough firewood for cooking during the harvest period. Harvesting requires the labour of all household members, including children who lend a hand after school. Men and women alike harvest rice with a sickle (*sasabi*), and the subsequent threshing is equally a joint activity of both sexes. The rhythm of hand threshing requires that two people work at one threshing table; the first (usually a man) beats each sheaf two or three times and hands it over to his partner (usually a woman), who dislodges the remaining grains. If the field is relatively dry, the rice is winnowed immediately to remove the coarsest chaff and the bulging sacks are then carried on people's heads to the village. Subsequent drying and second winnowing is done by the women at home. Another traditionally female job, hand pounding, has been taken over by a local rice mill. The mill is owned by a well-to-do widow and is operated by several male relatives.

Since all the rice in the village ripens more or less at the same time, the months of planting and harvesting are a time of labour shortages. As noted above, one way to overcome these labour peaks is to arrange for a work party. Usually one field after the other is planted or harvested by such a party, each member being host for the others once. As a rule, the host household cooks for all the members of the work party. It is obvious that households which participate in cooperative activities must have sufficient members, both men and women. According to the villagers, because of the growing out-migration of household members, the practice of working on each other's fields (*marsiadapari*) has declined (see also Wolfs 1988:102). Many people prefer to employ paid day-labourers over the obligation of working in turn for others. Most people devote their energy primarily to their own fields, some seeking extra employment only when they are otherwise unoccupied. In 1988 a day's hoeing or harvesting by a man was paid Rp 2500 plus lunch, while a woman earned Rp 2000 a day for transplanting or harvesting. I knew only one woman (a young widow), and no men, in Simatupang who relied entirely on agricultural wage labour.

Dry agriculture

It is only in Simatupang's lowlands that enough water collects to permit rice cultivation. The more elevated fields, found north of the village, are used for dry farming, or *ladang*. Although in Simarmata there have been rain-dependent rice terraces (*saba langit*) in the past, they have been abandoned or turned into dry fields due to lack of water. *Ladang* cultivation in Simarmata is concentrated on the narrow strip of land between the lake and the gradually rising slopes. The soil, especially in the upland area, has a low humus content and is easily eroded. Agriculture is wholly dependent on rainfall, and towards the end of the dry season (September/October) the first rains are anxiously awaited. The small streams coming from the central plateau only flow during the rainy season, while attempts to dig wells have failed because the groundwater level is too low. Hence, yields are generally poor. A windmill on the shore of Lake Toba, a gift from a successful migrant, is silent witness of a past attempt to pump water from the lake in order to irrigate the fields. It broke down soon after it was put into operation because, it is rumoured, it had been built on sacred ground.[14]

---

[14] People told me that the land was probably occupied by a ghost who did not want the

Dry-field agriculture differs significantly from wet-rice farming. Maize and cassava, for instance, can be planted, weeded, and harvested in a piecemeal fashion. There is a general need to coordinate planting and harvesting with the wet and dry seasons, but there are few of the strict constraints on the scheduling of cultivation like those in wet-rice farming. Harvesting can be accomplished over several days by a small group of workers.

On the whole, farming practices in dry agriculture have not changed much since the colonial period. Traditional tools like the *cangkul* (hoe) continue to be used. Organic manure, mainly animal dung and other organic wastes, is applied as a fertilizer on *ladang* in combination with chemical fertilizers. In Simarmata in particular, most farmers grow a little bit of everything to provide for the family's needs directly from the land, to reduce the need for cash, and to minimize the risk of losing everything in a bad year. Even if the land is not fragmented, a farmer may subdivide it into mini-lots to raise different crops. These subdivisions hamper agricultural intensification and mechanization, forcing villagers to retain their traditional technology.

The dry fields are planted with peanuts (*hansang*), red shallots (*bawang merah*), maize (*jagung*), cassava (*gadong*), and other tuberous plants. In Simarmata dry rice (*eme darat*) used to be the main subsistence crop, but since people have entered the cash economy it is easier to buy (*sawah*) rice at the market. Consequently, I only found a few households with *eme darat* fields. In Simatupang it is evident that due to the introduction of double-cropping, less attention is paid to the rather labour-intensive, but tastier, dry rice.

From the early twentieth century onwards, terraces have been constructed on the slopes to prevent erosion (Scholz 1983:78; Volz 1899). Cunningham (1958:73) also observed terrace farming in the nearby Meat valley, which he attributed to overpopulation. According to one villager the higher terraced fields in Simatupang were abandoned during the Second World War when the Japanese claimed the crops. Once the war was over it became more lucrative to migrate instead of re-opening the abandoned fields, similar to what has happened in Meat: 'Today, many of these terraced gardens and orchards have been abandoned by people who have migrated, and the remaining villagers prefer to maintain only the wet-rice fields on the valley floor' (Cunningham 1958:73).

On Samosir Island small-scale agriculture based on the cultivation of

---

windmill there. It was said that anyone who stole crops from a field in the vicinity of the mill was immediately struck by illness or other misfortune. Sherman (1990:178-9), however, claims that it is 'for lack of cooperatives [that] certain major capital investments in Samosir purchased by well-meaning emigrants, such as imported steel windmills for irrigation, were not maintained or used'.

shallots, one of the main cash providers, is the pivot of the village economy. Shallots were introduced by the agricultural extension service in the late twenties in an attempt to promote more commercial crops. Shallot production increased when, due to the economic depression in the 1930s, many male migrants returned from the plantations and invested their labour in cultivating cash crops (Oerlemans 1937:1; Welter 1935:37-8). Still today, shallots are mainly exported to urban centres on the East Coast, especially Pematang Siantar. However, due to competition in other areas which turned out to be even better suited to shallot cultivation, prices have severely dropped. Moreover, farmers complain about fluctuating yields since nowadays the dry and wet seasons can no longer be predicted.[15] In Simarmata many households depend on shallot cultivation, and a lean harvest can have direct consequences for the maintenance of the household, as the following example illustrates.

> Last rainy season, Nai Hilmen planted 10 *kaleng* (200 litres) of seed-shallots. The harvest amounts to 400 kg which was sold for Rp 350/kg. Cultivating the *ladang* for two months thus yields Rp 140,000. This money is primarily used for the schooling of the two eldest children in Pematang Siantar. Now that the dry season has set in rather early, Nai Hilmen worries about the next harvest, and her children's education is seriously at stake.

Many women have their dried shallots hanging on beams in the attic, waiting for prices to become more favourable. Whenever the household needs cash, some of the stock is sold.

While red shallot is an important crop, for most farmers the subsistence production of rice and cassava is a necessary precondition for cash-crop production in that it guarantees survival even in the case of losses or unexpectedly low returns from cash crops. Cassava as a staple food is an important supplement to the daily rice meal, especially for poor people. It is an easy crop to grow: cuttings of the best parts of the stem are simply put in the ground and the plant can be cultivated the whole year round, even on poor soils. It takes about six to nine months before the cassava plant is fully grown. The women collect the tubers, not all at once but bit by bit,

---

[15] Vagaries of weather occur all over Southeast Asia and are probably connected with large-scale deforestation. As a matter of fact, in the distant past the central elevated part of Samosir used to be covered with trees, which regulated the water supply to the lower areas. According to early reports, early in this century a large area was already deforested. While agronomists would attribute such a state to over-swiddening, there is little evidence to suggest that population density was ever high enough to attribute this clearing to agriculture alone (although population density was doubtless higher in the past). Rather, Hirschfeld (1979) attributes the deforestation to the construction of *adat* houses, for which large tracts of forest were cut down. Furthermore, this lumbering was followed by large-scale livestock grazing, so that cleared land would have little chance to revert to forest.

depending on the condition of the plant and the needs of the household. The nutritious leaves are used as well; they constitute one of the few vegetables that the villagers eat regularly. Until recently, cassava used to be grown exclusively for subsistence and was mainly intercropped with peanuts or planted on the borders of a field to fence off one area from another. But in response to relatively favourable prices, I witnessed farmers planting whole fields with cassava tubers. In Simatupang in particular, until late at night women could be heard chopping the roots into chips, which were sun-dried the following days. Although slightly more labour is required to produce *gaplek* (peeled, sliced, and sun-dried cassava), the burden of transporting it to market is considerably reduced. In addition, the price differential is significant, with cassava selling for Rp 50 a kilogram and *gaplek* for Rp 200 a kilogram in 1988. A local middleman usually sends the *gaplek* in large bags to a factory on the East Coast where they are further processed into animal fodder and glue. Another locally made cassava product is fermented boiled cassava (*tape*), which is sold as a snack. Especially for poor farmers, cassava is a reliable crop: whatever its fate in the market, it can, if necessary, be consumed by farmers themselves.

During the last few years some better-off farmers in both Simatupang and Simarmata have profited from government grants to plant clove trees. Because of its low weight it is an attractive tree crop to grow on the slopes, although initially the amount of labour required to get it established is substantial. The work involves digging a hole, planting the sapling, manuring, fertilizing, spraying, weeding, and pruning. Not surprisingly, it was the affluent farmers who could best afford to take fields out of staple-food cultivation, spend money on nurturing the young trees, and wait out the long period from planting to first harvest. Cloves have a production cycle in which bumper harvests occur every three to four years, with insignificant yields in between. Initially the crop promised high prices and consequently clove production in North Tapanuli expanded enormously: from 5 tonnes in 1974 to 213.8 tonnes in 1984. Prices dropped from Rp 11,000 in 1982 to Rp 5,000 per kilogram (US$ 2.50) in 1988.[16]

In neither village could a clear-cut gender division of labour be discerned in dry agriculture, although it is women and girls, more often than men,

---

[16] Between 1982–84 and 1985–88 the real price of cloves in the world declined by 62 percent. The most recent fall in prices is said to be due to the private monopoly on clove trading set up by President Suharto's son, Tommy, in late 1990. 'By doubling the price of cloves paid to farmers [to more than Rp 7,000 or US$ 3.50/kg] and quadrupling the price charged to *kretek* makers, it greatly worsened an oversupply situation and depressing demand. [...] After being encouraged to grow more cloves, tens of thousands of farmers stand to suffer as a result of [the monopoly's] failures' (Schwarz 1992a:40). In April 1992 it was decided to lower the purchasing price of cloves paid by the monopoly by 25 to 50 percent in an attempt to reduce supply (Schwarz 1992b:58).

Woman on her way to the *ladang* to collect cassava, Simatupang

who can be seen bent over their hoes, shaking soil from the tubers or shallots. Women are most active in planting, weeding, and processing, including the tedious peeling and binding of shallots (*ikat bawang*). In the households that I regularly visited I observed women participating vigorously in decisions concerning what and how much to plant, whether to sell crops or to hold them for higher prices.

Muara is also an important mango-producing area. Twice a year men climb the trees to pick the ripe fruits, which are then sold by women at the local markets or sent to Parapat where tourists are willing to pay good prices. Income from mangoes sometimes adds substantially to the household budget, if one is fortunate enough to possess some trees. One woman told me that were it not for the mangoes, she would not be able to send her son to university.

Finally, most households keep pigs and chickens for both sale and personal consumption. In Simatupang some families also breed goldfish in parts of their *sawah* not suited for rice cultivation. Wealthier families keep a water buffalo or, more often, they share one with one or more other households. Apart from being used in agricultural production to draw ploughs, water buffaloes are important as a means of storing and augmenting wealth. Some women in Simatupang process buffalo milk into *susu kerbo*, a cheese-like substance, which they sell at the local market.

The above description portrays two poor agricultural communities with characteristics and difficulties typical of North Tapanuli. It is not surprising that inhabitants have tried to find new ways of securing their livelihood beyond village boundaries.

Land and labour in relation to migration[17]

To a neo-classical economist, it is the poorest and the landless who are most inclined to leave the village and try their luck elsewhere (for example, Stiglitz in Connell et al. 1976:19). Several studies have found that the largest migration movements and those who migrate for the longest periods are to be found among the landless, while those with the most (and the best) arable land do not leave. Others (Lipton 1982:206, for instance) have asserted that complete household migration is usually highest among landless labourers, while individual migrants tend to retain their land. In general, the greater the amount of land held and the fewer the number of siblings, the higher the probability that the children can – and therefore will –

---

[17] As stated in Chapter II, substantial land data were only gathered in Simatupang (in cooperation with Peter Bosch). Therefore, most information in this and the following section refers to the situation in Simatupang only.

remain near the family home on reaching adulthood. Is this in accordance with the migration situation in Simatupang? The question is: to what extent does the land situation of the household influence participation in migration? In other words, is there a relation between land deprivation and the propensity to migrate?

In the previous section we have seen that population pressure has resulted in shrinking landholdings. Under such circumstances one might expect a large number of migrants to come from landless or near-landless families. I therefore tried to relate the amount of land owned or operated to the occurrence of migration in the household. It appeared, however, that there was no significant correlation between participation in migration and land ownership. In other words, household members decided to migrate irrespective of the land situation. There is, of course, the possibility that those with little or no land had moved away as complete households, to farm in other rural areas for instance. Unfortunately, given the nature of the village census, I do not have information on these cases. If we consider only those migrants who moved away for the purpose of education, there appears to be a weak tendency for households with migrants to have more land (especially *sawah*) than households without migrants (see Bosch 1990:22-3 for more details). This is especially evident for households from which children migrate to pursue tertiary education: they own almost twice as much land as the average household (12.5 versus 6.2 *rante*). Not only do affluent households have more land, they also have more capital at their disposal to make up for labour deficits as a result of migration of one of their members.

These findings suggest that the opportunity for migration, which is a relatively expensive undertaking, will appeal most to the better-off households who can bear the costs of failure. Part of their land can be used as collateral to obtain credit, or they can pawn land to co-villagers (Philpott 1970:16; Connell et al. 1976:18). Differential access to land implies that better-off villagers (compared with very poor villagers) are more likely to send off migrants than a simple neo-classical model would suggest (Connell et al. 1976:28). The next example from Simatupang is a case in point.

> Ompu Delmi (63) has seven children. Except for the youngest son, who is studying in Medan, they all live in Jakarta. Four of them have attended university, while the others have at least graduated from senior high school. As far as I could gather, Ompu Delmi owns 30 *rante* (1.2 ha) of *sawah* and 12 *rante* (0.48 ha) of *ladang*. In addition, she owns the local rice mill. She cultivates only one dry field herself, while the rest is sharecropped by others. The total rental income from these plots is some 6,000 litres of rice annually, which is divided between her and her sons. Her husband, the eldest son in a family of ten, died three years ago. His two brothers had been civil servants in Jakarta and moved away at an early age, so there was no need for the family land to be split up. Consequently, Ompu Delmi could rely entirely on

the revenue from the land and the rice mill to finance her children's education. She and her husband never needed to mortgage land. The youngest son's education is currently being paid for by two of his brothers.

The evaluation of the extent to which land ownership of the household influences participation in migration is hampered by the fact that the apparent wealth of a migrant household may well be a result of migration itself, and, on the other hand, it may be that land-owning households after educating their children up to university level are left with only a tiny plot of land. In addition, I knew several households that had never owned much land, but could nevertheless send their children to university because they enjoyed a regular salary in the public sector, or had income from other activities.[18] Furthermore, in both villages I observed that the initial costs of migration and the financial risks involved are no longer major obstacles for participation, due to the development of a migrant network. These days, people planning to migrate borrow the money needed from relatives who have already migrated.

Having demonstrated a positive correlation between land ownership and the propensity to send children away for schooling, we shall now investigate the extent to which soil fertility may play a role in the decision to migrate. I assumed that households with fertile land (and thus relatively high yields) could finance the education of more children. At the same time, in a situation of land scarcity, it is likely that households with low-quality land would be more inclined to migrate. This last proposition has been checked by comparing the fields owned by residents with the fields left behind by migrants. There did not appear to be a significant difference between migrants' land and residents' land with regard to yield per hectare, quality of the soil, or amount of fertilizer used. There was, however, a slight tendency for fields near the village to be owned by resident operators, and fields further away to be rented or pawned from migrants. Nevertheless, soil quality of the various fields was more or less similar, which indicates that migrant households do not hesitate to give up good fields (Bosch 1990).

That high-quality *sawah* may be given up by the owner shows that migrants make a comparison between the opportunities in the village and those in the *pangarantoan*. The availability and quality of land is not an isolated factor, but only one of a number of factors that influence migration. Evidence from Simatupang indicates that households in the middle and highest income groups not only have better opportunities in the village but that their members are also well equipped once they have moved away. They are generally better educated and have personal connections in the

---

[18] On the whole, however, it appeared that the men who held positions in the public sector, such as teachers, owned more land than the average landowner.

urban areas. Members from very poor families are less likely to migrate, partly because of their greater difficulty in meeting the costs involved and partly because of their having few connections outside the village.

Impact of migration on land distribution and land use

Out-migration has freed considerable amounts of land for those who stay behind. Caretaking arrangements are usually made, which enable otherwise landless villagers, kin and non-kin alike, to work an extra plot of land. It is this increase in access to land through renting, pawning, and borrowing rather than direct economic aid that makes villagers value the migration of co-villagers positively. In 1988 in Simatupang 39 households (19 percent of the total) cultivated land belonging to permanent migrants. Table 6 gives an overview of land operated and land owned by Simatupang residents.

Table 6. Land operated and land owned by Simatupang households (in *rante*)

Type of land	Owned by locals (A)	Operated by locals (B)	Status unknown (C)	Operated but not owned by locals (B minus A)
Sawah	662	937	2	275
Ladang	719	933	33	214
Other	317	323	20	6
Total	1698	2193	55	495

Notes: 'Local' means 'Simatupang villager currently residing in the village'. Fields operated by non-villagers are not included in this table.

It appears that in Simatupang about 23 percent of all locally operated land (495 *rante* or 19.8 ha) is owned by non-residents, many of them former inhabitants who have moved away.[19] This tendency has probably compensated for the fragmentation of landholdings resulting from the custom of partitioning inheritance among sons. When a man migrates with his household, he generally entrusts his share in inherited land to a brother or cousin. Male kin are formally entitled to be caretakers so that the land continues to belong to the patrilineage. That is why Ama Jujur, introduced in Chapter IV, not only had access to his own inherited fields but was also allowed to cultivate the property of his brothers who had migrated. But there are also people

---

[19] A very rough calculation was made by Eijkemans and Van Rooy (1990:22) for the central part of North Tapanuli. They found that more than 75 percent of the land (including agricultural land, house land, and idle land, but excluding forest) was not owned by local residents. Besides the fact that my estimate applies to operated land only, the large proportion of absentee landlordism found by Eijkemans and Van Rooy is partly due to the authors' definition of 'ownership', which differs from mine: in line with legal regulations, they considered pawned land as 'not owned' by the operator, whereas I, following local speech, defined it as being (temporarily) owned by the tiller.

who, after securing permanent positions in the city, pawn their landholdings to the *parripe* (immigrant) clans who have no land rights in the village, or to other marginal households. Other migrants retain their holdings, but, as a source of regular income, lease them to villagers in need of land under rental or sharecropping arrangements. Over time these practices may have actually levelled differences in wealth, but unfortunately I have no data to prove this. In order to keep a close relationship with their ancestral land, villagers say that for migrants, sharecropping land is preferred to pawning. In reality, however, as seen in Table 7, pawning and sharecropping are practised to about the same extent.

Table 7. Migrants' land in Simatupang (in *rante*)

	Lent out without pay	Rented or sharecropped	Pawned	Total
Sawah	13	67	63	143
Ladang	38	29	29	96
Other	3	–	–	3
Total	54	96	92	242

Whether lent out, sharecropped, or pawned, a man's permanent rights to land permit him to return to the village at any time without encountering major resistance from villagers. His land rights are seldom contested, though conflicts may arise concerning the way his father's or grandfather's legacy was originally divided. Or, as in the case below, a migrant may find his land mortgaged without his knowledge.

> Amanta Togatorop left Simatupang in 1954 to attend a teachers training college. When I met him in 1988, he was principal of a primary school in Pematang Siantar. He told me he had lent his inherited land to his younger brother (Ama Palmer), who occupies the ancestral house in Simatupang. Two years before, Ama Palmer had pawned his brother's land in order to try his luck as a taxi driver in Jakarta. The enterprise failed, however, and Ama Palmer came home empty-handed. When his elder brother suddenly appeared in the village, he had not yet been able to redeem the pawned land. Amanta Togatorop was furious because, being the eldest son, he was responsible for the ancestral property. He planned to redeem the land as soon as possible and sharecrop it to a non-relative. Ama Palmer apparently felt ashamed of his conduct, because it was only through others that I found out about this.

The fear of losing land, or quarrelling with kinsmen about it, can induce migrants to pay regular visits to inspect their property. Interestingly, it is because of the potential unreliability of brothers as managers of the estate that some migrants prefer to entrust their land to female relatives. We shall come back to this in the following section.

Although more land has become available for the stayers, part of the yield from this extra land does not accrue to the villagers themselves but has to be returned to the migrants through renting and sharecropping arrangements. In Simatupang the total payment to migrants in 1988 was 8,500 kilograms of rice out of a total of 33,000 kilograms harvested on migrants' fields. The estimated total rice production was 350,000 kilograms per year, so some 2.4 percent went to migrants through sharecropping and rental arrangements.[20]

Almost 11 percent of the total farming area (operated land and fallow land) in Simatupang is officially owned by migrants. With families scattered throughout Sumatra and beyond, the claims of individual members are difficult to anticipate by the remaining guardians of the land. This has resulted in a reluctance on the part of the villagers to put it into really productive agricultural use. Instead of growing perennials like cloves, the guardians tend to grow annual crops like peanuts or shallots which involve low investments. For this reason, even on steep slopes annual crops are cultivated which, from an ecological point of view, would be better planted with perennials. Moreover, some of these dry fields are not operated at all. In Simarmata some fields had lain fallow for so long that no one remembered who had last worked them. While the owners had probably migrated or lacked the necessary labour, the land was not attractive enough to be tilled by remaining villagers.

Contrary to the findings of other studies (Connell et al. 1976; Griffiths 1988), very few circular migrants in Simatupang and Simarmata have invested their money in agriculture (irrespective of whether they owned land or not), and none of them have bought farm land in the village.[21] There are several reasons for this. First, land can only be 'bought' on a temporary base, which is probably not attractive. Second, in Simarmata in particular, the land is said to be rather unproductive. Finally, there is the villagers' own desire to break their dependence on the land. After their return, very few circular migrants want to take up field work again. This is in accordance with other studies (for example Corner 1981; Lipton 1982:210), which indicate that villagers seem to use remittances for consumption purposes or for investment for getting out of the village (through education for instance), rather than for the improvement of agriculture. One circular migrant in Simatupang tried to introduce a mechanical thresher but, to use his own words, 'the villagers are not yet prepared for it'. In Simarmata in particular, migration and the lack of local infrastructure take away any inducement to develop the land beyond subsistence requirements.

Likewise, the few migrants who have returned to the village are not the

---

[20] I should, once more, warn the reader that these figures on land ownership and yields are far from accurate and are only given as a rough indication.
[21] Instead of making their own farms more profitable, there were, however, some circular migrants who had bought rice land in east Sumatra which they rented out or operated themselves with wage labour.

innovators modernization theory would like them to be, bringing back to their home communities skills and knowledge to improve traditional agriculture. In both villages, there is a tendency for returned migrants to be the sick and the unsuccessful. Few of them have learned new skills, or if they have, they are rarely able to put them to use in their home village.

To summarize, limited land availability is not a 'push factor' in the migration process. Instead, it seems that for many households the more land they own, the more likely they are to send away members, often to study elsewhere. Permanent migrants move away irrespective of the quantity and the quality of their land, a process which has expanded the land market in both villages. However, since migrants can reclaim their land at any time, only annual crops are grown on their land, thus limiting cultivators in their choice of crops. Finally, I did not find any evidence of substantial investments in land due to migration. To the extent that remittances are sent to the villages, they tend to be spent on consumption or education.

Contradictions and continuity

If agricultural land has little economic value, if it is not a significant source of present or potential income, why do migrants not give it up? Permanent migrants do not plan to return to live in the village, nor will their children go back. It therefore seems puzzling that some migrants so vigorously defend their few *rante* of land and wooden house with none of the facilities that a town can provide. In fact, few migrants part completely with their land. The reason must be that 'ownership' of land, especially ancestral land, ensures one's status in the *marga raja*. Even urban Toba Batak still care about this social value of land.[22]

Toba Batak ideology holds that ancestral land should never be sold. Whereas resident villagers may resort to pawning their land out of sheer necessity, well-to-do urban migrants are proud to be able to point out their land (whether cultivated by others or not) on their return visits. Even after they die, they want to continue their relationship with the land. As a result, many migrants who have lived in the *pangarantoan* for decades are buried in the *bona ni pasogit* (ancestral homeland). Journalists in Indonesian daily and weekly newspapers keep the issue of ancestral land in the minds of the reading public, often in highly charged moralistic tones: 'While migrants from South Sulawesi have imported cloves upon their visits home, to the point that the area is now noted for its cloves, Toba Batak migrants bring

---

[22] A similar concern with the social significance of land is reported by Kato (1982:229) for the Minangkabau.

only dead bodies to their homeland. Instead of having developed into a flourishing farming area, Tapanuli Utara has become a graveyard.' (Hutabarat 1987.)

This cultural attachment to *adat* land is also the key to understanding why, until now, the area has not been attractive to private companies (Hutabarat 1988). During my research a land conflict occurred in Muara subdistrict. A development company tried to buy 300 hectares of communal land (*tano hatopan*) in order to build a university. Since the government is keen to increase productivity, there is a rule that land which has been lying fallow for more than five years, as in this case, can be appropriated by the government. With the prospect of financial compensation (*pago-pago*),[23] several village men considered selling their property to the development company. It was, however, the absent landowners, especially those holding salaried positions in the city, who categorically refused to renounce their land rights.[24] Reforestation by government agencies faces similar difficulties when attempts are made to plant pine trees on ancestral land.

In talking to migrants, the point that recurred time and again was the necessity to retain ownership of *adat* land that ran the risk of being commandeered by others if left without a close relative to look after it. The value of land is aptly summed up by Cunningham:

> 'Government officials, businessmen, and even Christian ministers will hold onto their plot of land, both as social security for themselves and as inheritance and a symbol of respect for their children. The value of land as the ultimate tangible base of society is primary in the minds of Toba Batak villagers. Not only does the ownership of land give security, it actually represents an affirmation of Batakhood, and a tie to the group which is no more to be severed than that of the marga or dalihan na tolu.' (Cunningham 1958:33.)

Even in cases of non-cultivation, the productive potential of family land is not forgotten and its possession can be considered a form of security against adversity. For migrant husbands in particular, attachment to land may lead to retaining the low-yielding (but relatively secure) farm that is then worked by the wife and children alone.

---

[23] According to Vergouwen (1964:153), *pago-pago* is only sealing money which accrues to the witness in land transactions. It is not the actual compensation given to the rightful people (the descendants of the village founder).
[24] For a comparable case in Porsea subdistrict, see Simbolon 1992. Rather than differentiating between migrants and stayers, Simbolon points out the diverging interests of male and female villagers in the use of 'fallow' land.

Feminization of farming?

'Women, who leave farming more slowly than their menfolk, take over a very important amount of the agricultural activities carried out just one or two decades ago by men. The agricultural population, or at least part of it, tends to take on the characteristics of a residual population: those who cannot leave remain in agriculture, which makes the agricultural population prone to dramatic imbalances in sex-ratios and age-ratios.' (Cernea 1978:112.)

Several studies have argued that the loss of a significant proportion of the younger, more able, and better educated men and women (especially the former, since past out-migration has been predominantly male) increases the dependence of rural communities on women and the elderly and tends to increase their conservatism and hamper the viability of social and political institutions at the local level (Corner 1983; Wood 1985:253). This trend has been observed in Europe, as recent studies in such widely separated countries as Portugal (Brettell 1986) and Romania (Cernea 1978) attest, as well as in developing countries (Chaney 1983; Gordon 1981; Mueller 1977; Smale 1980).

Southern Africa in particular has experienced large-scale male out-migration for a long time.[25] The proximity of the South African economy and the attractiveness of relatively high wages in its mines, industry, or construction work has encouraged a long-established and extensive movement of men from Lesotho, Botswana, and Swaziland. It is younger men in particular who have moved away, and the women and older men left behind are unable to maintain the original level of production. 'The growth of the absolute number of women engaged in farming and even more important, the increasing number of men leaving family farms, produce the phenomenon of the feminization of the agricultural labour force' (First-Dilič 1978:125).

Although the picture painted in the studies mentioned above is a familiar one, the 'feminization of agriculture' thesis does not apply to all regions that experience out-migration (Moore 1988:75). There are a number of cases, especially in Islamic countries practising female seclusion, where women's farm work has not expanded as a result of male migration (Islam and Ahmad 1984; Jetley 1984; Shaheed 1981). Once again, this shows that women should not be treated as a homogeneous group. For a proper characterization of the feminization of agriculture one should recognize the differences between women based on variations in culture, class, age, and social status.

In Chapter II it was demonstrated that among the farming population in Simatupang and Simarmata women are clearly overrepresented: for every

---

[25] Bush, Cliffe and Jansen 1986; Mueller 1977; Murray 1981.

100 female farmers there are only 72 and 60 male farmers, respectively.[26] In the following section I shall explore the extent to which the empirical findings of my research match the common assumptions of the feminization of agriculture thesis.[27] First, to what extent have women gained more access to land due to male out-migration? Second, has this out-migration resulted in increasing female participation in the management and performance of agricultural tasks? Finally, does the absence of male labour lead to agricultural stagnation?

The comparative advantages of women's disadvantages[28]

Earlier in this chapter, I discussed the limited access of women to land due to their subordinate position in the kinship system. Although women put a lot of hard work into the land and their rights are recognized when they sell its produce, the land itself seldom belongs to them. However, while living

[26] Age, sex, and marital status of farmers in Simatupang

Age group	Unmarried females	Unmarried males	Wives/ widows	Husbands/ widowers	Total females	males
15–19	2	3	–	–	2	3
20–24	7	10	5	2	12	12
25–29	6	2	15	12	21	14
30–34	–	–	28	25	28	25
35–39	–	–	31	18	31	18
40–44	–	–	16	12	16	12
45–49	–	–	15	10	15	10
50–54	–	–	23	10	23	10
55–59	–	–	14	10	14	10
60–64	–	–	9	7	9	7
Total	15	15	156	106	171	121

Age, sex, and marital status of farmers in Simarmata

Age group	Unmarried females	Unmarried males	Wives/ widows	Husbands/ widowers	Total females	males
15–19	11	8	1	–	12	8
20–24	2	1	5	2	7	3
25–29	1	–	9	5	10	5
30–34	2	–	14	9	16	9
35–39	1	–	10	5	11	5
40–44	–	–	13	10	13	10
45–49	–	–	16	8	16	8
50–54	–	–	7	4	7	4
55–59	–	–	15	7	15	7
60+	–	–	17	13	17	13
Total	17	9	107	63	124	72

[27] It is, however, difficult to realistically assess women's adaptations to male absence on the basis of fieldwork, since both villages have a long history of out-migration.
[28] I borrowed this title from Arizpe and Aranda 1981.

in Simatupang I noticed a slight tendency for fields to fall into female hands, a process which Stivens (1985) has referred to as 'feminization of land'.[29] In several cases, rather than entrust their property to male kin, Toba Batak migrants prefer their sisters or other female relatives to cultivate their holdings. The argument is that when the land is operated by a brother or another male relative there is a risk that this person may claim the land as his own (since it originally belonged to their common father or grandfather). An example is the case of Amanta Togatorop presented earlier.

From the viewpoint of the migrants, the safest guarantee of their stake in the land is to have a female relative cultivate it since, according to Toba Batak *adat*, she is not entitled to inherit land. In Simatupang there were at least twenty women who had been given the privilege of cultivating male kin's land in this way. Most of them sharecropped the fields, while some were allowed to operate them for free. Going back to Table 7, which gives an overview of migrants' land in Simatupang, we can extend the table a little further. Of the 143 *rante* of *sawah* land, 33.5 *rante* (or 23 percent) was acquired through relatives of the wife. Dry fields are more easily entrusted to female kin: 60 of the total of 96 *rante* (or 62 percent) were transferred to women. This transfer should not be confused with the *ulos na so ra buruk* (garment that never wears out) or the *juma parulos* (blessing-shawl field), a land gift which goes from the *hula-hula* to the *boru* and which is given permanently (see beginning of this chapter).

In a few cases, as a result of their brothers' absence, women may even acquire property rights. During my stay in Simatupang, one woman received land as a gift (*daon sihol*) from her dying father because no brothers were left in the village, all having been educated and holding well-salaried positions in the city.

In general, however, cultivating the land of brothers who have migrated provides women only with temporary access and not with permanent usufruct or property rights. This results in a seemingly paradoxical situation in which the patrilineal system denies women ownership of land, but because of this very lack of ownership rights they may have more (temporary) access to land. Yet, the following example shows that the economic position of these 'privileged' women ultimately depends on the goodwill of the migrants.

> After the death of both her parents, Donna (26 years old and still single), runs the household with her schoolgoing sister. She has two brothers, the eldest being a farmer in a neighbouring subdistrict, while the youngest is a student in Jambi. Donna

---

[29] In the matrilineal society of Rembau (Malaysia), usufruct rights to ancestral clan land were transmitted from mother to daughter (mainly rice land and orchards). With increasing male migration, women also obtained rubber land, which used to be men's domain (Stivens 1985).

is allowed to operate the ancestral land (1 *rante* of *sawah* and 3 *rante* of *ladang*) which has not yet been divided among the male heirs. In addition, she performs some wage labour in the village. It is Donna who pays for the education of both her brother and her youngest sister. Recently, the eldest brother pawned the single *sawah* plot, with the result that Donna now has to sharecrop someone else's field.

This case illustrates that women's access to migrants' land, just like *pauseang*, is merely another kind of male generosity. Although women have a right to ask, brothers can refuse, which gives the sisters little room for bargaining. Women are not very likely to win in such cases; less access to resources gives them fewer options to exercise power. Moreover, as discussed earlier, few Toba Batak women oppose the patrilineal inheritance rules. A brother might return to his land in the village after years of residence elsewhere and it would still be recognized (although sometimes reluctantly) by his family that he had the right, 'if he had the need', to claim his land. The following story was related to me by two disappointed sisters in Simatupang.

> Directly after marriage, Ama Nurita (now 42) left his home village and went with his wife to Rantau Prapat, where they bought about 25 *rante* (1 ha) of *sawah*. When, ten years later, they had four daughters and no son, they were summoned by a *datu* (traditional healer) to return to the *bona ni pasogit* (ancestral homeland). Ama Nurita is the youngest son of a family of five. Since his only brother is a teacher in Pematang Siantar, Ama Nurita as the only remaining son is entitled to the parental land: 4.5 *rante* of *sawah* and 1.5 ha of *ladang*. While away, his mother had allowed her three daughters (two of them widowed) to operate most of the fields. Upon his return, Ama Nurita mortgaged two plots to his sisters. In other words, they were allowed to continue the cultivation of his land but now had to pay for it.

Beasts of burden or competent managers?

A tacit assumption underlying the 'feminization of farming' thesis is that, prior to male out-migration, women played a relatively minor role in farming and that when the men migrate, women 'take over' their tasks (for example Connell 1984:970-2; Menon 1989:188; Van Velsen 1960:266). Boserup (1970:19-20) has demonstrated how European penetration in Africa resulted in women enlarging their share in agricultural work in the villages, because both colonial officers and white settlers recruited males for work in road building, in mines, and on plantations. The gender distribution of agricultural work was thus to some extent modified on the lines encouraged by the Europeans.

If we believe accounts of the time, there is some indication that a similar change in the gender division of labour occurred on Samosir Island. At the turn of the century, Dutch officials were surprised to discover that women in Samosir were not the productive agricultural workers they had encountered in the Toba area. Instead, Samosir women were found to devote themselves mainly to weaving cloth. One source even attributes the food deficiency on the island to the fact that women did not participate in agriculture (Haibach 1927:21-2). However, it seems that in the late 1920s, with the conscription of men for labour in lieu of taxes, with (mainly male) wage migration, and with the introduction of cash crops, women took on a greater role in preparing the fields and planting and tending the crops (Middendorp 1913, in Sherman 1990:30).

In Muara, on the other hand, as discussed in Chapter III, women were said to do almost all the work, in the house as well as in the fields (Burton and Ward 1827:512; Junghuhn 1847; Marsden 1811:382). This is why some authors even depicted Toba Batak women as 'beasts of burden' (for example Krause 1981). Women's active role in agriculture might be related to the combination of both dry and irrigated fields, which required more labour. Villagers told me that migration entailed few changes because the permanent migrants of the time were usually unmarried men. Husbands often arranged to be away only during slack periods of the agricultural cycle. When double-cropping became more common in the 1970s, however, and as agriculture as a whole intensified, these slack periods dwindled away and more men remained in the village. Male out-migration from Muara, then, resulted neither in serious labour deficits nor in a significant shift in the gender division of labour.

Table 8. Number of agriculturalists in *afdeling* Bataklanden in 1930*

	A Total population	B Adult population	C Active in agriculture	D C as % of A	E C as % of B
Male	256,454	126,070	99,351	39%	79%
Female	265,197	143,018	19,504	7%	14%

* The population of the *afdeling* Bataklanden, including the *onderafdelingen* Dairi, Samosir, Barus, Toba, Hoogvlakte van Toba, and Silindung, was 93.2% Toba Batak.
Sources: *Volkstelling 1930*, IV: table 13, p. 186; table 29, p. 228; S. van Bemmelen 1987.

Since the 1930 census paid ample attention to the subsistence sector and to its participants, we would expect to find quantitative evidence of women's active participation in agriculture. Surprisingly, according to Table 8, only 14 percent of adult women were considered to be agriculturalists. How can we explain this low figure, which is in sharp contrast with the picture we receive from the literature of the time? It seems that the low figure stems from the definition of 'agriculturalist'. The census states: 'An agriculturalist is defined as he who rents out or sharecrops his land to others, who rents or sharecrops another person's land, who performs wage labour (coolie)' (*Volkstelling 1930*, IV:89). According to this definition, the first criterion is owning land. As we have seen earlier, it is mainly men who are landowners, since it is they who can inherit land. The second criterion, sharecropping land, also practically excludes females, since Batak *adat* did not allow women to be legal persons (*rechtspersonen*, in Dutch). Therefore women could not be classified as 'sharecroppers', despite the fact that they were often the ones who actually cultivated the land. The final criterion is not relevant here since coolie labour was virtually nonexistent in Tapanuli. Remarkably, owner–operators are not mentioned as agriculturalists. This is probably an omission, which I detected in the other census volumes as well.[30] It is therefore not very surprising that so few female agriculturalists were counted in the census. The 14 percent women in Table 8 are mainly widows and divorcees who, as we have seen, enjoyed some economic autonomy.

On the whole, oral history and travel reports seem to give a more reliable picture of women's active participation in agriculture than do the official census figures. For instance, although sharecropping was officially a male enterprise, several sources mention that women could engage in sharecropping arrangements (for example Nasoetion 1943:104-5; Ypes 1932:411), buy and mortgage land, or take land into pawn (*Indonesische dorpsakten* 1933:97, 100-2).

The fact that women farmers were historically as viable as men farmers has probably prevented women's workload from increasing dramatically with male migration. The assumption that women 'take over' male tasks is based on the idea that men do a considerable amount of work on the farm. Since many traditional off-farm duties of Toba Batak men have diminished or disappeared, as discussed in Chapter III, the work men do should not be overestimated. When the division of labour between men and women is observed in the two villages today, it turns out that even when the husband is present most tasks are performed by women and girls. I would even argue that the division of work is an important reason behind male migration. Whereas women and girls are indispensable for the work they do, men's labour can be done without. In line with the prevailing gender ideology, women add men's tasks to their own workload, thus enabling their husbands (or brothers) to find employment elsewhere.

This is not to say that the effects of male migration on the labour division within a particular migrant household can be entirely ignored. The extent to

---

[30] The reliability of the census figures is openly questioned by the authors of the *Volkstelling* because it is presumed that in some cases the term 'agriculturalist' has been defined too broadly: 'Often the wife of an agriculturalist was also considered to be an agriculturalist, even when she did not own arable land and was only helping her husband with his farming activities. Also, women who worked without renumeration were erroneously considered to be workers.' (*Volkstelling 1930*, IV:89.) While in my view such a broad definition of 'agriculturalist' is wholly justified, the problem, of course, is one of internal consistency.

which a migrant's absence is felt depends much on the life cycle of the woman. If she does not have children, or they are still very small, a woman has to do all the work in the house and in the field herself. This situation may be alleviated once the children grow older and start to lend a hand. Women all agreed that, although it led to more work for them on the farm, men could make themselves more useful by finding employment elsewhere than by staying at home. As farmers' daughters they have been socialized to engage in agricultural production from early childhood; they are used to making many kinds of decisions; they are knowledgeable about traditional farming practices and can perform almost all the necessary stages in the agricultural cycle. Most of them can independently answer questions pertaining to crop varieties, cultural practices, yields, and problems in the field.

If the out-migration of men does not dramatically add to women's workload, to what extent does it entail greater managerial authority for Toba Batak women? Some authors suggest that migrants' remittances can be used to hire labour, to improve land resources, and to introduce mechanization. As a result, women may acquire new managerial skills (Hay 1976:106). In this connection, Van Reenen (1987) maintains that in the West Sumatran village where she conducted research, landed women with relatives who have migrated are in a rather favourable position. They have withdrawn from fieldwork and instead rely entirely on revenues from the labour of others. These others are not only their absent relatives (husband or sons), who contribute to the household economy by sending money home, but also the sharecroppers and wage labourers who work the land.

In the Toba Batak villages, migrants' wives do not necessarily have more money at their disposal than women whose husbands are at home. Whether remittances are sent depends on the level of the husband's income. but even when his earnings are considerable, it does not automatically follow that the wife has access to the money or that she will invest it in agriculture. Nevertheless, most households without an adult male, like Nai Rina's below, rely on wage labour, especially for ploughing.

> For almost ten years, Inang Rina's husband has exchanged his residence in Simatupang for living in Medan where he works as a market vendor. Apart from operating some *ladang* fields, mother and daughter cultivate one plot of *sawah* land (2 *rante*). Wage labourers are occasionally hired to do the heavy work (ploughing, hoeing, planting, and threshing). During the previous season, a co-villager and some companions had performed the necessary tasks. These workers are said to be partly paid from the husband's remittances (some Rp 100,000 a year).

With her husband away, a Toba Batak woman may decide which crops to plant, when and where to plant them, and whether to hire labour. She may also deal directly with the KUD (*koperasi unit desa* or village cooperative) to acquire seeds and fertilizer. Rather than calling these responsibilities increased managerial authority, I would say that they are, at most, an intensification of an already existing pattern. As related above, over the years most adult Batak women have been active farmers, irrespective of the presence of their husbands. It is therefore misleading to give the impression that wives of migrant household heads are suddenly thrust into managerial roles for which they are ill prepared. According to one of them, while it was difficult to handle all affairs on her own, management of the farm did not represent a major change because, as she put it, 'I was accustomed to hard work and knew what I had to do'.

What may be new is a woman's control over resources, mainly revenue from the land. She may now allocate this according to her own priorities. This applies especially to unmarried women, who on their parents' departure may take on the role of farm manager, as in the following case.

> Nai Togis's parents moved to Tebing Tinggi in 1953, staying alternately in Tebing Tinggi, where they had bought 2 ha of *sawah*, and in Simatupang, an arrangement denoted by the Toba Batak as *marduahuta*. From 1968 onwards they remained in Tebing Tinggi permanently, leaving Nai Togis, their eldest daughter who was then 15 years old, to farm the family land, together with two younger siblings and occasional wage labourers. Nai Togis was entrusted with 2.5 *rante* (0.1 ha) of *sawah* and 4 *rante* (0.16 ha) of *ladang*, cultivating rice, shallots, peanuts, and cassava. Her parents paid her a visit once in a while to collect part of the harvest and to see if everything was going well. Although Nai Togis would rather have continued her schooling, she says she felt proud at the time to have the responsibility of looking after her father's property. At 25, she married her present husband from Samosir Island. Because of the availability of productive land they set up their household in Simatupang, resigning themselves to the prospect of having to give up or rent the land once it is divided among Nai Togis's brothers.

Although some women may take on the position of farm manager and employer of wage labour, it should be remembered that the reason men have moved away is because local agriculture is marginal. In other words, women continue the work which men no longer consider suitable. Moreover, in formal transactions the migrant husbands or brothers generally continue to exercise a dominant role, in pawning land or in borrowing money from a bank, for instance.

In North Tapanuli there are several reasons why migration does not result in farm expansion or innovation among the stayers. First, as we have seen earlier, most of the migrants' wives are at a time in their life cycle when their families and domestic responsibilities are increasing. Second, whatever remittances are sent are mainly used for children's schooling. Investment in education is encouraged by the lack of productive investment opportunities in agriculture. Agriculture itself remains a risky activity, given environmental conditions and unpredictable crop prices.

Declining agriculture?

'Farms on which women are the decision-makers tend to be smaller, more isolated, and have less fertile soils than those operated by men. [...] The feminization of agriculture without concurrent institutional support has led to declining productivity in the small-farm sector, an increasing proportion of uncultivated land, and a retreat into subsistence agriculture by women forced to feed their children from their land without extension or credit.' (Momsen 1987:345, 347.)

Several authors assume that where agricultural production is increasingly left to women productivity will necessarily decline, or, at best, stagnate (for example, Meillassoux 1981). Several African studies have stressed the deterioration of farming in the many cases in which women must do the work almost unaided by men (Boserup 1970:81).[31] Women may be forced to take fields out of production or to work them inadequately. Inability (due to lack of labour) to engage in appropriate land management practices may result in erosion, salinization, and other forms of soil damage (Collins 1991:41). In the Caribbean, Chaney (1983) sees a clear link between the local food shortage and the plight of women left behind by migrants to support their families from the farm. For Malaysia, Stivens (1985:18) shows that the majority of land owned by women is unused. She argues that male migration has led to an almost total neglect of agriculture in some places, with the consequence that rice has to be bought with migrants' wages. The under-utilization of farm land on the island of Bawean (East Java) has similarly been attributed to the absence of much of the male population, who prefer non-agricultural activities elsewhere (Vredenbregt 1964:117).

The general explanation given for this possible 'neglect of agriculture' is related to the prevailing gender division of labour in agriculture. It may be difficult, for instance, for women and elderly persons to maintain irrigation ditches or terraces in an adequate manner (Dandekar 1986). However, in the two Toba Batak villages I found no evidence of such phenomena. In Simatupang, where irrigated rice fields are usually ploughed by men, most temporary migrants are present during land preparation, as well as during the peak periods of planting and harvesting. In Simarmata, where dry fields predominate, the tilling can be done by either sex. Although migration of adult males is more common in this village, it seems that there are few labour constraints because there are no clear labour peaks. According to one woman in Simarmata, the harvest would not have been better if her husband had been at home to help her. It was because of poor soil quality and lack of rain that her yields were low, not lack of labour.

---

[31] An exception is Hay's study (1976:106), which demonstrates that in Kenya in the 1930s women responded to male migration by innovative agriculture: they started to plant cassava which required less labour input. In this way, the women managed to maintain – although not necessarily to improve – their standard of living.

On the whole, all but a few migrant households strive to maintain production in agriculture at levels achieved prior to migration. Part of the monetary contributions made by migrants is therefore used to hire wage labourers whenever the household experiences a shortage of hands. As a result, most households manage to produce the same amount of rice and shallots as they used to. Occasionally, women indicate that yields per hectare have decreased slightly due to time constraints or (especially during the initial period of out-migration) lack of money to pay day-labourers. Although large tracts of land on the plateau are left idle in Simarmata, they do not necessarily belong to migrants whose wives have stayed behind. Some households have such poor plots, or the distance to walk to their plots is so far, that they feel it is not worth the labour investment. In other cases, the fields have lain fallow for so long that no one remembers who last worked them. The owners have migrated and, except as occasional grazing for livestock, the land is not attractive enough to be operated by remaining villagers.

A second explanation for a possible neglect of agriculture, mentioned by Stivens (1985:24), is that women are more likely to receive land that is difficult to cultivate. This is unlikely in Simatupang and Simarmata, given since the main reason for giving land to women is to prevent it from falling into the hands of resident male relatives. Nonproductive land would certainly not be attractive to the latter.

In fact, rather than assuming that male out-migration results in a deterioration of agriculture, I would suggest that situations of stagnating agriculture are likely to encourage male out-migration. Hence, a feminization of agriculture may be a result rather than a cause of unfavourable agricultural conditions.

Having reviewed the major assumptions in the 'feminization of farming' literature, I found that rigid labelling may obscure several underlying processes. First, it is not always possible to disentangle migration from other processes or conditions which may equally lead to a preponderance of female farmers. In North Tapanuli heavy demands on women's work are not solely the result of migration. The roots of the present gender division of labour can be found in the pre-colonial period when men were frequently occupied with warfare, jurisprudence, and ritual activities, leaving agricultural work largely to women. Today, resident men may also spend their time on activities that are not directly productive (including social, political, and ceremonial activity and gambling). In other words, out-migration of men has not resulted in a drastic restructuring of gender roles but rather in a reinforcement of traditional patterns.

Second, all but a few studies describing a feminization of farming assume an increasing dichotomy between women working in subsistence agriculture and men as dynamic actors in a cash economy. It is argued that, as a result, the women become dependent on the cash remittances of the male migrants. I have noted that in both Simatupang and Simarmata, besides growing their own food, women are actively engaged in cash-crop cultivation and marketing. At the same time, as discussed in Chapter VII, many migrants are not the steady cash remitters they are expected to be.

Third, most studies on feminization of agriculture present a rather unsophisticated picture of mobile men and immobile women (Palmer 1985; Shaheed 1981). In North Tapanuli the low status associated with farming encourages not only men to migrate, but we also see an increasing number of young women pursuing their own (urban-oriented) ambitions. It appears that if the climate is favourable to migration, not only male adults (as 'heads of household') will migrate, but male and female adolescents as well. Since the departure of population from agriculture is not only selective by gender but also by age, it is wives and mothers rather than daughters who are increasingly involved in agriculture.

To conclude, if 'feminization of agriculture' is simply defined as more women becoming actively engaged in agriculture (Cernea 1978:108; First-Dilič 1978:125), then the concept may conceal more than it reveals. Not only the numerical overrepresentation of women, but also the ensuing changes in gender relations should be taken into account. Moreover, any linear perspective must be avoided; in other words, researchers should be aware that one single event or process (in this case male migration) seldom results in one particular pattern (feminization of farming). Instead, various processes take place simultaneously, each in its own way contributing to a 'feminization'. Hence, a discussion of the 'feminization of farming' concept should be embedded in a historical, cultural, and regional context.

In this chapter I have argued that, for an increasing number of Toba Batak families, agriculture has come to be seen essentially as a holding operation: its purpose is to continue to provide the basic elements of subsistence – food for the family in the village and partly for the migrant members as well – and to guarantee a home and a place in the community that can be reactivated when necessary (Hay 1976:107-8). Despite their lack of land rights, women play a pivotal role in this process as cultivators and caretakers of family land. In North Tapanuli, the women staying behind are not only migrants' wives (as most other studies maintain), but are increasingly mothers of male and female adolescents who have turned their backs on agriculture. It is generally agreed that one of the most successful avenues to urban employment is schooling. While in the past the education of girls was hampered by their numerous tasks in agriculture, today females make up a large proportion of the student migrants. For almost half of the migrants from both villages, the reason for moving away is for further schooling. This may seem surprising given the marginal farm incomes in Simatupang and Simarmata. The following chapter will, therefore, try to shed some light on the question of why Toba Batak attach so much value to education.

CHAPTER VI
The education syndrome

'When I was a boy in Tapanuli and left to study in Singapore, walking the long way down to the coast, the women in the family moaned and cried, fearing that I would fall off the earth and never come back. Today, the women will moan and cry if a son does not have ambition and does not want to leave the huta (village) and go into business or to school.' (elderly migrant, cited in Cunningham 1958:78.)

Many families in North Tapanuli encourage their children to continue their education and seek jobs outside the region. The almost excessive concern of the Toba Batak for having their children educated is not a new phenomenon. Its origins can be found in large-scale Christianization from the late nineteenth century onwards. While initially education was exclusively a male privilege, during the last few decades school enrolment of girls has rapidly increased as well. Since there are virtually no jobs in the region that require high levels of education, young people who wish to put their education to good use are obliged to leave their natal village permanently. The lingering question, however, is to what extent family members back home benefit from the investment in education.

Early Western schooling: a male affair

Considering the vast Muslim majority of Indonesia, it is striking that the inhabitants of North Tapanuli, like those of Minahasa and Ambon for example, are mainly Christian. This is the work of European missionaries who, from the late nineteenth century onwards, actively converted the Toba Batak to Christianity. However, they did not limit themselves to preaching the gospel, but also saw it as their duty to provide the people with general education.

As discussed in Chapter III, the Toba Batak lived in relative isolation until German missionaries and Dutch administrators entered the area in the second half of the nineteenth century. The Rheinische Missionsgesellschaft gained its first foothold in Sipirok, South Tapanuli, in 1861. From here it advanced steadily northward, converting many people in the regions of Silindung (1863), Humbang, and on the southern and eastern shores of Lake Toba. In 1883 a mission station was established in Muara (Pelzer 1958:ii-iii). According to one source (Kraemer 1958:47-50), in 1876 there were some 2,000 Christians in the Batak highlands, and by 1958 this had increased to 273,000.

While at first sight it appears quite extraordinary that Christianity was embraced so easily, the fact that conversion went hand in hand with education makes this more comprehensible.[1] Until then only a small elite could read (or decipher) and write the Toba Batak script. The old Batak letters served as runic scripts for divination, augury, and healing purposes for priests (*datu*) (Pedersen 1970:88; Rodgers 1988:68).

Christianity and education would hardly have borne fruit had not the indigenous chiefs felt strongly that a Westernization of Toba Batak culture was in their own interest. The Batak wanted more than conversion to Christianity. Attracted by achievements in neighbouring areas, an increasing number of local chiefs invited the Rheinische Mission to come and establish schools. All educational facilities for the rank and file were in the hands of the missionaries. Throughout the Batak highlands small schoolhouses were constructed by local lineage groups. The *zendingsschool*, or regional mission school, emphasized religious instruction, but also included practical reading, writing, and arithmetic (Cunningham 1958:51). The brightest pupils were able to gain prestige in their village by becoming evangelists and teachers (*guru*) in mission schools.

The missionaries were very optimistic about the possibility of 'civilizing' the Toba Batak, but there are some doubts about people's real motives for getting involved with the mission. Although the Toba Batak were generally eager to build schools, what they wanted was improved material conditions and the opportunity to break out of the limitations imposed by their traditional isolation (Kraemer 1958:44). For the Toba Batak, education promised positions of power.

As a result, the Toba Batak achieved a high literacy rate, which rose from a modest 5.9 percent in 1920 to 12.4 percent in 1930.[2] While they were better educated than, for instance, the neighbouring Karo and Malay, there were still considerable differences within the Toba Batak area. In the 1930 census most literates were found in the *onderafdeling* of rural Silindung (21.8 percent). In the Toba area, which includes the present subdistricts of Laguboti, Balige, and Muara, the figure was much lower (14.3 percent), while on Samosir Island only 7.3 percent were able to read and write (*Volkstelling*

---

[1] Another key to successful conversion may have been the policy of not challenging Toba Batak *adat* directly.
[2] For comparison, the 1930 census gives the following literacy rates for other areas of Sumatra: Aceh 7.1 percent, East Coast 8.4 percent, West Coast 9.6 percent, and Riau 5.6 percent. In general, it was in areas where Christianity predominated, such as parts of North Sumatra, North Sulawesi, and Maluku, that the highest levels of educational attainment were found (Oey-Gardiner 1991).

1930, IV:74). While these discrepancies may be due partly to economic differences, they are also related to the activities of the missionaries which spread from south to north. As will be discussed later, differences in educational level between Muara and Samosir still exist today.

When the Dutch annexed Batak territory they decided to subsidize the system of mission schools and gradually establish government schools (Pedersen 1970:89), less out of idealism or a desire for educated officials than as an integral part of the strategy of 'pacification'. For ordinary villagers, simple three- to five-year people's schools (*sekolah rakyat*) sufficed, which from the beginning of this century onwards mushroomed in the Toba Batak area. At the same time, improved roads enabled children to actually attend school. The first records of the primary school in Simatupang, Muara, date back to 1934, making the current village school at least 65 years old. It was a so-called *volksschool* (in Dutch, people's school), subsidized by the mission.[3] At that time there were 88 pupils, of whom ten were girls (Verhoef 1934:126). Through the *volksschool* many children obtained at least the rudiments of a Western elementary school education.

Emigration and the resulting need for further education clearly demonstrated to many Batak that popular education by the missionaries had failed them in the new circumstances of life. They were quick to see that the Mandailing Batak, for instance, who enjoyed government education with Malay as a subject, were far better suited for the new labour market. In order to satisfy their ambitions, the Toba Batak transferred their expectations away from missions, which up to that time had a virtual monopoly on guiding and educating the Batak, and turned henceforth to the government. In government schools the Batak trusted that they would receive adequate education for the jobs and minor administrative posts they desired in order to keep up with other groups of people (Kraemer 1958).

While the activities of the Dutch government raised expectations among the ordinary Batak, disillusionment was bound to develop before long (Cunningham 1958:37; Myers 1984:40). Few Toba Batak were allowed to attend education beyond *sekolah rakyat*. The Dutch restricted further education to the sons of local chiefs who were to be trained in the language, outlook, and bureaucratic practice of the ruling power (Graves 1971:251). This was provided in expensive Dutch–native schools (Hollandsch-Indische School or HIS), primary schools with a European curriculum, taught partly in Dutch. The first Dutch–native primary school was established in 1914 in Tarutung; the first school for secondary education (MULO)[4] opened its doors

---

[3] The monthly school fee was 9 cents per person (Verhoef 1934). A second primary school was built in the 1960s.
[4] MULO stands for Meer Uitgebreid Lager Onderwijs (extended primary education).

in 1927 (S. van Bemmelen 1992:146). Knowledge of Dutch was an essential condition for higher education. Most *anak ni raja* (descendants of local chiefs) showed considerable enthusiasm for this Dutch-language education, which suited their changing role. Only privileged ones were accepted at high school and a few of them continued their studies at universities in Java and Holland.

With the colonial government imposing restrictions on warfare and indigenous lawsuits, as discussed earlier, education offered a large number of men an attractive alternative. Descendants from ruling *marga* became leaders at the various administrative levels in the positions of *kepala negeri*, *demang*, and so on.[5] The Netherlands East Indies needed large numbers of clerks who had to be able to speak both Malay and Dutch in order to mediate between the colonial state and indigenous peoples. They were especially necessary when the state bureaucracy further expanded after 1900. Apart from the old district officer, new functions were created, like those of medical officer, irrigation engineer, agricultural extension worker, schoolteacher, and policeman (B. Anderson 1988:106; Castles 1972:202-25; Drijvers 1941). In the early decades of this century it seems to have already been the ideal for every Batak family to have at least one child in government service, if only as a minor clerk (Verhoef 1934).

The newly founded schools gave numerous young Batak the opportunity to turn away from farming as a source of livelihood. An increasing number of Toba Batak were eager to continue their studies beyond the village. Those who could read, write, and speak Dutch left their homeland for employment with the government as teachers and lower-level administrators, or with Western estates and business concerns as clerks and bookkeepers. White-collar positions came to be highly regarded in Batak society. 'Education was the "golden plough", the means of escaping from the drudgery of work in the rice fields and the monotony of village life' (Bruner 1961:511).

The demand for educated brides

> 'It goes without saying that healthy social development is impossible if women remain uneducated. They do not need to be equal to men in all aspects, in Batak society even less than in ours, but one may insist that all girls finish primary education at mission or government schools.' (Joustra 1918:305.)

With a slight knowledge of the prohibitions and constraints imposed on women's lives, missionaries like Joustra believed that Toba Batak women

---

[5] The Dutch followed a more restricted policy than, for instance, the British, who gave properly qualified Indians access to responsible posts in the administration (Myrdal 1972).

were servile, degraded, and overworked, and that an important part of their mission would be to improve the lot of these women, lifting them from ignorance and dependence to a state of knowledge and dignity.

Notwithstanding their good intentions, it soon became clear that the first mission schools were attended exclusively by boys; Toba Batak parents appeared to be reluctant to send their daughters to school (Kraemer 1958:66). This can be attributed to a number of factors. As discussed in Chapter IV, among the patrilineal Toba Batak a woman marries into another clan in which traditionally only her labour and her fertility counted. Any investment by her parents to educate her would therefore be seen as useless.

But perhaps a more important reason for parents' negative response is to be found in the gender division of labour (S. van Bemmelen 1989:22). As argued in the previous chapter, women's role was crucial in both household and farming activities. Daughters were expected to assist their mothers. They took care of younger siblings, they cooked, fetched wood and water, and helped in the fields. Mothers therefore had a lot to lose if their daughters were absent during the day in order to attend school. Most of them only agreed to send their daughters to school if the lessons were given in the evening. The missionaries made serious efforts to have vacations coincide with periods of the year when girls were most needed as helpers in the fields.

Another hindrance to educating girls was the Batak gender ideology's prescription of separate male and female realms. While parents might agree to let their daughters attend the first two years of the *volksschool*, the girls had by then reached the age that they were supposed to be separated from boys until they got married. This gender segregation also limited occupational possibilities for women, which was another disincentive to educating girls. There was a prejudice against office jobs for young women since it was considered indecent to work side by side with men not belonging to the same family. Apart from *bibelfrau* (in German, religious teacher), only nursing and teaching were considered suitable occupations for educated Toba Batak women (Kruyt 1946:72; S. van Bemmelen 1989:21). These professions fitted in with the prevailing image of Western women.[6]

However, by limiting or even denying education to women outright, some elite families got into trouble. Because of the scarcity of educated Batak girls, an increasing number of male intellectuals living in Batavia or elsewhere outside Tapanuli married educated women from other ethnic groups whom they found more appealing. Such interethnic marriages were strong-

---

[6] In 1988 I noted that in Simarmata, much more than in Simatupang, a fair proportion of female migrants were nurses; this is probably related to the presence of Catholic nuns in nearby Pangururan, who have run a local hospital (*kesusteran*) since the beginning of this century.

ly disapproved of by the Toba Batak. The missionaries took advantage of this general discomfort by actively promoting education for Toba Batak females. An increasing number of parents realized that educating their daughters ensured them of a 'good match'.[7] As stressed by S. van Bemmelen (1992), at a time of profound change the right marital alliance was very important for preserving the status of the family and the *marga*.[8]

Given the gender ideology, many parents preferred their daughters to attend segregated rather than co-educational classes. The first girls' school was established in 1892, led by sisters of the Rheinische Missionsgesellschaft (Pedersen 1970:88-9). Soon more girls' schools were founded, for instance at Pearadja, Balige, and Ambarita. The first pupils to attend the girls' schools came from elite families. They were the daughters of missionary teachers, pastors, some local heads, and the first Christians who lived near the mission. 'In a particularly creditable way Batak girls were educated in order to provide Batak teachers and clergymen with civilized wives' (Janssen 1924: 366; see also Manderson 1978).

The attempt to generate suitable wives for white-collar men is also reflected in the curriculum at mission schools, which stressed domestic skills like weaving, sewing, and hygiene, in addition to writing and reading, and of course religious education. It was mainly a 'training for the home', although not all these lessons in feminine skills were taken seriously by the pupils. Nor did the old gender patterns change. The lives of most women continued to be centred on the land and child care, along with collecting wood and water and weaving cloth, rather than on refined embroidery or ironing.

Even after the colonial administration entered the educational field, schools continued to be dominated by boys. Employment opportunities for women were still limited – at best they could work as unpaid domestic servants at the missions or as poorly paid nurses. The proportion of educated women gradually increased, however. While in 1920 women constituted only 14 percent of the pupils of mixed primary mission schools, ten years later it was 23 percent, and it rose to 34 percent by 1938 (Kruyt 1946:72). From a report in 1928 it appears that the proportion of educated women was

---

[7] In twentieth-century India the education of women also appears to be a response to an increased demand for educated brides (Dandekar 1986:98).

[8] Toba Batak parents wanted to have a firm grip on the choice of their future sons-in-law, as they had done before. In some instances, however, the education of their daughters led to conflicts, since the latter learned to regard marriage as a matter of individual choice. Their insistence on their individual rights threatened the Toba Batak *adat* system as a whole, because it implied that marriages could no longer be used by the elders to regulate social and political alliances (see Dobkin 1968 for a similar situation in colonial Africa). Consequently, several families refused to send their daughters to mission schools for fear that they would not accept the husbands chosen for them.

higher only in West Sumatra, Menado (North Sulawesi), and the Moluccas (*Algemeen verslag* 1928:6-7).⁹ At the time of the 1930 census 3.6 percent of Toba Batak females had gained literacy versus 28.3 percent of the males (*Volkstelling 1930*, IV:76).¹⁰ Throughout the first part of this century, higher education for women was still extremely rare. It was only later, following a period of intense nationalism and the eventual attainment of national independence in the 1940s, that significant gains were made for females as well (Raharjo and Hull 1984:101).

The 'path to progress'

During the period of Dutch rule, education became the most important avenue for advancement, mainly through the bureaucracy. Securing white-collar jobs carried immense prestige for both the applicant and his family back home in Tapanuli. 'Education was not only a matter of individual concern. Characteristic of Toba Batak society was the mobilization of funds by the clan in order to provide the brightest boys with a good education.[...] In other words, the education of its members became part of clan identity.' (S. van Bemmelen 1992:147.) Since the Toba Batak thought they were lagging behind other groups, the Javanese for instance, Western education was seen as the main path for catching up. The key word in Batak society became *hamajuon*, or progress. Emulating European education and material wealth and attaining higher social prestige became the ultimate goal for the modern Batak (Kraemer 1958:67; Pedersen 1970:91-3).¹¹

Some people, especially missionaries, reported with dismay the enthusiasm for materialistic advancement among the Batak people (Pedersen 1970:91). They observed a poignant discrepancy between the intellectual development of the Toba Batak and their persistent material poverty. One of them wrote: 'To a people who almost fully depend on agriculture [...] the provision of a certain number of jobs to be filled by natives is not very helpful. It is even to their disadvantage in that it confirms them in the

---

⁹ The table on which these data are based gives the school enrolment of boys and girls in relation to the total population in 1927. For Indonesia as a whole this was 1 male student to 21 men and 1 female student to 97 women. For Tapanuli these figures were 1 to 13, and 1 to 43, respectively.
¹⁰ In line with their relatively low education, women held few skilled jobs. In 1930 ten women in Tapanuli were in government service, amounting to 0.03 percent of the female labour force. For men this percentage was 2.4. Outside the civil service, 65 women worked in the health sector (making up 28 percent of all health workers) and 45 women held a teaching job (3.2 percent of all Tapanuli teachers) (*Volkstelling 1930*, VIII:126).
¹¹ Notwithstanding the ambition for Western schooling, B. Anderson (1988:103) notes that colonial educational policy was exceptionally conservative: in 1940, when the Indonesian population numbered well over 70 million, there were only 637 'natives' in college, and only 37 graduated with BAs.

opinion that a well-paid job is the ultimate ideal of earthly happiness.' (Joustra 1918:18.) Critics foresaw that educated people would develop an aversion to agriculture. They tended to regard their schooling as a badge that relieved them of any obligation to soil their hands through manual labour (Joustra 1918:11-2). In all schools whose courses aimed at entrance to higher-level education, the emphasis was on 'academic' subjects.[12] The structure of the school system was such that the degrees given were considered the primary objective, serving as passports to government bureaucracy.

One article mentions this problem even in relation to educated girls (Anonymous 1936). Despite their aspiration to live in the city and marry an intellectual husband, many had no other option than to stay in the village. The article contends that, in order to prepare them for the life of a farmer, agricultural schools should open their doors to women. These schools only trained boys to become farmers or agricultural extension agents, even though farmwork depended to a large extent on women.

While missionary schools and Dutch-language schools gradually spread throughout most of North Sumatra, the Toba remained the best educated of the neighbouring tribes for a long time and were usually preferred by the Dutch for administrative positions in the residencies, for example as clerks or overseers on the plantations, in government service, and in all sorts of private enterprise (Viner 1979:88). Their greatest opportunities came with the Second World War and the struggle for independence, when the departure of the Dutch created a shortage of educated personnel. Many Toba Batak men became army officers or took over important positions from Dutch and Eurasian university graduates or from members of the Javanese aristocracy (Pelzer 1961:71). On the other hand, during the heyday of nationalism after 1945 many Batak lost their positions because they were seen as collaborators of the Dutch. Moreover, the educational facilities provided by mission schools and supported by the colonial government were not continued by the new national regime.

While some preferential treatment had initially been given to the children of chiefly lineages who cooperated with the Dutch, mass education grew significantly with Indonesian independence after 1949, when regency officials instructed villages to construct schools and made attendance mandatory for all children. Schools were seen as the main way for poor families to 'escape' the rice-farming village for high-prestige salaried work in a bureaucratic urban setting.

To summarize, although today's North Tapanuli is one of the economically backward districts of North Sumatra, it has a long educational tradition.

---

[12] A notable exception was a large industrial school at Laguboti run by the Rheinische Mission (Pedersen 1970:89).

Due to the efforts of German missionaries the Toba Batak had the invaluable advantage of more educational facilities than were available for many other Indonesian groups. Long before independence they had developed an ambitious drive for education, both elementary and higher, because in their eyes it meant social and economic advancement and the key to personal mobility. This explains why a considerable number of Toba Batak men were able to leave their home area to occupy positions in government bureaucracy. As we shall see below, it is only relatively recently that women have joined their male schoolmates beyond primary school.

Education in the 1980s

The value of education is universally acknowledged in Simatupang and Simarmata. From the age of six or seven virtually all children go to the local primary school (*sekolah dasar* or SD). Those who complete their six-year primary education successfully, as most do, can go on to junior high school (*Sekolah Menengah Pertama* or SMP) in neighbouring villages. Subsequently, pupils can continue in senior high school (*Sekolah Menengah Atas* or SMA). For Simatupang, the nearest SMA is in Pasar Muara, four kilometres away; children from Simarmata who want to attend SMA have to go to Pangururan, a distance of 12 kilometres.

The 'hunger for education' in Simatupang and Simarmata can be found among all classes of the village community. This is the more remarkable since the situation in poor homes seldom stimulates pupils to concentrate on their school assignments. The family usually lives in a one-room house, often without a table or a chair. Reading and writing rarely have a place in family life and the necessary materials are not readily available. When the sun sets, there is no other light in most houses than that of an oil-lamp. I have watched youngsters barely settle down with their homework before being called to run an errand, answer a question, get a glass of water for their father, call other siblings from play; usually several interruptions follow each attempt to complete an assignment.

While secondary education has become more easily available to local teenagers, for those from poor families it is still a privilege rather than a right. But increasing land scarcity, the limited reliability of agriculture, and the realization that many job opportunities require at least senior high school have led more families to encourage both sons and daughters to get as much education as they can – if they have the funds. Many young people have rejected the idea of becoming farmers or performing other manual labour. Instead, a survey I held among 227 third-year SMA students in Muara revealed that they picture themselves in offices, working as clerks, or in higher, better-paying positions as government officials.

According to the village census, a large proportion of migrants from both Simatupang and Simarmata have moved away explicitly to continue their education. Table 9 shows that almost half the migrants from both Simatupang and Simarmata left the village for the purpose of education.

Table 9. Educational migrants from Simatupang and Simarmata (as a percentage of total migrants)

Type of education	Simatupang			Simarmata		
	M	F	average	M	F	average
Junior high	–	–	–	16%	8%	12%
Senior high	26%	29%	27%	38%	32%	35%
Tertiary	30%	15%	22.5%	2%	1%	1.5%
Total	56%	44%	49.5%	56%	41%	48.5%
	(134)	(100)	(234)	(100)	(54)	(154)

Notes: Senior high school includes general high schools (SMA) and vocational high schools; tertiary education includes universities and academies. Absolute figures are given in brackets.

It is striking that a large percentage of migrants move away to attend secondary school elsewhere. Despite the fact that junior and senior high schools are available within the region, some upper- and middle-class villagers prefer to send their children to urban schools, in Pematang Siantar or Medan for instance. These schools are considered to be of higher quality and provide a better stepping-stone to a position in the public sector. For this reason, several families have one or more children living in town. This is especially evident in Simarmata. Teenagers with a peddling father often join him in town in order to attend an urban school. The relatively large percentage of Simarmata youngsters who migrate to attend senior high school is related to the absence of an SMA within commuting distance of the village.

While children attending secondary school can usually choose whether they want to leave the village or not, those who aspire to tertiary education all have to migrate. A recently built university within the district (in Siborong-borong) is supposed to attract local Toba Batak students. Indeed, some parents from Simatupang encourage their children to attend this university because of its proximity and because board and lodging are cheaper. Its educational level, however, is said to be lower than that of other institutions. Moreover, the survey I held among SMA students in Muara revealed that one of the driving forces for migrating is to gain experience (*pengalaman*) in a different (preferably urban) environment.

As in other Indonesian areas, most migrants are better educated than

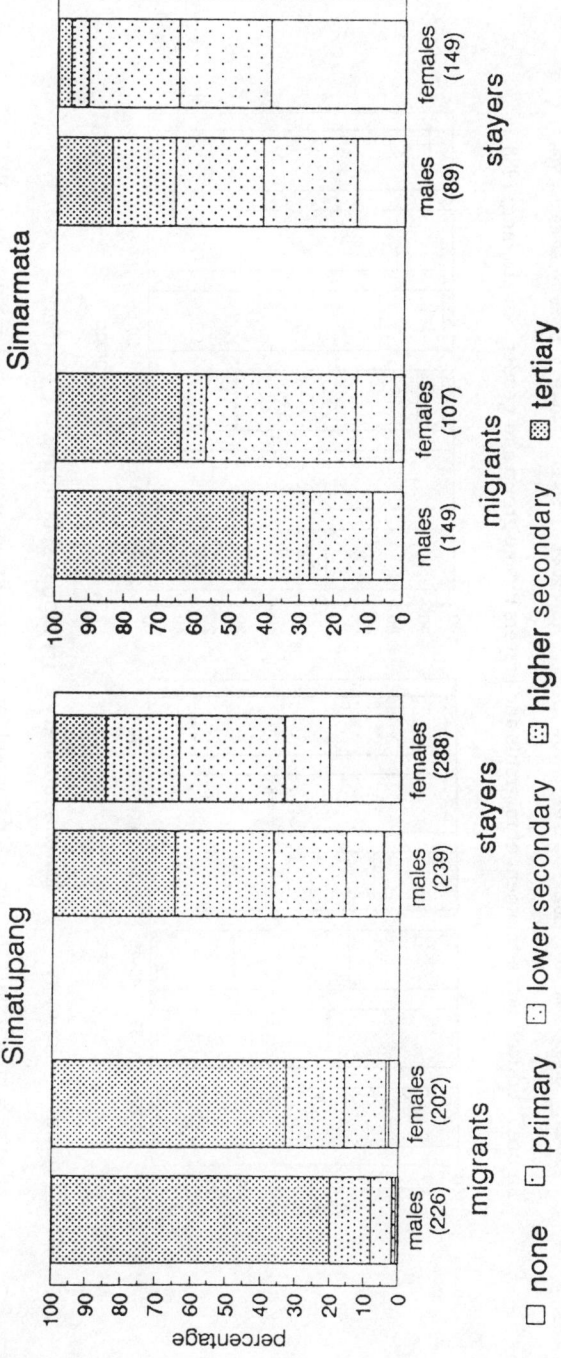

Figure 6. Educational level of migrants and stayers

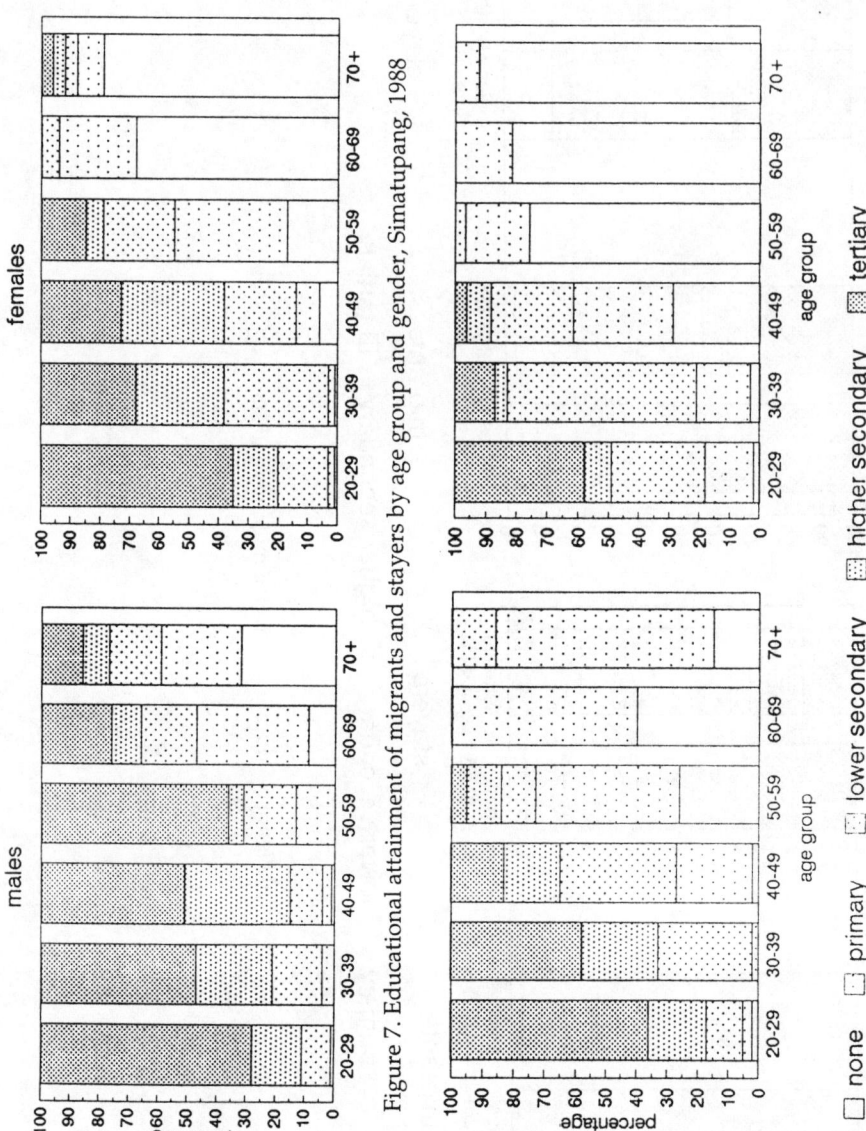

Figure 7. Educational attainment of migrants and stayers by age group and gender, Simatupang, 1988

Figure 8. Educational attainment of migrants and stayers by age group and gender, Simarmata, 1988

□ none   □ primary   ▨ lower secondary   ▨ higher secondary   ▨ tertiary

those who remain behind (Aklilu and Harris 1980).[13] Education elsewhere not only draws village youth away in the first place, but helps to keep them away once they have left. This can be concluded from the fact that there are relatively few highly educated persons in the village (Speare and Harris 1986:228). These trends are illustrated in Figure 6, which compares the educational level of migrants and stayers in Simatupang and Simarmata. In Simatupang 79 percent of male migrants were said to have continued their studies beyond high school, while only one percent had left with not more than primary education. In the less affluent village of Simarmata, 55 percent of male migrants were reported to have received tertiary education, while nine percent had only completed primary school.

As elsewhere in Indonesia, very few graduates practise their profession in rural areas, because no appropriate positions exist. But even if jobs were available, once they have lived in Medan or Jakarta to attend university, they no longer wish to come back, especially if they are able to find work or marry in the city. Even the migrants who leave to attend high school have no intention of returning to the village, whether or not they finish their education.

Boys and girls

Both Table 9 and Figure 6 suggest that education is no longer the male prerogative it used to be during colonial times. To compare school enrolment of boys and girls over time, I have placed men and women in separate age groups. Over the years, there have been marked improvements in the absolute educational level of men and women. While today girls get almost the same support from their parents to follow an education as boys, in Figures 7 and 8 we see that this was not the case for the older generation.

As can be expected, the number of individuals having no schooling increases with age. This tendency is especially marked for women. Several adult women, for instance, told me they had attended primary school when they were young, but every time a new sibling was born they were called home to help. When they returned to school they sometimes felt so stupid and ashamed that they dropped out for good. One woman from Simatupang (aged 58) explained: 'In the old days people didn't send their daughters to study because they felt they didn't need it as much. My brothers finished the fourth grade, but no one felt that we daughters had to. But I think that daughters should be educated as well as sons. I am illiterate (*buta huruf*), but I know that education is valuable, that it means rising out of ignorance.'

---

[13] Similar patterns have been found in most other studies of rural-to-urban migration in less developed countries (Hugo 1979; Pryor 1979; Speare 1975).

Overhearing this conversation, her husband commented: 'If parents do not allow their sons to continue their studies, they will soon turn restless, they get into mischief or they start *mangaranto*. It is different with daughters; they will feel pity (*kasihan*) for their parents and help them in the fields.'

Today, an increasing number of families claim not to discriminate in education between sons and daughters, but allow those perceived as 'bright' (*malo*) to continue their studies. This was already noted in the fifties, but a tight purse – not unusual in village households – may 'force' parents to deviate from the ideal of equal treatment:

> 'Whenever economic resources allow it, there is no hesitation in sending them [the girls] as far in school as possible. The abilities or capacities of girls are normally not belittled, and, in several instances, Batak fathers expressed great regret that finances have allowed them to give education only to their sons, who must become providers.' (Cunningham 1958:46.)

Boys and girls today spend the same amount of time in primary school, unlike the male-biased pattern seen in their parents' generation. However, girls are still less likely to attend secondary school, as seen in Table 10.[14]

Table 10. School attendance by gender, Muara subdistrict, 1986

	Male	Female	Total	Sex ratio (males per 100 females)
Primary school	2656	2527	5183	105
Junior high school	1081	928	2009	116
Senior high school	391	328	719	119
Passed final exam of senior high school	132	103	235	128

Source: *Kecamatan Muara dalam angka* 1986.

---

[14] When attempting to measure school attendance by boys and girls, we are hindered by the poor quality of statistics at subdistrict and district levels. Most figures give no breakdowns on class or gender. As a result, figures by gender could only be computed for Muara subdistrict. School attendance in Muara is slightly more egalitarian than that in the province of North Sumatra as a whole, as shown in the following table. The three age groups in the following table correspond roughly with the three levels of school in Table 10.

Sex ratios (males per 100 females) of the school-attending population by age and province, Indonesia, 1980 and 1985 (adapted from Oey-Gardiner 1991).

	1980			1985		
	7-12	13-15	16-18	7-12	13-15	16-18
North Sumatra	107	123	132	106	119	139
West Sumatra	104	104	101	103	98	110
Indonesia	106	127	152	106	116	130

The gender bias in Table 10 is a result of parental preferences in village households. To learn to what extent parents actually live up to equal treatment of the sexes (as most of them claim), in Table 11 I compared the total number of years of education sons and daughters had received.

Table 11. Educational level of sons and daughters within households

	Simatupang		Simarmata	
education of sons > education of daughters	49	52%	42	74%
education of sons < education of daughters	10	11%	3	5%
education of sons = education of daughters	35	37%	12	21%
Total	94	(100%)	57	(100%)

Note: This table gives only a rough indication of parental preferences. In order to assess educational attainment I counted the number of years children had been educated. Only households with both sons and daughters who had completed their education are included.

Especially in Simarmata, the favouring of sons over daughters is striking (74 percent), which may be partly due to the lower living standard in this village compared to Simatupang. It appears that in both villages parental preference for giving sons priority over daughters in higher education has resulted in males being better educated than females. This is not because of any stereotype concerning differential aptitudes of girls and boys, but continues to be related to the gender division of labour. Parents make more domestic demands on girls, and as a result they have less time than their brothers to devote to studying. Parental and familial assessments of possible returns on investment in their children's education also help explain continuing gaps in school attendance and achievement between men and women. Such assessments affect the family's decisions about who is 'entitled' to investments in education (Sen 1990). In this, as in most other societies, the issues of education and employment are linked to one another and to the larger question of how gender hierarchies are constructed and perceived in the society.

The preference for educating sons before daughters is based on parents' expectation that in a male-dominated society boys will benefit from their education by attaining well-paying jobs. Moreover, given their position in the kinship system, they are more likely to make the investment profitable by contributing in the future to the family or even to the entire clan. At the same time, a daughter's education is expected to yield a poor return for parents' investment, since after marriage whatever income a daughter earns goes primarily to her husband's family. While this may be the preferred gender ideology, in the following chapter it will be shown that more than a few educated women, even among those who are married, support their

Simatupang youth on a grazing field

siblings in town. It remains to be seen whether the gains from investing in education are greater for males than for females. Whereas in the past the education of daughters was a reflection of the concern of better-off families to secure a suitable son-in-law (that is, one earning a good salary), today it is increasingly acknowledged that educated daughters as individuals might find well-paid employment, a trend also noted for other developing countries (Connell et al. 1976:63).

Girls and their mothers frequently point out the value of education for a woman in case someday the death of her husband or a separation oblige her to earn her own living. In the past it was the provision of *pauseang* (a gift of land by the father) and the possibility of levirate marriage (that is, marriage with her husband's brother) which provided for a woman – at least in a rural setting – in the event of the death of her husband or a separation. The question of her own efforts would not normally have arisen. With increased female migration it is more often recognized that women may become breadwinners. Moreover, they are expected to provide something towards the education and maintenance of younger siblings, as in the following example.[15]

> Nai Meida (36) is a migrant from Simatupang who works as a secondary school teacher in Medan. Her father died some ten years ago. Although Nai Meida never sent any money back to her rural family, she did support three younger siblings as they in turn came to the provincial capital for further schooling. The first who came to join her was a sister attending secondary school. Nai Meida paid her tuition and they shared domestic activities. Subsequently, her brother came to Medan to continue his studies, again financed by Nai Meida. At present another brother enjoys free board and lodging while attending a technical school. Nai Meida's husband has been unable to work for several years. By teaching at two schools a day (one in the morning, the other in the afternoon) Nai Meida provides for her husband, their five children, and her schoolgoing sibling.

While secondary education has become more easily available to village youth, university entrance exams are often a serious obstacle to pursuing higher education. Males who fail the exams are more likely than females to take them again – or they are sent to the more expensive private institutions which are said to accept anyone who has the money. Girls, on the other hand, have less expectation of success because of the lack, until recently, of female role models, and they have been conditioned by the frequently expressed opinions of older villagers that there is no use in educating them beyond the secondary level.

Males usually claim that their families expect them to achieve academic success. A typical statement is: 'Their hopes are on me'. Failing the exam

---

[15] Unfortunately, the available data do not permit an estimate of the significance of female migrants' remittances in relation to other income sources.

while lacking the money to attend a private institution can smash the dreams of many a boy and result in frustration. They had envisioned themselves as government employees with regular salaries, and find themselves confronted with the prospect of becoming farmers like their fathers. Many then decide to migrate anyway and look for jobs in the private sector. Males had, and continue to have, greater mobility and freedom to seek such work without parental opposition. Although some female drop-outs also migrate, many are persuaded to stay at home to help their mothers in the field and weave *pandanus* mats.

Notwithstanding the obstacles, a fair proportion of women have made it into tertiary education. As shown in Table 9, 15 percent of female migrants from Simatupang left for that purpose. Most parents are hesitant to educate their daughter beyond the BA (*Sarjana Muda*) level, not only because of the costs involved but also because the range of acceptable marriage partners will narrow. As in many other societies, marriages in which the wife is more educated than the husband are disapproved of, and this encourages parents and daughters alike to stop education at a stage at which it is still possible to find a husband at a similar or higher educational level (Boserup 1970:122; Vatuk 1972:80). Or, in the words of a woman from Simatupang, 'a wife should work at a job slightly inferior to that of her husband, or perhaps equal in status, but never higher'. She is a primary school teacher in Medan, while her husband has a well-paying government job.

Job opportunities

During the colonial period most white-collar jobs were held by men. After independence many of these positions, including typing and other secretarial and clerical jobs, were redefined as 'women's work', while men took on the more prestigious occupations which had previously been the exclusive domain of the Dutch. Notwithstanding increased job opportunities for women, we have seen in Chapter III (Table 4) that the proportion of female migrants who have office jobs is only one-fifth to one-third that of male migrants. This situation is not peculiar to migrants from Simatupang and Simarmata but is a reflection of the national situation. Office work is still a male prerogative in Indonesia, just as it is in many other developing countries. There is one notable exception. Far from being a male monopoly, the teaching profession seems to be open to both sexes (see also Inglis 1983; Manderson 1978). At the national level women even outnumber men in the teaching profession although, significantly, men continue to dominate senior administrative positions within the schools. Women are less likely to be employed at secondary and tertiary levels than at the primary level. This is consistent with a study by Hull (cited in Raharjo and Hull 1984:113), who found that whereas in Yogyakarta 29 percent of primary school teachers were female, only 16 percent of high school teachers were, and even at the primary level only 10 percent of the principals were female. One reason why women have been able to get teaching jobs fairly easily has been the wide expansion of schools, particularly the government primary schools (SD Inpres). The recent slowing down of this expansion means many young graduates have greater difficulty finding employment.

I surveyed job preferences and plans for future residence among third-year students at the senior high school (SMA) in Muara.[16] Most of the students did not see much future in staying in the region. They were willing to remain in North Tapanuli only if they could obtain white-collar jobs there. Lacking this opportunity, virtually all wished to migrate. In replies to the question concerning absent relatives and their places of residence, it was apparent that students planned to make use of their connections outside the village and district.

As far as career goals are concerned, most girls aspired to become secondary school teachers. One teachers training college in Medan is even jokingly called *sekolah namboru* because of the large number of Toba Batak girls related by kinship ties. As in most other societies, female students tend to choose subjects of a generalist rather than a specialist nature. They prefer to be educated in a literary or academic manner, rather than in the fields of science and technology, as boys tend to do. Moreover, quite a few male SMA pupils aspire to a job in the army or the police force. These job preferences may seem unrealistic given their parents' low educational attainment and their generally limited household resources. More than 80 percent of all pupils hoped to get a government job as *pegawai*, while a similar percentage of their parents are farmers. The term *pegawai* is used by villagers to refer to all kinds of white-collar employees including clerks, teachers, and government administrators. Applicants often need personal connections with employees in influential positions who can help them secure a job, as in the following case.

> Rebecca (24), an SMA graduate from Simatupang, left for Medan a few years ago to live with her elder brother. She failed the entrance exam for a state university and therefore had to look for employment. Her brother, who works as a senior high school teacher, managed to find her a job at a health institution, but she resigned within a few months because she did not like the work. She thereupon took typing lessons to increase her chances on the labour market. Again through her brother's mediation she found employment as a clerk at a senior high school, a branch of his own school. While her salary is only Rp 32,500 (US$ 16.25) a month, she prefers this work to better-paid factory employment because 'it brings more status'.

---

[16] I wish to thank the school head for permitting this survey to take place and the teachers and students for helping me carry it out. The survey took place in July 1988.

To summarize, even though many families have low revenues from agriculture, education has become a key ingredient of Toba Batak life, and both girls and boys leave the region to look for further education or training. Some will succeed in finding an office job, while others lack the financial backing to enter the white-collar labour market. While income disparities do exist, parental strategies turned out to be relatively uniform across the different socio-economic groups, varying not in kind but only in degree. Below we shall focus on the repercussions of the 'education syndrome' for the rural family.

Financial drain

> This afternoon I went to see Ama and Nai Dompak. Nai Dompak was chopping *gaplek* (cassava chips) in front of the porch. Her husband had just returned from the primary school where he works as a teacher. Soon our chatting was disturbed by the postman, who entered the village on his motorbike and delivered a letter. It was a message from their eldest son, Dompak, who is a student in economics in Bengkulu, requesting Rp 1 million (US$ 500!) to take an exam. Taking a quick look into the interior of the house, I was puzzled how these people could ever raise such a huge amount of money. (Based on field diary Simatupang 3-3-1988.)

While Indonesia has made significant efforts towards providing public school education beyond primary school for all children, families must make considerable investments to make possible their children's education. In 1988 the annual fee for junior high school was Rp 5,300, while parents with children in senior high school paid double that amount. In addition, books have to be bought and one or two uniforms. Those who live outside the region to attend school or university need much more. The costs for tuition, rent, clothes, and food are estimated at Rp 400,000–500,000 a year.[17] Hence, migration for tertiary education – with its heavy costs, uncertain outcome, and delayed returns – is inevitably linked to higher incomes (Lipton 1982:198) and, as discussed in Chapter VII, to land ownership. This is illustrated in the following example.

> Ompu Jonar (aged 58) has ten children, three of whom still live at home in Simatupang. Being one of the descendants of the ruling *marga* and his father's sole heir, he owns 13 *rante* (0.52 ha) of *sawah* land and 4 *rante* (0.16 ha) of *ladang* land. The rice fields are worked by casual wage labourers, usually less-affluent neighbours, earning Rp 2500 a day, while the dry fields are cultivated by his wife. Since Ompu Jonar holds a position as school inspector, he has a regular salary of at least Rp 200,000 a month. He is also one of the few people in Simatupang who ride a

---

[17] In Muara subdistrict 61 percent and in *kabupaten* North Tapanuli 88 percent of the money received through postal orders was sent to dependent migrants, presumably for educational purposes (*Tapanuli Utara* 1986:134). A similar calculation for four villages in West Sumatra revealed that only 11 percent of the money received from migrants was subsequently sent off to people living outside the region (Van Reenen 1987).

motorbike and who have built themselves a brick house. His four eldest sons have all attended tertiary education and hold well-paying government jobs, the eldest working at the forestry department in Central Sulawesi. The next three children are studying in Medan. With two others from Simatupang they occupy a house their father bought some fifteen years ago. A quick calculation reveals that virtually the complete salary of Ompu Jonar is spent on education and living costs of these three children. Apart from being school inspector, Ompu Jonar holds two other important posts. He is *voorganger* (lay preacher) at the local HKBP church and chairman of the village cooperative.

While it is commonly believed that successful migrants will contribute to their siblings' education, the above example shows that this is not necessarily always so. It seems that those who have ample means to educate their children and provide them with a job can usually do without remittances. The situation of Ompu Jonar's neighbours, who have fewer resources, forms a poignant contrast.

> Jumina's parents own 2 *rante* (0.08 ha) of *sawah* land and 4 *rante* (0.16 ha) of *ladang* land. Apart from revenues from the land, Ama Jumina earns additional income by performing casual wage labour (for Ompu Jonar among others). After graduating from SMA, the eldest daughter, Jumina, initially stayed in the village. Despite her pleas, her parents did not allow her to continue her studies. They wanted to save money to send the other children to senior high school as well. Feeling bored with village life, Jumina soon left for Medan where she started to look for a job. When I met Jumina, she was living with Ompu Jonar's children in Medan without paying rent (*manumpang*) and had not yet succeeded in finding suitable employment. It is clear that she lacks both the money to 'buy' a job and the relatives to intercede for her. Being the first child, there are no remittances from an elder sibling, nor will she probably be able to help her younger siblings in the future.

When the family is short of money, the resources the family is willing to allocate to the schooling of girls is determined to a large extent by the educational needs of their siblings. Eldest daughters, like Jumina, are often expected to forego their chances for higher education so that younger children, especially males, can continue beyond secondary school. Younger siblings are generally better off. Not only are there no more relatives left to sacrifice for, but there is also a chance that older migrant siblings will send remittances, enabling them to continue their education longer.[18] Most parents in Simatupang and Simarmata try to offer equal educational opportunities to all their male offspring. However, in some households with limited resources there is a preference for concentrating investments on one

---

[18] Whereas according to other studies (for instance Greenhalgh 1988:56; Strange 1981:96) the eldest daughter in a family is most likely to be denied education, I did not find evidence for this. My survey among third-year SMA students in Muara indicates that (at least up to this level) eldest daughters were not underrepresented. Of the 109 girls surveyed, 29 percent were eldest daughters, 42 percent were middle, 27 percent were youngest, and 2 percent were only daughters.

son, often the first, with the expectation that in the future he will help finance the schooling of the younger siblings.

Instead of supplying a child with land upon marriage, as used to be the custom, parents now try to provide a child with education and a white-collar job (Fegan 1983). In order to finance their children's education many households have pawned part of their land, as discussed in Chapter V. A primary school teacher in Simatupang explained to me that she had not received *pauseang* because her parents had financed her study. For this woman land and education seemed to be viewed as interchangeable, but this does not hold for all household members. One man in Simatupang, a youngest son, complained that he could not continue his education because not only had his parents used up their savings for the education of his siblings, but they had also pawned most of their land. He was thus injured twice, receiving neither education nor land.

Besides pawning land, parents may also sell a water buffalo, in 1988 worth about Rp 300,000, or other livestock. Clauss (1982:7) recounts that Simalungun families that 'can afford to do so usually give each child whom they want to get higher education his [sic] "personal" water buffalo, to be sold later to pay education and "job promotion" expenses'. Also in North Tapanuli water buffaloes are often explicitly kept as 'education insurance' for children. When asked for the reason for the decline in the number of water buffaloes in Simarmata, a woman replied '*Kerbau diganti oleh sarjana*' ('Water buffaloes have been replaced by university graduates').

While most households in Simatupang have valuable rice land which can be mortgaged, in Simarmata a number of families are able to shoulder education costs only through the husband's peddling activities. Interestingly, a considerable number of the students live with, or in the vicinity of, their trading fathers in town. One of the features of a 'split' household is that small expenses like exercise books, pens, or pocket money for the children at home usually come straight from the mother's purse, while larger expenses are borne by the migrant father.

Parents are expected to make great personal sacrifices for their children. Even if it entails real personal deprivation, parents are seen as having the duty to provide their children with as much education as possible. I know many women, mothers as well as wives of migrants, who, regardless of the level of their own literacy, scraped together money from selling mangoes, cultivating shallots, or weaving *pandanus* mats. While ignorant of her son's branch of study, one elderly woman told me that she had sold what little wealth she possessed in the form of gold a few years ago to finance her son's education. The details differ, but many village women, through their industry and their secret savings, make it possible for their children or siblings to continue their education. Appeals are made to them regularly, for example through the Medan bus driver handing over a request to send a certain amount of money the following day.

Because lodgings in town are expensive, most families can only afford to send their children to an urban school provided they stay with a relative. If the rural family also provides rice for the urban relatives, food costs decrease substantially. Several children are able to attend high school with the financial help of a migrant sibling, male or female, like Nai Meida mentioned earlier. Other students may have their university fees paid by an uncle (either paternal or maternal) or they may live in his household. This is not always one-sided generosity but can be advantageous to the urban relatives as well. One woman, originating from Simatupang, told me that she lived with a cousin and his family (twelve children!) while attending teachers training college. Although she had paid a small amount of rice for board and lodging, she was treated no better than a maid. She complained of having to get up at four o'clock in the morning and sweep the house. From the stories I gathered, it seems that girls in particular are expected to return a 'favour' to their urban relatives.

Having examined the substantial costs involved in educating one's children, we shall now turn to the parents' expectations as to how those who stay in the village may benefit in the future.

Security and status

In a society like Indonesia where there are no state pensions (except for certain government employees) and where all savings and financial investments are extremely insecure in the long run, parents depend on their children for support in their old age. Toba Batak children are taught from an early age that if they have any *akal* (intelligence) and ambition they will migrate so that they can help the family back home. Parents believe that investing in a son's education in particular is worthwhile, for economically successful sons lose face if they are miserly in supporting their family. In any case, parents do not have much choice, for most children openly dislike the hard physical labour of tilling the soil.

Most families strive to have at least one son finish tertiary education and they expect him to acquire a position in the civil service or in the commercial sector. Irrespective of the salary, a white-collar job provides security and income, and it is therefore preferred to jobs in the non-formal sector, which generally provide low and irregular wages (Oey-Gardiner 1991:66). A government job is also aspired to because of the fringe benefits and opportunities for receiving bribes. Moreover, many government employees have some free time and the inside knowledge necessary to take part in business outside office hours.

For villagers, remittances from family members who have migrated are by no means the only form of repayment for educational investments. They can also profit from having relatives in the urban public sector who can act as intermediaries between the villagers and the government apparatus (Von Benda-Beckmann and Von Benda-Beckmann 1987). There are also other benefits, such as assistance in finding jobs and housing for those coming to town, socio-political advantages that could accrue to wealthier parents arranging profitable marriages for their children, and more generally the prestige of having a university graduate (*sarjana*) in the family.

Although children who have migrated cannot be forced to repay the financial and social costs of their education, they are under moral pressure to 'remember' their relatives back home (Anonymous 1976).[19] When bidding farewell to her son who left to study in Jakarta, one mother said: 'You are my hope, my son, the hope of all of us. Now you go away to seek knowledge; you should not forget us.'

In some cases migrants have their own preferences as to how to spend their money. As discussed in Chapter IV, many Toba Batak males who have reached positions of prominence have shown a desire to sponsor feasts or construct tombs to commemorate their forebears. In the villagers' eyes this may not be altogether dysfunctional, since it brings prestige to the entire clan (Sherman 1990:52).

Risks involved

Almost all village youth want to obtain an education in the hope that they may leave the highlands and find employment in an office. Most villagers fail to recognize that this path to success is no longer as functional as it was in the past. As long as only a minority are literate, it is taken for granted that an educated person is entitled to a job in the public sector. It is not surprising that this attitude tends to survive long after the majority have become educated (Dore 1976). Sending children to school is not only costly; nowadays it is also risky. A surplus of those seeking office jobs is inevitable when the number of children enjoying secondary and tertiary education is increasing by leaps and bounds. Consequently, many people with twelve or more years of schooling behind them will not manage to secure a place in the government apparatus, and it is questionable whether they will obtain access to private enterprise, since this sector is usually not interested in

---

[19] A comparable situation has been described by Greenhalgh (1988) for Taiwan. Given the importance of patrilineal kinship ties and the persistence of extended patriarchal family households in Taiwan, both sons and daughters were forced to repay their 'debt' to their family.

young people with general education only.[20] As large numbers of students complete SMA, employers begin to require still higher levels of education for the same jobs. For instance, I met several women who found a job as salesgirl in one of the many shops in Medan, but at some department stores a tertiary education is already required because university graduates are considered to be more 'civilized', as one Simatupang girl regretfully discovered.

Once having lived in an urban environment, it is doubtful whether these young migrants will decide to return to the village and become farmers. After years at school, young people find it difficult to adjust to manual work in the fields. The curricula in schools seem almost totally irrelevant to the needs and concerns of the rural workforce, or the rural community at large. As children climb the educational ladder, their attention is inevitably directed towards the towns. As a result, some young men end up driving a *becak* (tricycle cab) or doing all kinds of miscellaneous jobs in town rather than return to the village.

Even for university graduates it is difficult to find employment, and many have to accept jobs other than the ones for which they were trained. Although graduates may have to wait years to find positions to which they consider themselves entitled, tertiary education is still seen as the high road to permanent employment. With the large number of college graduates in Indonesia, a diploma alone will not assure one of getting a job unless one 'knows the right people'. Others seek government positions far away, in some cases migrating as far as Sulawesi or Kalimantan.

It seems that women in particular have trouble finding suitable employment because they have less freedom to look for a job on their own. For example, my assistant in Simarmata was a graduate from a teachers training college and had been waiting to get tenure at a junior high school for more than two years. Her parents had called her back to the village in order to assist them on the farm.

Even those who eventually manage to secure a job in the public sector will not always be in a position to help their family back home. Teachers and clerks are underpaid, and advancement in government positions is not as rapid today as it used to be. In other words, parents can never be sure of a son's loyalty and promise of support, as in the case below.

---

[20] Vocational schools attract far fewer students than the general SMA. In 1990 only 33 percent of all male students at senior high school in North Sumatra attended vocational training, compared to 42 percent of the female students. When compared to the other Sumatran provinces, only the percentages for Aceh were lower (27 and 36, respectively) (*Penduduk Indonesia* 1990:139-40). Apart from a preference for general education, the relatively low percentage of students at vocational schools may also be related to the distance involved and (for the technical schools) to the higher costs for buying materials and tools, a complaint I heard in both Simatupang and Simarmata. Whether vocational schools are less widespread in North Sumatra than in the other provinces, I do not know.

Ompu Eriza has nine children, the younger two still living at home. Having limited resources, she and her husband concentrated their educational investments on their first son. They pawned their productive land, which after ten years has not yet been redeemed, with the result that they have to rent and sharecrop from others. The parents hoped that by educating this son, the younger children could later reap the fruits. The son finished teachers training college in Medan some ten years ago and found employment at a senior high school. His monetary salary amounts to some Rp 85,000 (US$ 42.50) a month, with which he has to support his wife and children. He has never sent his parents money, and consequently his younger siblings have not been educated beyond secondary school. Two brothers are factory workers in Belawan (Medan), while one has become a farmer in East Sumatra. Ompu Eriza is disappointed in her eldest son ('we get small thanks for our pains') and, stereotypically, blames her daughter-in-law for being stingy.

In sum, despite their limited resources poor households spend most of their reserves on their children's education. The need for social security induces a 'wait and see' attitude on the part of parents with respect to the earnings and loyalty of educated children. As we have seen, wealthier households (like Ompu Jonar's mentioned earlier) have a wider range of options for risky but potentially profitable schooling of their children.

The education syndrome

Having come to the end of this chapter, the notion 'education syndrome', as used in the title, merits a brief explanation. As I have argued, the Toba Batak have an almost excessive concern with education as the only possible means to advancement. To many villagers, education has become an obsession, and being forced to give up schooling often results in frustration. Some people have even literally fallen victim to the 'education syndrome': they have gone mad because the household's financial resources did not permit them to pursue their intellectual ambitions.

When I met Ama Rajiman (55) for the first time, I was shocked. He lay on the floor in a dark corner of the house, with one foot locked to a tree trunk. His face was ashen and he stared around wildly. His wife, Nai Rajiman, warned me that he could be dangerous. Ten years ago he raped her, with her youngest daughter (named Sedih or 'Sad') as the result. When I entered the house, Ama Rajiman asked me in perfect English 'What's the time?' Then Nai Rajiman related to me the background of her husband's lunacy. When he was a boy he attended teachers training college; he wanted to become an English teacher. Before completing his education, however, his mother was no longer willing to pay his tuition fee. Her son begged her to give him the money 'sampai menangis' ('until he cried'), but she stuck to her guns and sent him to the fields. When he married Nai Rajiman he was already frustrated, but his insanity became clearly manifest after the birth of their second child. In one of his lucid moments he commanded his wife to send all their children to school, no matter how high the costs. Nai Rajiman operates 1 *rante* (0.04 ha) of *ladang* (her husband's inheritance) and 1.5 *rante* (0.06 ha) of *sawah* (owned by her migrant brother-in-law). Their eldest son, an SMA graduate who occasionally sent remittances from Jakarta, suddenly died a few weeks ago. All hope is now on the youngest son, who attends university in Siborong-borong.

Another woman, aged 25, was said to have gone mad after her mother sold her golden jewellery to finance her daughter's teachers' training. During my stay in Simatupang she was kept inside the house in a cage. Although there is no hard and fast proof that these cases of mental illness are due to an 'education syndrome', the mere fact that the villagers relate the two is revealing.

However, rather than suggesting that those who aspire to education suffer from an incurable trauma, I use the term 'education syndrome' as a metaphor, denoting a detrimental, self-perpetuating process. Education has become an end in itself which, rather than encouraging local development, actually undermines it in ways that serve to increase, rather than reduce, economic and social disparities between urban and rural areas. Those who have secured a steady salary thanks to their educational achievements have not strengthened the village economy, but their example has merely encouraged more people to aspire to education. As such, Toba Batak education has become deeply embedded in the local value system and is thus self-perpetuating in social terms. Decades of student migration have fostered the attitude among Toba Batak villagers that education is the key to prosperity and success, whereas the lives of those who remain behind are marked by poverty and failure. The education syndrome is the outcome of the high expectations of attaining jobs in the urban sector, over against a lack of investment in North Tapanuli.

The notion of an 'education syndrome' may be somewhat exaggerated, focusing mainly on effects on the local economy and production-related issues. I am aware that the concept leaves little room for the acknowledgement and appreciation of the positive side of education for the individuals involved. Without the possibility of educating their children, many households would have been confronted with far worse living conditions, or household members might have left the village altogether in order to join the unskilled labour force. Moreover, the label 'education syndrome' gives the villagers little credit for their creative solutions to rural poverty, for example by making use of a dense migrant network.

It is nevertheless correct to conclude that migration for education has contributed little to strengthen and diversify rural employment and investment opportunities. On the other hand, it is also doubtful whether economic developments would have been more positive in the absence of migration for education. Betting exclusively on formal general schooling makes people vulnerable to fluctuations in the white-collar labour market. This vulnerability is indeed exemplified by the considerable number of educated people who have not been able to secure a suitable job, resulting in frustration and discontent. While better-off households may use their connections outside the village and their money to secure their children degree and a job, poor households are much more restricted.

Whether they are relatively well-off or destitute, all families face a general social responsibility to provide their children with the means to establish their own independent households. With insufficient land resources and a lack of rural employment opportunities, Toba Batak families increasingly opt for education as a possible means to economic advancement. It is true that most Toba Batak children now attend secondary school. Yet, as Corner (1983:56) observed in Malaysia, 'it is equally true that those from disadvantaged homes have a high probability of becoming "drop-outs" before attaining a level of education sufficient to equip them for a productive role outside agriculture, while their role within agriculture is constrained by the paucity of land'.

Despite the fact that women have been catching up rapidly, joining their male counterparts at secondary school and even beyond, it is obvious that in poor families the education of sons is given priority. One of the results is that in both Simatupang and Simarmata there is a relative surplus of adolescent women who, together with wives and mothers, tend to remain at the helm of the family economy back home. These three categories of women will be the subject of the next chapter.

CHAPTER VII

Wives, sisters, and mothers

Nai Datir (42) lives in the most remote upland *huta* of Simarmata, the hamlet where she was born and raised. Her parents are still alive and reside a few houses further down. Her father, Ama Anwar, has been a hawker (*parjaja*) in East Sumatra for over thirty years, during which period her mother stayed in the village to care for the seven children. At age nineteen Nai Datir married her present husband from a neighbouring village. Since her father was absent most of the time and her only brother had migrated permanently to Tanjung Karang (Lampung), the couple were offered some land to operate for free. They thereupon decided to reside in her parents' *huta*. In 1970, after five years of marriage, Ama Datir followed his father-in-law to East Sumatra in an attempt to augment the family income by engaging in trade. In 1976 his family joined him there, but in due course they all returned to Simarmata because the enterprise failed. By the time the children went to secondary school, however, money again became a serious problem. Ama Datir therefore resumed his hawking activities, this time in Jambi. In the meantime Nai Datir continued to cultivate 4 *rante* (0.16 ha) of *ladang* land and to support the seven children (between 5 and 17 years old) with her revenues from shallots, cloves, maize, and cassava. When I met her husband in 1988, his wife had recently called him home: '*Ai na hupaksa do ibana mulak. Umtago ma di huta ibana karejo*' ('I forced him to come home. It's better that he just works in the village'). During his two-year stay in Jambi he had come home twice, handing over only Rp 50,000 (US$ 25). The eighth child had just been born, while the two eldest sons had recently left the household. One of them is attending university in Tanjung Karang. His parents pay his tuition, while his mother's brother (*tulang*), by now a rather successful trader, provides free board and lodging. The second son attends teachers training college in Pematang Siantar. Nai Datir hopes that once these sons have finished their education they will be able to help their parents and younger siblings. Her husband confides that he plans to migrate again, but he doubts whether his wife will agree.

The example of Nai Datir shows that women staying behind hold different positions in relation to household members who have migrated: they may be daughters,[1] wives, sisters, or mothers. They share with the migrant's wife not only the possible gains resulting from the household's increased prosperity, but also the concerns arising from the migrant's absence, and a heavier workload. It is important to distinguish between wives, sisters, and mothers, since in each case a woman's expectations, benefits, and sacrifices

---

[1] In this study daughters in migrant households are not discussed as a separate category. Their position – in terms of health, education, and workload – did not differ significantly from daughters in non-migrant households.

may be different. In this chapter I will argue that the relationships between migrants and female stayers is based to a large extent on complementarity and mutual interdependence. At the same time, however, these intra-family relations are not immune to conflicts and tensions that reflect hierarchies and internal power relations between genders and generations.

Cooperative conflicts and perceived interests

The *gender* division of labour in Toba Batak households becomes manifest in a *spatial* division of labour, whereby women tend to remain within the home and village area, whereas men frequently move beyond the village in their roles as providers of family income. This pattern is an extension of the basic division of men's and women's tasks and responsibilities (see also Chant 1991:60-1).

As stressed throughout this study, migration is not only about the people who move and their characteristics, but also about social and economic arrangements that permit certain members to leave the village. These arrangements have been viewed in contradictory ways in assessing migration. On the one hand, recent migration studies, especially historical-structural approaches, have recognized that the sustenance and reproduction provided by rural relatives to migrants in the urban areas are essential for the success of the migrants. On the other hand, the people who give this economic and emotional support are typically not regarded as contributing to migration and are often classified as 'residual' population, 'left behind' in the countryside. It is important to take an integrated view of the pattern of activities within *and* beyond the rural household that together constitute the migration process. Urban–rural relations can then be seen as mutually beneficial or cooperative.

Others (for example, Meillassoux 1981), however, have argued that the so-called productive migrant activities of husbands, brothers, and children may be parasitic on the work carried out in the rural household, such as farm labour, housework, and the care of children: 'Women are tied hand and foot to the place where they live – men may escape their responsibilities in the towns. The migrant system therefore deepens the age-old exploitation of women and the weak.' (Bush et al. 1986:293.) So although there is some degree of cooperation, relations between household members may also be strained by conflicting interests inherent to the gender division of labour. Because of these opposing tendencies, Sen suggests that household relations can best be understood in terms of 'cooperative conflicts':

> 'The members of the household face two different types of problems simultaneously, one involving *cooperation* (adding to total availabilities) and the other *conflict* (dividing the total availabilities among the members of the household). Social arrange-

ments regarding who does what, who gets to consume what, and who takes what decisions can be seen as responses to this combined problem of cooperation and conflict.' (Sen 1990:129.)

Sen goes on to argue that individuals within the household are motivated not only by their individual well-being but also by their perceptions of obligations and legitimate behaviour which family members should ideally live up to. I have been inspired by this approach. Applying Sen's ideas to North Tapanuli, we see that cooperation between Toba Batak relatives is based on strong patrilineal kinship bonds, while at the same time conflicts may arise about who within the household is entitled to migrate, the amount of remittances sent home, or the extent of support given to newcomers in the city. Such contradictions are rarely resolved through coercion but rather through bargaining and negotiation.[2] In the case of Toba Batak migration, the gender division of labour makes it fruitful for the parties to cooperate, but the particular way these fruits are divided reflects the 'bargaining powers' of the respective parties. In the context of this study, possible sources of bargaining power are ownership of and control over land, access to employment and other income sources, and access to external support networks. Inequality between family members in respect of these power sources – often based on gender and age – gives some members a weaker bargaining position than others.

Perception plays a vital role in shaping these bargaining powers. How women see themselves and how they value what they do may in part determine the outcomes they attain. Yet, given the nature of gender divisions inside and outside the household, perceptions of individual interests are not always clear and unambiguous. In Toba Batak society the family identity may exert such a strong influence on women's perceptions that it is not easy for them to formulate their personal interests (see also Ardener 1975). While men's strategies are usually geared towards both collective and individual needs, women's strategies are mainly focused on the present and future situation of their children, and generally have a collective character (Beneria and Roldán 1987:136). For instance, when I asked women what migration meant for them, they answered in terms of the well-being of the family more often than did men. This is not surprising given that in a patrilineal society a woman's social status is mainly derived from her husband's status. Moreover, having children, and particularly sons, is in the self-interest of all mothers in a society that measures a woman's position by her reproductive performance. Potentially contestable

---

[2] The bargaining approach was developed by neoclassical economists and is used by feminists to describe intra-household dynamics.

issues are dismissed to the realm of what Bourdieu (1977) calls 'doxa' – that which is part of 'undisputed tradition'.

There appear to be numerous inequalities within families which are generally taken for granted. The unquestioning acceptance of inequalities in the allotment of land, education, and mobility may stem from a socialization stressing family welfare above personal interests (Sen 1990:126). Nevertheless, it is worthwhile to distinguish between the subjective perception of individuals and a more objective notion of their respective well-being. A confrontation of statements on personal satisfaction or relative independence with quasi-quantifiable variables such as land ownership or educational achievements may reveal attitudes and mechanisms that sustain traditional inequalities (Sen 1990:133). It is important to note that issues seen as 'doxa' can change over time, for example through structural changes in the economy, through shifts in cultural meanings, or through processes of emancipation. I now turn to the different relationships between migrants and female stayers as illustrated by the case of Nai Datir above: marital relations, sibling relations, and mother–child relations. As far as possible, each section will deal with the perceived interests and contributions of men and women, cooperative conflicts within the household, and the bargaining powers of the respective parties.

Marital cooperation

The villagers of Simatupang believe unanimously that husbands should not migrate alone for any length of time, as they are 'apt to misbehave and to neglect their family'. The idea of extended separation from one's husband, as in Simarmata, strikes Simatupang women as utterly unthinkable. Consequently, in only thirteen households (or 6 percent of the total) had the husband been away during the previous year, usually for not longer than a few weeks. They migrated in the slack period to search for better opportunities for earning cash. In addition, there were three households in which the husband was more or less permanently absent, but the villagers attributed these cases to fragile relationships prior to the husband's departure. The situation in Simatupang is different from Simarmata, where migration of husbands is more easily accepted, or, as one woman put it, '*Umtago ma laho mangaranto. Ndang tartaon be na marpogos on*' ('It is better that he leaves than that we remain in poverty'). During the previous year (1987) the husband was reported to have been absent most of the time in 39 households (or 12 percent of the total). While it is tempting to view husband migration in Simarmata as part of a household survival strategy, most hawkers frankly say that they dislike farming.

In some of the literature on circular migration, women's loneliness while husbands are away has been stressed as a major problem (for example Gordon 1981; Jetley 1984). Although several wives in Simarmata (especially the younger ones) had mixed feelings about their husband's departure, only a few of them said they would like their husbands to remain at home. They did not complain of loneliness during his absence and they rarely wrote their husbands about day-to-day problems (see also Wolfs 1988:101).[3] Indeed, some older women rather pointedly commented that they were relieved to be without the tiresome bother of a man.

Because of the long tradition of peddling husbands in Simarmata, most women are used to the situation in which men spend the greater part of the year away. The husband usually moves out during the early stages of the household's developmental cycle, when the couple must provide for a growing number of children. The majority of male circular migrants in Simarmata had started their business when they were between 25 and 35 years of age; at the time of research their average age was 43. In the meantime, as providers for the rural household, the wives depend on agriculture, and may occasionally receive remittances from their husbands. The wives fulfil crucial productive and reproductive roles in relation to the land, their homes, and their children. These are not merely supportive roles but are central to the life of the migrants, the maintenance of the farms, and the continuity of their families.

With remarkable consistency, many village women describe farming as 'drudgery' and dwell upon the difficulties in making ends meet. According to them, however, these realities have to be endured to 'better one's life' and to 'arrange better conditions'. In most conversations about the husband's migration, what invariably surfaced was a sense of resignation, acceptance, and necessity. While some women made jokes about their status as *janda hidup* (living widows), they put the separation into a perspective quite typical of many Toba Batak women: 'What can we do? We need money... People have to earn a living.'

Daily life in the village must continue whether men are present or not. Children study, work and play, get sick and recover, and sometimes even die while their fathers are away. Only a few activities, like baptisms, funerals, and marriages, are postponed or deliberately planned so that husbands may attend. But if necessary a woman will replace her migrant husband – after consultation with neighbours and relatives – as in the following example.

---

[3] Since many of the wives are functionally illiterate, they have to depend on neighbours or their children to help them read and write letters.

When Nai Satria's daughter in Medan announced her intention to marry, both Nai in Simarmata and Ama in Padang were informed. However, since by the time the preparations were due, Ama Satria had not yet replied, Nai Satria had no choice but to go off to Medan to undertake negotiations with the groom's family on the necessary arrangements. Feeling insecure about the proceedings, she had asked advice from a male neighbour about the *adat* rules concerned. When, one day later, her husband finally arrived in Medan, Nai Satria felt relieved and happily turned the responsibility over to her spouse.

In their husbands' absence it is women's responsibility to maintain social and kin obligations.[4] The wives of hamlet heads (*tunggane ni huta*) in particular play an important role in this respect. They represent their husbands on several occasions within the *huta*, such as marriages, alienation of land, and the farewell ceremony of a migrant. They also make visits of condolence when someone has died, and they welcome a newborn baby. Even when a married son lives in the village, it is usually the wife who represents the family. The range of activities engaged in by women throughout the year thus clearly extends beyond the household and the farm. The presence of women as a source of information back in the village is crucial for migrant men. Both partners acknowledge women's ability to run the household and the farm, at least tacitly. Women are not timid with government officials, or with outsiders who come to the village for special purposes, such as itinerant salesmen or foreign researchers.

One could, therefore, argue that the migrant and his wife are mutually dependent: the migrant needs a stable place to which he can return and children who can support him in his old age; the wife relies on her husband for access to land and additional income. It is not only a question of economic dependence; husband and wife may also be emotionally attached. During the days before Christmas I observed several wives waiting anxiously for their husbands to return; some of them were clearly disappointed when their spouse did not get off the bus. A picture emerges of the migrant and his wife having complementary roles which together form an integrated whole. Let us see to what extent this picture relates to women's reality.

Perceived contributions of husband and wife

While it has become clear that husband and wife both contribute to the migration process, by pooling labour and money, we may wonder how they themselves view their respective contributions. Migrant men often boasted about their hardships in trading and belittled the daily worries of their

---

[4] Some migrant husbands who return home regularly continue to hold important functions in the village. For instance, one man from Simatupang who worked as a schoolteacher on Samosir Island came home about once a month and then acted as a deacon in the local HKBP church.

wives who, in their eyes, merely have to keep the household functioning. The women who stay behind are associated with a static pattern of life, while the men who move back and forth view themselves as dynamic actors with more experience in the outside world.

Nevertheless, several women noted that upon their visits home their husbands did little, while the women continued with their usual work and also had to be available for their husbands. The migrants sometimes lent a hand, but also enjoyed plenty of leisure time. 'If my husband comes home for a week or two and he wants to be the boss, fine,' says one woman. 'You know, men usually expect you to be at their beck and call: Is dinner ready? Have you polished my shoes? I have more freedom when my husband is not around. I am used to running the household on my own.'

Clearly, in the villagers' eyes, migrating has more prestige than staying behind, but this does not imply that women are powerless. They are able to influence the ideas, feelings, and wishes of their husbands, in order to bring them into greater accord with their own interests. As mentioned in Chapters III and IV, it is not rare for a wife to push her husband to try his luck elsewhere, sometimes mobilizing her urban relatives to pave the way for him. Some women regularly remind their husbands of the lengths to which they go to enable them to migrate. The effect of these complaints is to keep the men aware of their dependence on their wives, of how they must in their turn and in their own way sustain the family by reciprocating what the women do for them. For some women, especially those with adolescent sons, the ability to create and maintain such a sense of obligation is an expression of their power. Although not all women are equally assertive and persevering, many have very strong personalities and openly criticize their husbands. For instance, during an interview with a couple, when the husband could not answer my questions on the children's education accurately, his wife blamed him for only being interested in *porkas* (lottery).

Most women actively support their husband's departure. One woman told me that she had prepared a ceremonial meal to send her husband on his way: a red cock, *kue Batak* (Batak cake), and *jeruk purut* (indigenous lemon), served with red flowers and banana leaves. During the ceremony, the guests were asked to give their *pasu-pasu* (blessing) for the husband's undertaking (see also Vergouwen 1964:88-92). Some wives even back their husbands financially, for example by pawning some jewellery, by breaking into their secret savings, or by simply skimping on their daily food. Women feel it is their duty to help. If there are no savings, land or a water buffalo may be sold in order to raise sufficient starting capital – to the detriment of the household's economic resources. After the actual migration, wives' involvement increases, and can extend to several years of shouldering responsibilities and making sacrifices.

Simarmata women on their way to a ceremony

There is some ambiguity as to what women actually do to make migration possible and how they see themselves. They play an integral role in male migration, often without acknowledging their contribution. The 'perceived contribution' has to be distinguished from the real effort. Sen (1990: 139-40) stresses that in terms of time, women invest large amounts of work to enable their husbands to migrate. Nevertheless, their economic contribution is perceived to be rather modest. The bias is related, of course, to the relative weight attached to earning a cash income and engaging in subsistence activities. Because women trivialize the importance of their own work, the ambiguity remains dormant.

Apart from the complementarity of their labour, the couple's separate earnings may be pooled for the collective needs of the household. I observed a difference between migrant and non-migrant households. In most non-migrant households the married couple obtain a joint income from agriculture, and in general, it is the women who sell the agricultural produce and their *pandanus* mats to middlemen, or who are petty traders themselves. As a result, women hold the purse strings and retain effective control over all expenditures, even those of the men. For example, the money men need for socializing in coffee shops is usually provided by the women. It is expected that a woman will always grant her husband some pocket money, even if the budget is very tight, but she may not give as much as he wants. Men may fuss or grumble, but it is the woman who determines how much will be given (Krause 1981:63). It appears that many women are as adept at bargaining and negotiating with their husbands about drinking money as they are with middlemen over the price of shallots. Both sexes agree that women are in a better position than men to allocate resources on a daily basis.[5]

With male migration a different situation develops. Ideally, men bring home part of their revenues from the *pangarantoan* to meet the cash needs of the household. The earnings are handed to their wives, who manage the household and the farm and support the husbands during their visits to the village. As demonstrated by Whitehead (1981:100-2), in these situations substantial gender differences may arise in the couple's respective earnings. In the first place, despite the fact that most women sell some agricultural produce, men usually have larger cash incomes from their migration activities. Some women told me how much they had received from their husbands, and others did not. They seemed likely to divulge the amount when it was low or barely adequate, complaining that their husbands earned so

---

[5] After the installation of the drinking-water supply in Simatupang (discussed in Chapter II), when 'water groups' had to be set up, it was decided that the treasurer of each unit had to be a woman. The argument was that women are more trustworthy than men and less inclined to be corrupt.

little, but they were much more reluctant to reveal higher amounts. Apart from the level of their respective cash incomes, another fundamental difference is that migrants' and wives' earnings are earmarked for different purposes. Basic needs – food, clothes, medicine – are covered by the wives; so-called extras – mainly higher education, clan rituals, and occasional gifts – are met from migrants' earnings. As one woman put it, 'My husband is hawking cloth in Padang, but my children and I still have to eat, don't we?' In some cases, this division of responsibilities can certainly bear fruit, as the following example shows.

> In 1969 Ama Bonggas (now 48) went off to Kisaran (East Sumatra) to hawk cloth. His wife stayed behind in Simarmata with five small children, the eldest being eight at the time. Ama started his business with money from the shallot yields. After three years he could build himself a house in Kisaran and some years later he purchased a secondhand motorbike to facilitate his hawking activities. He also bought some rice land in Kisaran which is operated by others. He earns some Rp 200,000 a month, half of which is used to support two sons who are in university. Four other schoolgoing children have joined him in Kisaran. By cultivating 5 *rante* (0.2 ha) of *ladang* (*pargadongan*) Nai Bonggas is able to support herself and her two youngest daughters.

Interestingly, several women said they had refused to follow their husbands to the migration area because they did not want to be economically dependent. But even when women stay in the village, their *relative* independence may be threatened by the larger opportunities for men to expand their commercial activities. Women who stay behind have less scope for increasing their incomes because the prevailing farming system sets limits to agricultural intensification. Few women seemed to regret these diverging income levels, but instead felt proud because their husband's success enabled their children to study.

When asked why more men than women migrated, most villagers referred to the male role of breadwinner. As discussed in Chapter IV, this principle among the Toba Batak is supported ideologically by patriarchal values. It is also an important component of official state ideology (Pancasila) which promotes the idea that men are responsible for women's economic and physical welfare. Confronted with this principle of male responsibility, several women (especially those who had been abandoned) openly mocked it. Men send home too little, too infrequently, to their rural families. True, town life is expensive, but women suspect, and with some reason, that town entertainments take up a disproportionate amount of the earnings which should be sent home to finance school fees and clothes for the children or improvements for the farm. Most women consider this freewheeling as a 'typical male' attitude which cannot be changed. Women witnessed a sharp contradiction between the generalized ideal of male responsibility and the necessity of hoeing the fields on their own.

There is no assurance that migrant husbands will send remittances. Although the majority do, many women take into account the possibility that they will have to provide for the household on their own. One of them summarized her position as follows: 'I don't rely on my husband. If I get some money, well and good; and if I don't, I just try to make money for myself by selling shallots and cloves or by weaving mats.' Another woman, a mother of three small children whose husband has been a migrant for two years, commented: 'The only advantage of my husband's migration is that he can now buy his own cigarettes'. Some women had a very clear perception of the situation:

> After her husband had hawked cloth in Sibolga for ten years, Nai Amson (55) recently called him home to Simarmata. He returned 'without a *rupiah* in his pocket', and neither had their children been able to study beyond SMP, 'so what's the use of migrating?' According to Nai Amson many Batak men use the pretext of peddling just to be independent and to roam about (*jalan-jalan saja*), while their wife and children in the village live on the verge of starvation. She boasts she would not mind if her husband had taken a second wife; she would probably not have been worse off. Now that Ama Amson has returned, he regularly slips off for a few days without informing his wife. 'I don't get angry. It's no use questioning him afterwards.'

Marital conflicts

In her essay on domestic budgeting, Whitehead (1981) discusses the important links between patriarchy and property relations that shape the 'conjugal contract', that is, the terms under which claims on products and income, produced by the labour of both husband and wife, are divided to meet their personal and collective needs. Elaborating the concept, Beneria and Roldán (1987:137-8) stress that no single, static marriage contract exists; instead marriage involves continuous renegotiation of the terms of interaction and exchange between spouses. Similarly, among Toba Batak migrant households, it is not only the respective contributions of migrants and their wives which make up the conjugal contract, but also the partners' attitudes towards each other, their evaluation of the marital situation, and their life experience (whether young, recently married, or older and more sceptical). The discrepancy between what a woman expects and what she receives can lead to marital conflicts.

The effects of such a conjugal contract can be examined in Pidie, an area in Aceh, in northern Sumatra (Jayawardena 1977; Siegel 1969:45; Snouck Hurgronje 1906, I:361-2). Within their marital relations, women are said to be in a strong bargaining position because, due to the bilateral family system, they own and manage individual property. In the average situation a woman has enough resources to support herself and her children, and due to matrilocal settlement further sustenance can be expected from her natal family. Her husband is in a less favourable position because he lives among his wife's kin and often depends on her resources. A viable option for him is to migrate. Migrants are expected to send back money, textiles, and other articles; neglect of these duties may lead women to renounce and divorce their migrant husbands.[6] Jayawardena (1977:29) mentions a lawsuit in which a woman demanded a divorce from her husband who had not sent her remittances for nearly two years. She refused to have him back unless he compensated for the neglect. In the village Siegel (1969:117) studied, 39 percent of all marriages ended in divorce. Fourteen of the 22 divorce cases were related to financial conflicts, and in each of these cases it was the woman who took the initiative to split up. In West Sumatra women who have been living without their husbands for long periods are also said to be likely to initiate a divorce, but unfortunately, the available studies do not pursue the issue (for instance Hugo 1975; Naim 1971:7).[7]

Interestingly, when talking to Toba Batak women, the amount of the remittances sent by husbands seldom appeared to be a source of conflict. Few migrants tell their wives how much money they make. Their wives interpret this withholding of information as a sign of the husband's independence and they seem to accept it. Why do Toba Batak women comply with these seemingly asymmetrical exchanges of income and responsibility?

The gender ideology underlying Toba Batak kinship rules plays an important role in shaping the conjugal contract. As discussed in Chapter IV, in the patrilineal and patrilocal Batak society women are dependent on their husbands to gain access to the most important means of production, land. In case of an official divorce they are apt to lose both their children and their access to land. Hence, they have little to win but everything to lose. In this connection, Sen (1990:135) speaks of a 'breakdown position', which indicates a person's vulnerability or strength in bargaining. 'If, in the case of a breakdown, one person is going to end up in more of a mess than it appeared previously, that is going to weaken that person's ability to secure a favorable outcome.' The concept of bargaining can be extended by bringing in the idea of 'threat'. In these terms, it can be argued that Toba Batak women have a weak bargaining position because they cannot credibly threaten their husbands with divorce if the latter do no fulfil their obligations (as can, for example, Acehnese or Minangkabau women).[8] As discussed in Chapter IV,

---

[6] On the island of Bawean a woman was even reported to have asked for divorce because her husband had never migrated and therefore could not be considered to be grown-up (Subarkah et al. 1986).
[7] Undoubtedly, the greater stability in marriage among Toba Batak is also related to the development and the influence of Christian law and Christian morals (Vergouwen 1964:248).
[8] When asked whether she enjoyed more freedom when her migrant husband (who was a notorious gambler) was not around, one woman in Simatupang replied bitterly: 'A Batak woman is only free when her husband is dead'.

the position of women without sons is even worse, and they are often advised to follow their husbands to the *pangarantoan* as soon as possible. Of the nine women in Simarmata who had been abandoned by their migrant husbands, three did not have sons.

The prolonged absence from wife and children poses a serious threat to marital relations. It gives men the opportunity to engage in gambling (*marjuji*) or to start liaisons with other women (*marboru-boru*), a fact some of them tend to boast about rather than try to hide.[9] While it is a public secret that migrant men may have adulterous affairs while away (although this is denied by most wives), the wives in the village must of course be careful not to engage in a relationship with another man – a double moral standard prevalent in most societies. The threat of gossip seems adequate to keep wives from having extra-marital liaisons.[10] But the wives who ventured to talk about this all agree that, unlike men, women can easily do without sex for a year.

I found nine women in the Simarmata region (a quarter of all husband migrations) and three women in Simatupang who had been deserted by their spouse. As mentioned earlier, this is exactly why many Simatupang villagers do not trust long-term male migrants. As a rule, the separations were the result of 'falling in love with someone else' rather than of specific conflicts, or the breaking of the conjugal contract. Most women said that their spouses had simply withdrawn from the scene, the wives had received no word of them since, except perhaps through rumours that they were living with another woman (*isteri gelap*, or secret wife).[11] One woman bitterly commented: '*Ai husuru do ibana mangalului ngolu, hape mangalului boru-boru do niula*' ('I had ordered him to look for a living, instead he looked for a wife'). She lives in an old shack with her three children, cursing the day she helped him set up his business in Bukittinggi. 'Looking back, I wonder how much I benefited from his trading. Until he went away, that is for the first three years of our marriage, we used to stint on everything and save so that he could accumulate starting capital. Now I find that all the sacrifices I have made have gone totally unrewarded through no fault of mine. Life would have been better if he had not migrated at all. Do not forget that it was largely with money from my savings and jewellery that he could even think of leaving the village.' Most

---

[9] Circular migrants who have lovers in the *pangarantoan* are called *panjeji*. They are said to catch venereal diseases (*padi-padi*) easily, but in the villages I found no evidence of this.
[10] Vergouwen (1964:267) notes that a married woman who has been left by her husband for a long period sometimes has extra-marital intercourse, but it is not often committed openly.
[11] Polygamy is no longer possible among Christian Toba Batak. However, the male children of an *isteri gelap* (illegal wife) are accepted as heirs if there is no son by the first legal wife.

men are in their early thirties when they abandon their wives. When they get older the wives feel more confident because they think their husbands are no longer appealing to other women or, as one of them said of her 54-year-old spouse: '*ndang langku be*' ('he is no longer wanted').

While conflict and tension do not appear to be obvious reasons for deserting one's wife, what then? I would suggest that this situation is a result of estrangement, or living in two different worlds. Upon the migrants' visits home, one of the first things that struck me was the difference in experience between the husband and his village wife. The men have come to know different parts of the country through their work on plantations, agricultural pioneering, or trading activities. One of the results is that fewer Toba Batak females than males are able to speak Indonesian. Most of the women have never visited their husbands in the *pangarantoan*, because it is often too far and they do not want to be considered suspicious.[12] One 45-year-old migrant told me: 'I do not expect my wife to share my experiences or to listen to my stories. These are men's business which do not interest her. As long as she is satisfied in the village and looks after the children, what else can I desire? If I want to discuss things, I go to the *lapo* (coffee shop) where I can meet my mates.' Not only is there a difference in experiences, there is also a striking contrast in outlook. It is common to see a visiting migrant in his Sunday best, smoking brand-name cigarettes, while his wife wears worn-out clothes and chews betelnut.[13] In spite of the wife as well as the migrant husband maintaining that they are satisfied with their situation, the prolonged separation of a couple sometimes leads to extra-marital relationships of the husband, a phenomenon also noted for other parts of Indonesia (Hugo 1993; Lineton 1975; Naim 1985).[14]

Of course, there is also the possibility that migration is sought as a solution to a bad marriage, as Lineton proposed in her study on South Sulawesi: 'Marital breakdown is commonly expressed in the emigration of the husband, a solution to marital discord which creates far less disharmony within and between the kin-groups of both than divorce or the taking of a

---

[12] When children had joined their fathers (often for educational purposes), the women visited their husbands once in a while. Although not readily admitted by the wives, sending children to live with their father seemed an effective strategy for keeping the husband from extra-marital liaisons.

[13] Such differences in appearance are not only the result of male migration. In the early 1930s a Dutch administrator noted: 'Zien de ongehuwde vrouwen er frisch en verzorgd uit, in den huwelijken staat vervallen zij snel, verzorgen zich in het geheel niet meer en zien er spoedig oud en afgewerkt uit' (While unmarried women look clean and immaculately dressed, when married they quickly look dishevelled, no longer take care of themselves, and soon look old and used-up) (Verhoef 1934:43; see also Krause 1981:63).

[14] In the 1930s Vergouwen (1964:256-7) noted that Toba Batak husbands who went to the East Coast sometimes never showed their face again, after which the wife and her relatives would insist on a divorce.

second wife would have done. Bad relations between siblings, or between father and son, are also often resolved by the emigration of one or more of the parties involved.' (Lineton 1975:185.) One abandoned woman in Simarmata indeed suggested that her husband may have used the pretext of migration in order to leave her. He drank a great deal and sometimes became violent when drunk. Although the woman resented her husband's irresponsibility and the drain upon household resources that his activities entailed, she said they never had serious conflicts prior to his departure.

In general, in cases where migrant husbands have deserted their wives, the man is criticized while sympathy is with the woman – unless she is childless. 'The idea is that a woman [...] has given him all that he could desire of her, she has contributed to the building up of his "house" and therefore she should not be at the mercy of any inclination of his to get rid of her' (Vergouwen 1964:254). Abandoned women may even be supported by their family-in-law, as in the following case.

> Nai Rintu is 41 and lives with her two schoolgoing daughters in an upland *huta* in Simarmata. Although her husband was born here, he spent his youth in East Sumatra where his father hawked cloth. In 1965 his parents returned to Tapanuli and shortly afterwards his father died. Being the eldest son, Ama Rintu was then urged to marry his *boru ni tulang* (maternal cross cousin), although the couple did not know each other. They went to live in Tebing Tinggi, where Ama Rintu resumed his father's trade, while his wife cultivated 10 *rante* (about 0.5 ha) of dry fields. During this period Nai Rintu gave birth to five children, two of whom survived. When his trade dwindled Ama Rintu decided to try his luck in Aeknabara, southeast of Tebing. He did not want to take his family along because it would have been difficult to rent land there. For two years he came home regularly, providing his wife with some Rp 120,000 in total. When she was pregnant with her youngest child she learned that her husband had a relationship with a Javanese woman in Aeknabara. Soon after that, the rental contract in Tebing was terminated as the owner needed the land himself. Nai Rintu felt compelled to return to Simarmata, where she was offered help by her husband's family. Her mother-in-law provided her with a house and with some land to cultivate for free. The eldest son, Rintu, went to live with his father's brother in Medan where he attends university, but all study costs are borne by his mother. Ama Rintu has six children with his second wife and no longer supports Nai Rintu or her children. Nevertheless, Nai Rintu prefers not to dissolve the marriage. This would place her in the position of a divorced woman who may have difficulty in remarrying and who has no means of sustenance of her own.

As stressed earlier, there is a need to distinguish between a person's perception and a more objective notion of a specific situation. Women told me they did not have conflicts about remittances or extra-marital relations. They either accepted their husband's independence in these issues or they painted a nicer picture of him than he really was. What criticism they did utter was often disguised in mild terms: the women used indirect methods to express their indignation. In her study on marital relations in the Netherlands, Komter (1989) found a similar situation of latent conflict. Women tend to anticipate possible negative reactions by their husbands and to resign themselves to the current situation in order to prevent disruption or outright conflict. Komter suggests that even the avoidance of conflict can be seen as a form of power. Among the Toba Batak, it seems that the reason for not antagonizing a husband is not just to keep harmony in the household, but is related to a woman's weak bargaining position in negotiating a more favourable situation. Any open resistance to her husband's activities would probably only work against her. If her recurrent criticisms led to the husband's abandoning her, the wife would then be considered the instigator, thereby losing the sympathy of her in-laws. In general, where access to land is controlled by male kin, women rarely initiate conflicts during their husband's absence, because such action could deprive them of essential access to land (Bourque and Warren 1981; Margolies and Suarez 1978; Mueller 1977). In addition, the fact that in case of divorce a Toba Batak wife has no rights over the children has far-reaching effects in maintaining marriages in spite of long periods of separation (see also Sibisi 1977:168). In other words, in conflict situations, the bargaining power of women is weakest when they live in patrilineal societies and when they work primarily for the farm or business of the household head, because their lack of access to cash creates 'systematic biases in the perception of who is "producing" what and "earning" what within the household' (Sen 1990).

In sum, it can be concluded that village wives often actively support their husbands in migrating. While not all women perceive their contribution as crucial to the migration enterprise, some of them appear to be very outspoken and confident. Ultimately, however, given their position in the patrilineal kinship system, when it comes to a conflict situation, whether open or covert, women have little bargaining power. Below, we shall investigate the position of another category of women who can be directly affected by migration: migrants' sisters.

Sibling solidarity?

> 'Many boys and men who are out of the village – schooling, travelling, working, pioneering, or trading – have mothers, sisters, or wives who remain at home, raising children and tilling the soil. In most cases, the women provide a good portion of the wherewithal for males who are attending school or engaged in other enterprises. Sisters thus occupied are by no means unconscious dupes. Many view themselves as helping their brothers and their parents. Some seemed to refuse offers of marriage to continue doing so.' (Sherman 1990:199-200.)

When I asked adult women in Simatupang and Simarmata to list their siblings with their occupation and place of residence, it became clear that many brothers had moved away from Tapanuli for schooling, employment, or trade. Why did these brothers leave, while their sisters continue to work the land?

One way of conceiving gender differences is to focus on 'entitlements'[15] of household members. Papanek defined entitlement as follows:

> 'the social consensus about the value of specific categories of persons as expressed in the norms governing "who gets what and why". [...] the term "entitlement" refers to the socially and culturally recognized rights of specific categories of persons to particular resource shares. [...] The concept of entitlement to resource shares embodies the ideas of distributional justice shared by members of a family and can therefore be seen as a central part of its moral basis.' (Papanek 1990:170.)

Papanek argues that the greater entitlement of one person often becomes the increased responsibility for care by another. In a migration-oriented society a man's entitlement to migrate may translate into increased responsibility for his caretaker, usually his wife, mother, or sister. In this respect, Papanek (1990:173) refers to a 'culture of female sacrifice'.

In the patrilineal Toba Batak society, sons are entitled to more strategic resources – landed property, education, a good occupation – than daughters. This can be understood by looking at the different roles and functions of males and females in the Toba Batak kinship system. As discussed in Chapter IV, sons are long-term members of the family who have the obligation to care for their elderly parents, whereas daughters are temporary members who migrate upon marriage. Therefore, parents may allow sons more freedom to leave the village and find a good job, even if, in the short run, it means loss of labour or income to the family. Historically, adolescence for boys is a period in which they are exempt from social norms. Among young males, especially if they have completed secondary school, there is a strong tendency to despise and refuse work on the land. Rather than helping their parents, they often hang about in local coffee shops. Consequently, most parents merely view their adolescent sons as additional mouths to feed and their migration is therefore generally encouraged, but with the expectation that they will provide for their parents in their old age. At the same time, most parents seek to keep daughters at home, which is frequently explained in terms of preserving their reputation.[16] A closer look suggests that a more fundamental concern of parents is control over their daughters' labour.

---

[15] The concept of entitlement was initially used to analyse the different claims to goods and services in households experiencing famine and deprivation (Sen 1976).

[16] There were three women in Simarmata, aged 23–24, who had finished teachers training college in Medan. In anticipation of getting a job, they had been called home. It was their parents' contention that rather than roaming about in town, they had better assist their mothers in the village. When one of them was offered a teaching job in Jakarta, her mother refused to let her go because she considered it 'too far'.

> Being the youngest daughter and still single, Wasti's (30) parents are anxious to keep her at home. Her four sisters and one brother are all married and have left Simarmata. It is obvious that Wasti's labour is crucial to her parents' livelihood. While her parents spend most of their time running a modest coffee shop, all agricultural and household activities fall on Wasti's shoulders. She sells her shallots at a nearby market and is fairly independent in managing the household budget. Part of her earnings have been invested in her brother's education. Both her brother in Bandung and a sister in Binjei have proposed that Wasti move in with them and start her own business, but her parents do not want to let her go. Wasti pities her parents and that is why, so far, she has not packed her bags. In confidence she tells me, however, that she is planning to go to Bandung next year to start her own *warung* (shop).

So far, Wasti's responsibility towards her parents appears to have prevailed over her wish to work in Bandung. In this respect, Wasti is one of the Toba Batak daughters described by Sherman (1990) above, who seem resigned to their role as supporters. Their relationship with other household members is characterized by cooperation rather than conflict. Indeed, I met several young women in the villages who almost effaced themselves, like Donna for example, who was introduced in Chapter V.

> After the death of her parents Donna (26) saved every *rupiah* to finance her youngest brother's schooling. Although she does not know her brother's field of study, Donna has paid the annual tuition fee of Rp 160,000 (US$ 80) and Rp 300,000 (US$ 150) for his board and lodging for four years. She speaks bitterly of her eldest brother who migrated many years ago. He has not contributed a single *rupiah* to the education of Dalmok, the youngest brother, and does not even fulfil his *adat* obligations. When Dalmok married in 1987 it was Donna who took a bus to Jambi with five *kaleng* (100 litres) of rice and 25 kg of pork. Donna does not know how she will finance her sister's education in the future. She therefore asked Dalmok and his wife to acquit themselves of this task on the pretext that she would like to marry.

A sister who helps her brothers migrate may also be rewarded for her efforts. Donna's brothers allowed her to cultivate the family land so that she could support herself and her younger sister. It should be remembered, however, that brothers can reclaim the land at any time. So, rather than interpreting Donna's case as sibling solidarity, it could equally be argued that modest improvements in women's resources serve to mask the fact that the brothers are advancing at their sisters' expense. In other words, sisters may not *perceive* their situation to be disadvantageous. To the extent that sisters would want to oppose their dependency, they find themselves with little bargaining power anyway, since they are not legally entitled to the family property.

Of course, not all sisters in Simatupang and Simarmata are exploited by their migrant brothers, nor are they necessarily pitied as 'those left behind'. For a number of women, staying in the village appears to be a deliberate choice.

Heti (about 38) is the youngest daughter of a family of seven. While her elder siblings enjoyed only primary education, Heti attended economic senior high school (SMEA) in Tebing Tinggi. She worked in Belawan (Medan) for two years, but returned to Simarmata after an unhappy love affair. In the meantime her parents had both died. Heti then moved from one place to the other, staying alternately with her siblings in Padang, Tanjung Karang, Bandung, and Jakarta and lending a hand in the household. The last couple of years she has joined her eldest brother's family in Simarmata. She runs most domestic affairs while her brother and sister-in-law do some work in agriculture. If she needs money, she asks her brother, who never refuses her requests. Outside the house she leads an active social life. She supports and even initiates church activities, teaches catechism classes, and sings at Sunday masses. She no longer expects to find an administrative job because, she says, employers prefer to have young people. Neither has she ever considered becoming a trader, like so many of her fellow villagers. She regards herself as being too sensitive for the coarse language and aggressive behaviour necessary in trading activities. When she was younger she wanted to become a Catholic nun, but her mother did not consent because 'it was a woman's duty to marry and bear children. My mother should have known that I am still unmarried!' Heti hopes to find her *jodoh* (life companion) one day and get married because, 'that's what people expect you to do'.

On the whole, it seems that while giving their brothers a chance to succeed, more and more sisters become aware of their own restricted mobility. While landed property remains the exclusive entitlement of sons, another vital resource, education, has become increasingly available to women as well. The higher the social or educational aspirations a woman has, the greater the probability that she will migrate. In general, adolescent women have adopted a far more defiant stance towards their brothers' privileges. One girl, a student in Medan, said: 'It is the parents' duty to give their children the opportunity to leave the village, sons and daughters alike'.

Women who have migrated may actively assist their younger siblings. As discussed in Chapter VI, they can provide cheap and secure housing for newcomers. They can finance their siblings' education or help them find a job through their own or their spouses' connections. In short, they prevent their village parents from having to worry, knowing their children are supported within the family network.

While some village women may still perceive themselves as 'helpers' of their relatives, it seems that once women challenge their traditional position and migrate, their bargaining power vis-à-vis their male family members will increase. The mechanisms by which women have enhanced their status include education, a process that is usually associated with the advancement of women's position (see Boserup 1970). Although daughters are still less entitled to education than sons, to some extent education and access to the urban labour market have removed women from patriarchal control and given them independent means of support.

While young women have the possibility of 'voting with their feet', for an elderly woman one way to increase her status is through her children. And the more sacrifices a mother makes to enable her children's successful out-migration, the higher her expectations will be.

Motherhood and migration

> 'A woman, especially an old one, who must hoe her own land is a sad sight, but no disgrace stems from her having to do this work. If economic necessity has forced all children to leave in search of their own fortunes, disgrace may well be felt though, because of the fact that she has no family to help her.' (Cunningham 1958:41.)

Some authors have proposed the term matrifocal or matricentric for those societies 'in which women's work of whatever kind is done in or near the home, while men's pursuits periodically take them far from home' (Schneider and Gough 1961:556). 'Matrifocality presumes an emphasis on the mother–child bond and implies the capacity for mother–child units to function effectively on their own' (Tanner 1974:153). Although the financial contribution of men, be they husbands, brothers, or sons, is important, women can effectively support and care for their children with very little input from men. Matrifocality is usually associated with matrilineal descent (for instance, the Minangkabau), but even in societies with patrilineal or bilateral descent, mothers may have a central place. For example, when discussing gender relations among the bilateral Acehnese, Siegel (1969:55) notes that 'although men tried to create a role as husbands and, especially, as fathers, women thought of them as essentially superfluous'. The term matrifocality has been generally used to denote kinship systems in which the role of the mother is culturally and structurally central. In these societies the relationship between the sexes is relatively egalitarian, and both women and men are important actors in the economic and ritual spheres (Tanner 1974:131). Even where the matrifocal family is formally patriarchal, meaning that higher status and respect go to the father, the mother is dominant in ordinary family affairs.

Despite the strong patrilineal kinship rules, Toba Batak women are often depicted as strong, independent, forceful characters, somewhat dismissive of men, who play a powerful role within their families. Without labelling Toba Batak society as matrifocal, it is obvious that the women do have a central position in the household. This position appears to be related to the large variety of women's reproductive and productive activities, which may even be increased by the out-migration of household members. It is also the mother whose personal assets are often a principal source to be tapped for raising the capital needed to finance migration expenses. The central position of the mother is particularly felt by her sons. As Schrijvers (1985: 212) observed in Sri Lanka: 'the greater indulgence shown towards sons is on the one hand a mechanism with which women are taught their second place while they are still little girls. On the other hand, by spoiling and admiring her son, a mother can effectively make herself indispensable and keep him emotionally dependent on her.' The Batak have many popular songs about migration in which they express longing for their village and their carefree childhood, and love for the mother they left behind (Nasution 1987). Because a son is expected to give his mother social and economic security (see Chapter IV), a woman will easily overindulge him and make him emotionally dependent on her.

As discussed in Chapter IV, in the 'patriarchal bargaining' (Kandiyoti 1988) motherhood is the main avenue to whatever control and authority a woman may gain. A woman's status is linked especially to that of her son and, particularly in later life, to the care and respect he shows for her. In the past, the reproductive success of a Toba Batak woman was defined in terms of having mature male sons resident with or near her, as others have argued for South Asia and Malaysia (Cain 1988; Wong 1991). A mother had access to her son's labour and, in addition, she could delegate part of her work to her daughter-in-law. Landed property was dispensed in such a way as to guarantee the care of the older generation. If a son did not fulfil his obligations, he ran the risk of being disinherited by his parents.

Today, when a son wants to migrate, the parents can no longer credibly use disinheritance as a threat. With the continuing decline of smallholder agriculture, employment opportunities elsewhere have become more attractive even for landed sons. The following example shows that the outmigration of a son may cause tensions between individual aspirations and kinship obligations. It also shows the crucial position of daughters-in-law in providing for parents' old age.

> Despite his parents' wish to keep their only son in the village, Ama Lamsar (32) left Simarmata at the age of 20. He went to Padang, where he engaged in hawking. Two years later he was called home to marry at his parents' instigation; directly after the wedding ceremony he returned to Padang. His parents summoned his wife to remain with them in Simarmata and to cultivate the 6 *rante* of *ladang* land. Because of domestic tensions, however, Nai Lamsar followed her husband to Padang within a year, against the old couple's wishes. For seven years they lived in Padang, where they had four children and recently built a house. But a year ago Ama Lamsar was called back to Simarmata because his father was dying. After the funeral (which cost him Rp 2 million) he resumed his trading activities in Padang, again leaving his wife and children behind to nurse his sick mother. When I asked Ompu Lamsar (a shrivelled but sharp old woman) about the possibility of joining her son's household in Padang, she definitely rejected this idea: she had always lived in Tapanuli and felt afraid of moving to an urban area. Her daughter-in-law added that after her death she wanted to be buried in the family grave. The transport of a corpse from Padang to North Tapanuli would be too expensive.

Elderly woman whose children have all migrated, Simatupang

While the out-migration of Ama Lamsar involved extensive negotiation (with his wife as a bargaining asset), for an increasing number of Toba Batak parents it has become normal and right that their sons leave the village to make money elsewhere, either as traders or, ideally, in a professional career. A 50-year-old woman said: 'It is enough for me to suffer in the village. I don't want to see my son suffer as a farmer.' Another woman expressed a similar reaction to her son's migration. She said: 'Even seeing him around the village frustrates me. There is no reason to stay here where there is no future.' She had great hopes for her children and was supportive of their desire to continue their studies outside the region. She wanted them 'to become something big'. Whether they are physically present or not, sons are expected to support their parents in their old age; not to do so is aberrant behaviour subject to disapproval. For example, one son, a university graduate working for an oil company in Pekanbaru, was openly blamed by his mother for not sending any remittances, although his alleged salary was some Rp 250,000 per month. Whereas in the past landed parents could bind at least one son (usually the first-born) to them by holding out the prospect of inheriting land, today parents have little bargaining power to enforce a son's loyalty.

At the same time, other traditional mechanisms used by parents to keep their sons effectively in check are no longer relevant. For instance, in the past Toba Batak sons were dependent on their parents' resources to pay a bride-price. Today it is possible to marry without making any initial payment, and on the whole bride-prices have decreased. Moreover, sons who have their own salary no longer need their parents' assistance to obtain wives, which weakens parents' control over them.[17]

As discussed in the previous chapter, parents increasingly try to provide their children with education instead of land. They may go to great lengths to enable their children to migrate successfully. Some women have to accept prolonged separation from their husbands, who contribute to the children's schooling with the proceeds from hawking. Toba Batak motherhood is closely aligned with subjugation of self-interest and a predominant focus on 'children and their future'. The ideology of maternal altruism (Whitehead 1981) encourages women to devote their earnings to meeting collective rather than individual needs. However, a mother's aspiration to have successful children is not based only on the wish for her children to have a more prosperous life than she herself has had. Legendary for their hard work and self-sacrificing thrift, Toba Batak mothers nevertheless hope to receive financial support from their children. This was stressed by one woman who in rather direct terms explained: 'We have children to be

---

[17] A similar process has been described by Hoddinott (1992:562) for western Kenya.

assisted, at home and in the fields, and when they have become adults they can pay back what we have invested in them.'

Analogous to the concept of conjugal contract mentioned earlier, it may be useful to focus on 'intergenerational contracts', or expectations regarding mutual obligations that guide relations between parents and children (Greenhalgh 1988:40; see also Wong 1991). According to Greenhalgh, in traditional China these obligations included obedience (filial piety) and large contributions to the family economy, and differed considerably between sons and daughters. The intergenerational contract described by Greenhalgh has also been referred to as generalized exchange (Sahlins 1972:191-6). In contrast to balanced exchange, in which one item is directly reciprocated for another of the same value, generalized exchange produces a counter-obligation which need not be equivalent in value and may be fulfilled at a much later time. This is the kind of exchange that is said to characterize all family relations (Becker 1981:172-99; Sahlins 1972:196-204).

It seems that the Minangkabau of West Sumatra see a direct link between the intensity of a mother's care and her children's moral performance. If a mother cares for her children properly, the expectation is that the children will 'repay' this by living up to their obligations. If the successful migrant forgets his poor village mother, 'he may lose all he has' (Tanner 1974:145), effectively being punished for his negligence. Migrant sons are constantly reminded of the fact that their activities are only worthwhile if they are in the service of the family (Postel-Coster 1985:158). This moral pressure usually results in material benefits for the family back home (Chadwick 1991:80).

In Toba Batak society, 'contracts' between parents and their sons are based on generalized reciprocity with a specifically moral emphasis. Although the migration of young people cannot be considered part of a joint household strategy prompted primarily by individual job expectations, once a salaried job has been secured counter-obligations certainly exist. These may include economic support of younger siblings coming to town, or sending remittances to elderly parents in the village. Sons who have migrated to rural areas usually come from relatively poor households; they are therefore less likely to send money, and when they do, they remit a smaller part of their earnings (see also Lipton 1982:210).

Prosperous parents, who are in a better position to finance education and job acquisition and who have more urban connections, have more to offer their sons than do poor parents. Consequently, well-to-do parents who can provide their sons with an education or a job can exercise more social control over them, while parents who are not in a position to do so may find themselves in a relatively weak bargaining position. Having no access to a means of living (education or a salaried job) young men increasingly go their own way and are not easily disciplined by family pressure, as in the following example.

> When I first met Nai Mansun, she had just returned from Palembang where she had gone to fetch her eldest son, Mansun (27). Her husband had died the previous year, but despite Nai Mansun's repeated requests, her son had not come home. At Easter she wanted to tend her husband's grave, and she went all the way to the south to force her son to pay his father his last respects. After completing SMA, Mansun had not been allowed to continue his studies. Four years ago he left for Palembang where he has been working for an oil company. During this period he never returned, nor did he send any remittances.

This case shows that the poor 'lose' their children and thus their ability to increase resources, whereas the wealthy can 'bind' them by means of their resources in property (Wong 1991:201).

When daughters migrate, parents' expectations of future benefits from them are much lower. Unlike sons, daughters have no traditional obligation to support their parents in their old age, since they will marry into another family. In the past, a mother's workload gradually decreased as her daughters grew older and could help out more in the household. These days, the mother's workload remains heavy. Daughters can no longer be mobilized to give a hand, because they first go to school and shortly afterwards migrate to continue their studies or look for a job. The migration of daughters means that the responsibility for domestic and agricultural labour falls, as never before, upon the mother alone. That is why, in some cases, mothers actively oppose a daughter's departure, especially when she is the only one left.

In an increasing number of households, however, mothers want to give their daughters a chance which they themselves were denied. These women chatted at length about their daughters living in urban areas providing their siblings with board and lodging or sending money home to educate their siblings. One woman was clearly disappointed because her daughter had to stop teachers training college due to becoming pregnant.

It is the ideal of many elderly women to have a successful son in town, but also to have sons and daughters living nearby who can assist with domestic and agricultural work. If all their sons remain in the village, then parents have to get along without cash remittances. If the sons all migrate, the household may run short of labour. If the elderly couple can rely on a daughter's labour by delaying her marriage, or can rely on the labour of a daughter-in-law, then the problem is solved. Yet, the best option for parents is to put their eggs in more than one basket: having mature children in town as well as in the village enables the parents to receive remittances *and* to be assisted with daily tasks, as in the following case.

Having some grandchildren around is the ideal of every elderly woman

VII Wives, sisters, and mothers

Ompu Jonker boru (55) has ten children: four sons and six daughters. Her husband (74) is the second son of a family of six and the only one left in Simatupang. Their children have all left the parental household. The first son and daughter have become farmers in Simatupang, while the second daughter married a farmer in a neighbouring village. The mother and two of the daughters regularly work together cultivating their fields. The old couple concentrated their investments on the education of the second son, Rajabun. He studied law in Medan, for which his parents had to sell 3 *rante* (0.12 ha) of rice land, three water buffaloes, and a dozen pigs. Rajabun currently lives in Timor Timur where he has a job in a financial office. After they completed their secondary education, he asked a younger brother and sister to join him in Timtim and paid their tickets. Through his influence they found employment in a bank and a village cooperative (KUD), respectively. Another sister, also an SMA graduate, has an administrative job with the railway service in Medan. The three youngest children also live in Medan in a house built by Rajabun. Two are studying at private universities, while the youngest is still in SMA. For his parents' house in the village, Rajabun has recently financed the installation of electricity and the construction of a storage container for water. Each month he sends his mother a money order for Rp 50,000, and the other son in Timtim also occasionally remits money. In addition, Rajabun finances the schooling of his youngest siblings.

Ompu Jonker's lot contrasts sharply with that of another elderly woman in the same *huta* who has no children. Her house is a bamboo shack without light or water and she supports herself by renting a tiny plot from a neighbour.

This chapter has focused on the relationships between migrants and women remaining at home. I have argued that the 'women left behind' are not a homogeneous group: besides class differences, wives, sisters, and mothers each have their own interests in a migrant's enterprise and perceive their situation differently. While stressing the complementarity and mutual interdependence of these different relationships, based on close family ties and kinship obligations, I have also indicated that in some situations the out-migration of a family member may involve extensive bargaining because of the divergent interests of movers and stayers. To what extent the women staying behind benefit, depends to a large extent on the family's economic resources. Well-to-do households can provide their children with education and a salaried job, thereby creating a counter-obligation to remember the family back home. Landed brothers can leave part of the estate to a sister, thereby increasing the latter's access to land. And husbands who are successful in the *pangarantoan* can send home remittances or finance children's education. So some women are flourishing, resting on the laurels of their good work, while others have not been quite so fortunate. It has become clear, however, that for many women the migration of a family member entails a 'wait and see' attitude: they cannot be sure if and when they will reap the fruits of their sacrifices.

Simatupang villagers in front of a traditional Toba Batak house

CHAPTER VIII

Conclusion

'If women will no longer stay in the rural areas where sub-subsistence conditions prevail, who will keep even the skeleton of agriculture together, especially when the older generation of grandmothers at present taking care of the next generation is dead and buried?' (Bush, Cliffe, and Jansen 1986:299)

This study has focused on women who stay behind in the countryside while their close relatives migrate. I have emphasized women's crucial contribution to farm and hearth, without which migration of household members would be impossible. In a symbolic sense, land and women in the village have always represented security to Toba Batak men as they travelled in search of a livelihood. Together, productive land and able-bodied women working on the land have meant that if opportunities elsewhere failed, one could always return to the village and find shelter, food, and a well-established network of social relations.

While numerous scholars have analysed who migrates and what causes migration, there has been little in-depth study of the role of non-migrant women. Most of the existing literature assumes that migration is a rational response to a given range of resources and choices and that, as such, the family as a unit, including women, benefits from such migration.

It is only relatively recently that an examination of the impact of migration has included not only the people who leave, but also those who stay behind when their husbands, children, or other relatives migrate. In the literature highlighting the 'women staying behind' the migration of men is considered to result in either subordination or emancipation of their wives. Depending on the author's theoretical orientation, male migration is depicted as increasing women's economic and social dependence on men (see for example Menon 1989) or, instead, it is assumed that women actually gain greater economic and social freedom through male out-migration (for example Colson 1970), since it gives them more 'autonomy' (Wojno 1986) and 'status' in the family and community (Cernea 1978). Furthermore, it has been argued that, in a situation of circular migration, the migrants and the stayers are mutually dependent (Mueller 1977; Murray 1981). Migrants (whether temporary or permanent) depend on their wives, mothers, and other kin who remain at home to assume primary responsibility for the reproduction and socialization of the next generation.

However, the argument of 'mutual dependence' does not take into account different levels of dependence. For example, both sexes may depend on migration for survival or upward mobility. Yet most women also depend on men, who are the landowners and the main cash providers (Brown 1983: 387). In other words, none of these studies deals with the complex interaction between women and men: taking into account both the difference in their entitlements to essential resources and the difference in their responsibilities based on the gender division of labour.

This study has focused on the people involved in migration in two locations, one in Simatupang in Muara subdistrict, the other in Simarmata in Simanindo subdistrict. In these villages various types of migration have been found, be it in different combinations: the permanent migration of adolescents or whole households, and the temporary migration of individual husbands. The conditions described in these two villages are not necessarily the same as those in other places, although they seem to accord reasonably well with what is to be found in the region as a whole, according to the 1990 census.

In this last chapter I want to come to grips with the question of the extent to which village women win or lose when their close relatives migrate. The answer to this question must be seen in the context of the prospects, now and in the future, of farming. Before I deal with this issue, I shall review some of the findings and summarize the contradictory position of Toba Batak women.

Each chapter in this book discusses a separate but related issue in connection with migration; together they constitute the 'building blocks' of my analysis. These blocks are: the male-dominated migration pattern dating from pre-colonial times, the family and household structures as mediators in the migration process, the agricultural situation as a possible deciding factor, and the importance of education for achieving 'success' in the *pangarantoan* and for supporting the family back home.

Toba Batak migration started slowly and rose significantly during the early twentieth century with the introduction of a cash economy and large-scale plantations. The Ethical Policy of the colonial government opened the door to schooling and hence also to migration, because all schools beyond secondary level were outside Tapanuli. I have related the predominance of men in these early migration patterns to the 'traditional' division of labour between men and women. With the construction of roads, increasing education for girls, and shifting norms regarding proper female behaviour, increasing numbers of women have engaged in migration as individuals.

In the past there seems to have been a certain 'logic' to who migrated and who stayed on the land and looked after the children. Because of the marriage and inheritance rules as laid down in the Toba Batak kinship system

(Chapter IV), certain family members were 'pushed' out while others were induced to stay and cultivate the land. Where once migration had been undertaken by the weakest in the clan, the losers in family quarrels over the partition of the land, it has now become an avenue for the strongest (the educated or those to be further educated), leaving the weak behind. Successful migrants are confronted with a variety of claims and kinship obligations imposed by the rural stayers.

Women figure prominently in the migration process, often arranging the departure of migrants in such a way that ties with remaining kin are solidified and strengthened. Despite the mutual cooperation between relatives, I have argued that Toba Batak migration cannot be reduced to a mere aspect of household strategies. The behaviour of some migrants is evidence that the allocation of family labour is not always a careful collective decision taken for the benefit of the household as a whole. Especially where young male migrants are concerned, the adventurous nature of a move to other areas adds to their desire to migrate permanently from their home village. In these cases, the out-migration of household members may clearly endanger the continuation of the farm.

In the past, the general scarcity of fertile land was a major factor inducing the Toba Batak to migrate, either to supplement their agricultural income on a temporary basis or to stay away permanently. The situation in North Tapanuli today is that an increasingly low esteem is attached to farming. To the extent that households have land at their disposal, the proceeds are generally invested in children's education and not in increasing the viability of the family farm. This is not to say that Toba Batak are willing to part with their landed property. On the contrary, while the economic value of ancestral land may have declined, Toba Batak, especially those who have migrated, feel very strongly about its cultural value.

Here again, women appear to play a crucial role: due to their position in the household and kinship structure, women are considered to be the best persons to continue cultivating the land of their male relatives and thereby to maintain strong ties with the *bona ni pasogit* (ancestral homeland). In spite of this, there has been no permanent shift in the patriarchal family structure: notwithstanding women's central role in farming and the departure of male heirs, their access to land has not been anchored in inheritance rules, but remains contingent upon the goodwill of men. Nevertheless, many rural women form the linchpin in the migration process, linking migrants and stay-at-homes. While the rural household as such seldom benefits from migration, it functions as a 'transfer point': any money that enters the household is handed over to the future generation in the form of education or to deceased ancestors in the form of graves and ancestral monuments (*tugu*).

Work in agriculture is despised by most Batak youth, and notwithstanding the scarcity of formal jobs, villagers hold firmly to the idea that education is the only way to progress. They invest large sums of money in their children's schooling, sometimes skimping on food and other daily necessities. Although this strategy does not always bear fruit, and runs counter to the viability of the village as a whole, alternative investment opportunities in the region are scarce.

Those who have left North Tapanuli are by and large the skilled, the educated, and the economically active. Those who remain behind are those who are in many ways deprived. They are the less educated and are found in the economically less productive age group. More women, small children, and old people stay behind, while the young and the strong leave for cities throughout Indonesia.

From the discussions I had with village women it became clear that the effects of migrants' absence can be both negative and positive. Migration not only entails extra responsibilities and burdens, but can also enhance the decision-making power and influence of the women who stay behind. In some cases, the absence of brothers gives women the opportunity to cultivate more land; in other instances the migrants' remittances may lead to upward mobility, if not for the women themselves, then perhaps for their children. 'Women who remain in the villages when men migrate for short periods, or for some years, do not necessarily suffer catastrophic declines in their standard of living. One should avoid romanticizing the ability to cope, just as much as one should avoid excessively sentimentalizing their plight.' (Standing 1983:i)

Marginalization and power: a paradox

Many households in Simatupang and Simarmata have difficulty making ends meet. As a result of both land fragmentation and soil degradation, most incomes are below the national average. While adolescents and adult men can search for alternative employment outside the village, the maintenance of the farm and the care for the young and the aged usually curtail the mobility of wives. Married women are numerically overrepresented and they do most of the agricultural work. This situation may be defined as 'marginalization': women are left behind in agriculture, which is less remunerative than most other economic activities. Women are not just marginalized because they have to perform labour-intensive or undervalued activities, but also because they are burdened with additional tasks which impede their participation in the wider society.

Apart from women's marginal position in the rural economy, prevailing cultural conceptions regarding their role and status reinforce the general picture of women's subordination. Toba Batak women are disadvantaged in traditional *adat*. They themselves give numerous examples: a daughter is not entitled to her father's inheritance, and when divorced a woman cannot share in the couple's joint property. If childless or sonless, she can easily be abandoned by her husband. And if she has children, she must leave them with her in-laws if there is a divorce. If her husband migrates there is no guarantee of financial support. And, finally, if he starts a relationship with another woman, the wife may be abandoned.

Yet men's authority within kinship and household arrangements co-exists with remarkable independence for women within their own sphere of domestic responsibilities and economic activities. Women's self-determination becomes especially evident when husbands migrate. Although I do not want to present an overly optimistic picture, the ability of rural women to run the farm and to give active support to the migration of their kin is evidence of the inadequacy of viewing them as passive victims of migration (see also Hart 1991:115). Although they often stressed the problems they had in making ends meet, Toba Batak women in everyday life are hard-working, hardy, and stoical. Scarcely educated, they are sharp of perception and tongue. Their talking, laughing, joking, and quarrelling provide vivid evidence of their active roles. They often influence family decisions, for instance regarding their own and their children's marriages. Whether their husband is present or not, they can take the initiative to recruit wage labourers, and as a rule they hold the purse strings. Moreover, they can 'send' their husbands to the *pangarantoan*, exert moral pressure on their migrant sons to 'remember' their mother, or force a daughter to stay at home.

Indeed, when living in Tapanuli, I was struck more by the general competence of women in providing for the needs of their families than by the difficulties they experienced in the migrants' absence. A woman staying behind has considerable day-to-day autonomy[1] and makes all major decisions regarding production in the fields and in the house. However, her autonomy extends only as far as her husband allows it. She does not feel confident of the relationship with her husband to the extent that she would risk open confrontation. Her autonomy, then, is limited by the fear of being abandoned.

Both within and beyond the household there are contradictions and constraints on the position of women, such that, because of their social and reproductive responsibilities and labour, and by virtue of being 'good' mothers, whatever 'power' (or, more accurately, influence) women have is ultimately subject to the power of men within households and male-

---

[1] 'Autonomy' as it is used here refers to control over one's personal life, activities, and revenues from labour.

dominated institutions in the wider society. The concept of 'power' can be broken down into three analytical components: material control, moral authority, and potential or actual use of physical force. It is far from clear whether the influence older women undoubtedly exert as the linchpins of extended families, within which women therefore have some degree of moral authority, can ever be converted into something as substantial as power. Lack of a material basis for this influence limits the scope for influence to turn into power.

Although this influence has neither a material basis nor an ideological legitimation, we may nevertheless call it informal power (Schrijvers 1985:204). When looking for the manifestation of this power, we find that Toba Batak women have always been forceful characters who have acquired strength through specific functions in the household. Women's roles in the market, management of domestic production, and other responsibilities figure prominently in daily life. The fact that Toba Batak women tolerate the situation, although reluctantly, does not mean that they are passive victims of their husbands' whims. If they do not resist, they have their reasons. Even without being openly disobedient, women find ways in which to attain certain objectives even against the wishes of their husbands: 'The trick is to avoid quarrels and open conflict as much as possible' (Schrijvers 1985:217). As we have seen, this strategy seldom poses a fundamental threat to the basic structure of gender inequalities, either materially or symbolically. What it does represent, however, is a constant process of testing and renegotiation of power relations between women and men.

In attempting some general concluding remarks, I fear that I have provided a rather homogeneous picture of the women staying behind. It is therefore important to stress that some women have less room for manoeuvre than others to attain their objectives. As indicated in the previous chapter, a quarter of the wives staying behind have been abandoned by their migrant husbands. Especially if they have small children, these women find themselves in a vulnerable situation, raising their children without the emotional and financial backing of the father. Because of the increased individualization of households, kin support is not always received. More daughters than before are beginning to move away from the life their mothers had. They acquire an education, and try to find a job so they can earn an income of their own. Without openly challenging the basic structure of property and domination, they are in a position to achieve economic independence away from the family farm. Yet because these women migrate from the village, there is little feedback to the rural community from this sort of emancipation.

The paradox of power is perhaps most clearly illustrated by the position of Toba Batak women in agriculture.

'What freedom is working the land?'

To any visitor, the active role of Toba Batak women in agriculture is striking. I had assumed that I would find evidence of a 'feminization of farming' in the fate of the women left behind in North Tapanuli. I had expected the women who sustained the families and the tiny plots of land to be subject to unrecognized exploitation by their own men whose relative freedom and occasional flings in the city they can never share. I had half expected that while women themselves might not perceive this as exploitation, many of the injustices they suffered would be traceable to the insensitivity of men. However, what emerged in the course of the study and the interviews with the women is a far more complex picture.

Although Toba Batak women do not *control* economic resources such as land, they have the task of *managing* these resources in their husband's absence so that they can feed, clothe, house, and educate the children. Hence, there is a sharp contradiction between their responsibility for making ends meet and their limited control over resources. Some studies argue that, through the migration of family members, women seem to acquire 'new power' with their increasing workload and the new decisions they have to make during the absence of males. This power is said to be manifested in the public sphere in the course of women's dealing with institutions such as cooperatives or banks (Khafagy 1984:19-20).

It is important to acknowledge the structural limitations that restrict the potentially emancipating aspects of a 'feminization of farming'. Even though it is true that women take over productive functions and assume 'public roles' during the absence of male family members, this is not equivalent to the acquisition of 'new power'. Historical developments have contributed to the fact that males are offered better chances in a variety of non-agricultural sectors. They can refuse to till the soil while their wives and female relatives remain behind, with limited chances of leaving the village. Whereas males can afford to abandon agricultural work, this option is not equally available to married females.

Whether they have the full responsibility for tilling the land while males are away, or whether male migrants continue to exercise control, the fact remains that, for access to land, Toba Batak women are dependent on men: husbands, brothers, or sons. Through the migration of male kin, some women enjoy increased access to land, but it is as custodians and not as owners in their own right. Migrant men maintain their land through the non-remunerated work of their wives or other female relatives. Toba Batak women, then, are caught in the contradictions of institutions which both protect and oppress them. Attachment to the land secures women a basis for subsistence production, but at the same time they are tied down to the land as mere caretakers.

To evaluate properly the changes in the position of women, one has to take into account the social significance of the new forms of gender differentiation – resulting from shifts in the gender division of labour and the confidence acquired by men who migrate and come into contact with the wider world. These changes relegate to women the socially devalued status of the 'left behind' and the *pangula* (workers). Women continue the work which men consider unsuitable. It is true that for some women the cultivation of rice and the sale of shallots yield enough cash to support themselves and their children. They do not need to depend on the unreliable remittances of their absent husbands. Yet the fact that these women can successfully support themselves may induce migrant men to neglect their responsibilities towards the family back home.

In conclusion, if we looked only at the active economic role of women who remain behind, we would surely stress their courage and persistence in their relatives' absence. What this emphasis would not reveal, however, is the fact that a feminization of agriculture is often accompanied by a structural devaluation of agriculture, and thus a devaluation of women's work. It devalues women since they are left in the 'traditional' sector and excluded from the 'modern' world of men, which entails migration.

Glossary

All important Indonesian, Batak, and Dutch terms used without explanation in the text are listed in this glossary. Batak and Dutch terms are indicated by the abbreviations (B) and (D), respectively; the remaining terms are Indonesian. Words quoted from poems and sayings are not included.

adat	customary law and tradition
ama (B)	father (of)
anak	child (or son)
balai desa	community meeting hall
boru (B)	wife-receiving clan; daughter
cangkul	hoe
dalihan na tolu (B)	three stones to hold a cooking vessel over the fire; metaphor for *boru, hula-hula,* and *dongan sabutuha*
datu (B)	Toba Batak medico-religious specialist; traditional healer
demang	head of a subdistrict in the colonial hierarchy
desa	village
doli-doli (B)	Toba Batak male adolescents
dondon (B)	to pawn land
hula-hula (B)	wife-giving clan
Huria Kristen Batak Protestan (HKBP)	Batak Protestant Association
huta (B)	hamlet or part of a village
kabupaten	district
kampung	village; clusters of *huta*
kecamatan	subdistrict
kepala kampung	elected head of a village
kepala negeri	appointed head of a conglomeration of villages
KUD	*koperasi unit desa* or village cooperative
ladang	dry field (as opposed to *sawah*), often used for raising cassava
mangaranto (B)	to travel in search of work; to migrate
marga (B)	patrilineal clan
marga raja (B)	*marga* which holds the agricultural land of an area under its authority; ruling clan
nai (B)	mother (of)
namboru (B)	father's sister; the term is also used to refer to an older woman if a child does not know the relationship

negeri	administrative district composed of several *kampung* and located within a *kecamatan*
ompu (B)	grandmother or grandfather
onderafdeeling (D)	subdistrict
pandanus (Latin)	reed-like grass
pangarantoan (B)	migration area, destination area of migrants
panjaean (B)	gift from father (usually land) upon the setting up of one's own household (*manjaen*)
pargadongan (B)	dry field, *ladang* (especially for cultivating cassava)
parripe (B)	outsiders, immigrants (i.e. those who do not belong to the ruling clan)
pauseang (B)	land given by parents to their daughter at her marriage as dowry, or some time after that, as at baptism of children
raja (B)	local chief
rante	measure of area; 0.04 hectare
sawah	wet-rice field
SMA	senior high school (Sekolah Menengah Atas)
tugu	ancestral monument
volksschool (D)	popular school
voorganger (D)	lay preacher

Bibliography

Adamse, C.J.
1913 Memorie van Overgave van de onderafdeeling Toba. [Available at the library of the Koninklijk Instituut voor de Tropen, Amsterdam.]

Aklilu, B. and J. Harris
1980 'Migration, employment and earnings', in: G. Papanek (ed.), *The Indonesian economy*, pp. 121-53. New York: Praeger.

Alexander, J. and P. Alexander
1979 'Labour demands and the "involution" of Javanese agriculture', *Social Analysis* 3:22-44.

Algemeen verslag
1928 *Algemeen verslag van het onderwijs in Nederlandsch Indië*. Deel II. Batavia: Ruygrok.

Amin, S.
1974 *Modern migrations in West Africa (Les Migrations en Afrique de L'Ouest); Studies presented and discussed at the Eleventh International African Seminar, Dakar, April 1972*. New York: Oxford University Press.

Analisa
1987 'Usaha tekstil di Balige kembali cerah', *Analisa* 23-9-1987.

Anderson, John
1826 *Mission to the East Coast of Sumatra, in 1823*. Edinburgh: Blackwood. [Reprint 1971, Kuala Lumpur/New York: Oxford University Press.]

Anderson, Benedict
1988 *Imagined communities; Reflections on the origin and spread of nationalism*. London: Verso. [First edition 1983.]

Anonymous
1935a 'Bertambah lama bertambah banjak djoemlah orang Toba jang pindah kenegeri jang lain', *Pandoe; Madjallah Opisil di Residentie Tapanoeli* 6:72-3.
1935b 'Makin sempit pintoe kedoenia kaoem boeroeh (makan gadji), makin dihargakan orang oesaha pertanian itoe', *Pandoe; Madjallah Opisil di Residentie Tapanoeli* 7:84-7.
1936 'Soal pertanian semakin penting dikalangan pemoeda kita', *Pandoe; Madjallah Opisil di Residentie Tapanoeli* 4:43-4.
1976 'Bah! Alai sarjana!???', *Dalihan Na Tolu; Majalah Kebudayaan Batak* 7:5-7.

Ardener, S. (ed.)
1975 *Perceiving women*. London: Malaby.

Ariffin, J.
1978 'Industrial development in Peninsular Malaysia and rural–urban migration of women workers; Impact and implications'. Paper Tenth International Congress of Anthropological Sciences.

Arizpe, L.
1982 'Relay migration and the survival of the peasant household', in: H. Safa (ed.), *Towards a political economy of urbanization in Third World countries*, pp. 19-45. Delhi: Oxford University Press.

Arizpe, L. and J. Aranda
1981 'The comparative advantages of women's disadvantages; Women workers in the strawberry export business in Mexico', *Signs* 7-2:453-73.

Asselt, G. van
[1906] *Achttien jaren onder de Bataks*. Rotterdam: Daamen.

Auer, U.F.
1933 Memorie van Overgave van de residentie Tapânoeli. [Available at the library of the Koninklijk Instituut voor de Tropen, Amsterdam.]

Baca, R. and D. Bryan
1985 'Mexican women, migration and sex roles', *Migration Today* 8-3:14-8.

Baks, C., A. Ploeg and C. Slot
1985 'Over marginalisering', *Antropologische Verkenningen* 4-1:1-25.

Becker, G.S.
1981 *A treatise on the family*. Cambridge, Mass.: Harvard University Press.

Bemmelen, L.R. van
1931 Vervolgmemorie van Overgave van de onderafdeeling Samosir. [Available at the library of the Koninklijk Instituut voor de Tropen, Amsterdam.]

Bemmelen, S.T. van
1986 'Een adatrechtstudie in historisch perspectief; J.C. Vergouwen over Toba-Batakse vrouwen', in: J. Reijs et al. (eds), *Vrouwen in de Nederlandse koloniën*, pp. 52-78. Nijmegen: SUN. [Jaarboek voor vrouwengeschiedenis 7.]
1987 ' "Welsprekende" cijfers; De economische rol van Toba-Batakse vrouwen in de Volkstelling van Indonesië', *Jambatan; Tijdschrift voor de Geschiedenis van Indonesië* 5:25-40.
1989 'Zwart-wit versus kleur; Geschiedschrijving over Indonesische vrouwen in de koloniale periode', in: F. de Haan et al. (eds), *Het raadsel vrouwengeschiedenis*, pp. 11-46. Nijmegen: SUN. [Jaarboek voor vrouwengeschiedenis 10.]
1992 'Educated Toba Batak daughters as mediators in the process of elite formation (1920-1942)', in: S. van Bemmelen et al. (eds), *Women and mediation in Indonesia*, pp. 135-65. Leiden: KITLV Press. [Verhandelingen 152.]

Benda-Beckmann, F. von and K. von Benda-Beckmann
1987 'Verwantschap tussen dorp en staat'. Paper for the Eighth Conference on Tropical Asia, Amsterdam.

Beneria, L. and M. Roldán
1987   *The crossroads of class and gender; Industrial homework, subcontracting, and household dynamics in Mexico City.* Chicago/London: University of Chicago Press.

Bisilliat, J.
1983   'The feminine sphere in the institutions of the Songhay-Zarma', in: C. Oppong (ed.), *Female and male in West Africa*, pp. 99-106. London: Allen and Unwin.

Boer, D.W.N. de
1921   'Het huwelijksrecht bij de Toba-Bataks', *Koloniaal Tijdschrift* 1-3:76-97, 201-25, 354-72.

Bosch, P.R.
1990   *Hubungan antara migrasi dan kualitas tanah di desa Simatupang, Tapanuli Utara.* Medan: Lembaga Penelitian Universitas HKBP Nommensen. [Makalah Sesewaktu 6.]

Boserup, Ester
1970   *Woman's role in economic development.* New York: St. Martin's Press.

Bossen, L.H.
1975   'Women in modernizing societies', *American Ethnologist* 2:587-601.

Bourdieu, P.
1977   *Outline of a theory of practice.* Translated from the French by Richard Nice. Cambridge: Cambridge University Press.

Bourque, S.C. and K.B. Warren
1981   *Women of the Andes; Patriarchy and social change in two Peruvian towns.* Ann Arbor: University of Michigan Press.

Bovill, Kathryn
1987   *Toba Batak marriage and alliance; Family decisions in an urban context.* Ann Arbor, Mich.: University Microfilms International. [PhD thesis University of Illinois, 1986.]

Brandes, S.H.
1975   *Migration, kinship and community; Tradition and transition in a Spanish village.* New York: Academic Press.

Bray, F.A. and A.F. Robertson
1980   'Share cropping in Kelantan, Malaysia', *Research in Economic Anthropology* 3:209-44.

Brettell, C.B.
1986   *Men who migrate, women who wait; Population and history in a northern Portuguese parish.* Princeton: Princeton University Press.

Brown, B.
1983   'The impact of male labour migration on women in Botswana', *African Affairs* 82:367-88.

Bruce, J. and D. Dwyer
1988   'Introduction', in: D. Dwyer and J. Bruce (eds), *A home divided; Women and income in the Third World*, pp. 1-19. Stanford: Stanford University Press.

Bruner, E.M.
1959 'The Toba Batak village', in: G.W. Skinner (ed.), *Local, ethnic, and national loyalties in village Indonesia; A symposium*, pp. 52-64. New York: Institute of Pacific Relations.
1961 'Urbanization and ethnic identity in North Sumatra', *American Anthropologist* 63:508-21.
1970 'Medan; The role of kinship in an Indonesian city', in: W. Mangin (ed.), *Peasants in cities; Readings in the anthropology of urbanization*, pp. 122-35. Boston: Houghton Mifflin.
1972 'Batak ethnic associations in three Indonesian cities', *Southwestern Journal of Anthropology* 28:207-29.
1981 'Exchange theory and migration', in: R.W. Force and B. Bishop (eds), *Persistence and change; Papers from a symposium on ecological problems of the traditional societies of the Pacific region*, pp. 135-40. Hawaii: Pacific Science Association.
1987 'Megaliths, migration and the segmented self', in: R. Carle et al. (eds), *Cultures and societies of North Sumatra*, pp. 133-51. Berlin: Reimer.

Burton R. and N.M. Ward
1827 'Report of a journey into the Batak country, in the interior of Sumatra, in the year 1824', *Transactions of the Royal Asiatic Society of Great Britain and Ireland* 1:485-513.

Bush, R., L. Cliffe and V. Jansen
1986 'The crisis in the reproduction of migrant labour in southern Africa', in: P. Lawrence (ed.), *World recession and the food crisis in Africa*, pp. 283-99. London: Currey.

Cain, M.
1988 'The material consequences of reproductive failure in rural South Asia', in: D. Dwyer and J. Bruce (eds), *A home divided; Women and income in the Third World*, pp. 20-39. Stanford: Stanford University Press.

Castles, L.
1967 'The ethnic profile of Djakarta', *Indonesia* 3:153-204.
1972 *The political life of a Sumatran residency; Tapanuli 1915-1940*. [PhD thesis Yale University, New Haven.]

Cernea, M.
1978 'Macrosocial change, feminization of agriculture and peasant women's threefold economic role', *Sociologia Ruralis* 18-2/3:107-24.

Chadwick, R.J.
1991 'Matrilineal inheritance and migration in a Minangkabau community', *Indonesia* 51:47-81.

Chan, K.E.
1983 *Socio-economic implications of population ageing in a developing country; The Malaysian case*. Kuala Lumpur: Population Studies Programme, University of Malaya. [Mimeo.]

Chaney, E.M.
1983 *Scenarios of hunger in the Caribbean; Migration and decline of smallholder agriculture and the feminization of farming*. Ann Arbor: University of Michigan. [Michigan Working Paper 18.]

Chant, S.
1991 'Gender, households and seasonal migration in Guanacaste, Costa Rica', *European Review of Latin American and Caribbean Studies* 50:51-85.

Chant, S. and S. Radcliffe
1992 'Migration and development; The importance of gender', in: S. Chant (ed.), *Gender and migration in developing countries*, pp. 1-29. London/ New York: Belhaven.

Cho, H.
1984 'Republic of Korea; Those left behind', in: *Women in the villages, men in the towns*, pp. 187-246. Paris: UNESCO.

Clauss, W.
1982 'Village household reproduction; A case study from North Sumatra'. Paper for the joint seminar 'Households and the World Economy' at the Fernand Braudel Center, University of Bielefeld.

Cliffe, L.
1978 'Labour migration and peasant differentiation; Zambian experiences', *Journal of Peasant Studies* 5:326-46.

Colfer, Carol
1983 *On circular migration – from the distaff side; Women left behind in the forest of East Kalimantan*. Geneva: International Labour Office. [Population and Labour Policies Programme Working Paper 132.]

Collier, W.L., J. Colter, Sinarhadi and R. d'A. Shaw
1974 'Choice of technique in rice milling on Java', *Bulletin of Indonesian Economic Studies* 10-1:106-20.

Collier, W.L., Gunawan Wiradi and Soentoro
1973 'Recent changes in rice harvesting methods; Some serious social implications', *Bulletin of Indonesian Economic Studies* 9-2:36-45.

Collins, Jane L.
1991 'Women and the environment; Social reproduction and sustainable development', in: Rita S. Gallin and Anne Ferguson (eds), *The woman and international development annual*, vol. 2, pp. 33-58. Boulder: Westview.

Colson, E.
1970 'Family change in contemporary Africa', in: J. Middleton (ed.), *Black Africa; Its peoples and their cultures today*, pp. 152-9. New York/London: Macmillan.

Connell, J.
1984 'Status or subjugation? Women, migration and development in the South Pacific', *International Migration Review* 18:964-83.

Connell, J., B. Dasgupta, R. Laishley and M. Lipton (eds)
1976 *Migration from rural areas; The evidence from village studies*. Delhi: Oxford University Press.

Corner, L.
1981 'Linkages, reciprocity and remittances; The impact of rural out-migration on Malaysian rice villages', in: G.W. Jones and H.V. Richter (eds), *Population mobility and development; Southeast Easia and the*

Pacific, pp. 117-36. Canberra: Australian National University. [Development Studies Centre 27.]
1983 'The persistence of poverty; Rural development policy in Malaysia', *Kajian Malaysia* 1-1:38-61.

Couillard, M.A.
1982 'A brief exploration into the nature of men/women relations among pre-colonial Malayan people'. Paper presented at the Canadian Council for Southeast Asian Studies, Singapore.

Crummett, M.
1985 *Class, household structure and migration; A case study from rural Mexico.* Notre Dame: University of Notre Dame. [Working Paper 92.]

Cunningham, Clark E.
1958 *The postwar migration of the Toba-Bataks to East Sumatra.* New Haven: Yale University. [Southeast Asia Studies 5.]

Dandekar, H.C.
1986 *Men to Bombay, women at home; Urban influence on Sugao village, Decan Maharashtra, India, 1942-1982.* Ann Arbor: Center for South and Southeast Asian Studies. [Michigan papers on South and Southeast Asia 28.]

Dinerman, I.
1978 'Patterns of adaptation among households of US-bound migrants from Michoacan, Mexico', *International Migration Review* 12:485-501.

Dobbin, C.
1983 *Islamic revivalism in a changing peasant economy; Central Sumatra, 1784-1847.* London: Curzon.

Dobkin, M.
1968 'Colonialism and the legal status of women in francophone Africa', *Cahiers d'Etude Africaines* 8:390-405.

Dore, R.
1976 *The diploma disease; Education, qualification and development.* London: Allen and Unwin.

Drijvers, J.
1941 'Inheemsche rechtsgemeenschappen in de Bataklanden', *Koloniaal Tijdschrift* 30:656-75.

Eggink, W.
1923 Brief aan de heer M. Joustra te Leiden. [Royal Tropical Institute, Amsterdam, no. 783.]

Etienne, Mona and Eleanor Leacock
1980 *Women and colonization; Anthropological perspectives.* New York: Praeger/Bergin.

Eijkemans, Chris and Joost van Rooy
1990 *Evaluasi tanah dan keadaan pertanian pada sembilan kecamatan di Tapanuli Utara, Sumatera Utara.* Medan: Lembaga Penelitian Universitas HKBP Nommensen. [Makalah Sesewaktu 3.]

Fegan, B.
1983 'Establishment fund, population increase and changing class structure in Central Luzon', *Philippine Sociological Review* 31:31-43.

Findley, Sally E.
1987 *Rural development and migration; A study of family choices in the Philippines*. Boulder: Westview. [Brown University Studies in Population and Development 5.]

Findley, S.E. and L. Williams
1991 *Women who go and women who stay; Reflections of family migration processes in a changing world*. Geneva: International Labour Office.

First-Dilič, R.
1978 'The productive roles of farm women in Yugoslavia', *Sociologia Ruralis* 18-2/3:125-39.

Folbre, N.
1988 'The black four of hearts; Toward a new paradigm of household economics', in: D. Dwyer and J. Bruce (eds), *A home divided; Women and income in the Third World*, pp. 248-62. Stanford: Stanford University Press.

Freeman, Derek
1970 *Report on the Iban*. Second edition. [London]: Athlone, New York: Humanities Press. [First edition 1955, Report on the Iban of Sarawak; London School of Economics Monographs on Social Anthropology 41.]

Friedman, K.
1984 'Households as income-pooling units', in: J. Smith et al. (eds), *Households and the world economy*, pp. 37-55. Beverly Hills: Sage.

Gearing, M.G.
1988 *The reproduction of labor in a migration society; Gender, kinship, and household in St. Vincent, West Indies*. N.p.: n.n. [PhD thesis University of Florida, Gainesville.]

Geertz, Clifford
1963 *Agricultural involution; The processes of ecological change in Indonesia*. Berkeley: University of California Press. [Asian studies 11.]
1973 *The interpretation of cultures; Selected essays*. New York: Basic Books.

Ginting, N. and R. Daroesman
1982 'An economic survey of North-Sumatra', *Bulletin of Indonesian Economic Studies* 18-3:52-83.

Goldschmidt, W. and E.J. Kunkel
1971 'Structure of family peasant life', *American Anthropologist* 73:1058-76.

Gonzales, N.L. Solien de
1961 'Family organization in five types of migratory wage labor', *American Anthropologist* 63:1264-80.
1965 'The consanguineal household and matrifocality', *American Anthropologist* 67:1541-9.

Goody, J. and S.J. Tambiah
1973 *Bridewealth and dowry*. Cambridge: Cambridge University Press.

Gordon, E.
1981 'An analysis of the impact of labour migration on the lives of women in Lesotho', *Journal of Development Studies* 17-3:54-76.

Graves, Elizabeth E.
1971 *The ever-victorious buffalo; How the Minangkabau of Indonesia solved their 'colonial question'*. N.p.: n.n. [PhD thesis University of Wisconsin, Madison.]

Grawert, E.
1992 'Impacts of male outmigration on women; A case study of Kutum, Northern Darfur, Sudan', *AHFAD Journal* 9-2:37-60.

Greenhalgh, S.
1988 'Intergenerational contracts; Familial roots of sexual stratification in Taiwan', in: D. Dwyer and J. Bruce (eds), *A home divided; Women and income in the Third World*, pp. 39-71. Stanford: Stanford University Press.

Griffiths, Stephen
1988 *Emigrants, entrepreneurs and evil spirits; Life in a Philippine village*. Honolulu: University of Hawaii Press.

Grijns, M.
1986 'Marginalisering; Theepluksters in West-Java', *Antropologische Verkenningen* 5/4:55-73.

Guest, Philip
1989 *Labor allocation and rural development; Migration in four Javanese villages*. Boulder: Westview.

Guyer, J.
1988 'The multiplication of labor; Historical methods in the study of gender and agricultural change in modern Africa', *Current Anthropology* 29:247-72.

Haibach, W.W.
1927 Memorie van Overgave van de onderafdeeling Samosir. [Available at the library of the Koninklijk Instituut voor de Tropen, Amsterdam.]

Handschriften H 806
1920 Hoofdstuk 29; Inheemsche Landbouw. Manuscript H 806 kept in the Royal Institute of Linguistics and Anthropology, Leiden.

Harbison, S.F.
1981 'Family structure and family strategy in migration decision making', in: G.F. de Jong and R.W. Gardner (eds), *Migration decision making; Multidisciplinary approaches to microlevel studies in developed and developing countries*, pp. 225-51. New York: Pergamon.

Harris, J.R. and M.P. Todaro
1970 'Migration, unemployment, and development; A two-sector analysis', *American Economic Review* 60:126-42.

Harris, O.
1981 'Households as natural units', in: K. Young, C. Wolkowitz and R. McCullagh (eds), *Of marriage and the market; women's subordination in international perspective*, pp. 49-68. London: CSE Books.

Hart, Gillian
1986 *Power, labor, and livelihood; Processes of change in rural Java.* Berkeley: University of California Press.
1991 'Engendering everyday resistance; Gender, patronage and production politics in rural Malaysia', *Journal of Peasant Studies* 19:93-122.

Hay, M.J.
1976 'Luo women and economic change during the colonial period', in: N.J. Hafkin and E.G. Bay (eds), *Women in Africa; Studies in social and economic change*, pp. 87-110. Stanford: Stanford University Press.

Hefner, Robert W.
1990 *The political economy of mountain Java; An interpretive history.* Berkeley/ Los Angeles: University of California Press.

Hetler, Carol B.
1986 *Female-headed households in a circular migration village in Central Java, Indonesia.* N.p.: n.n. [PhD thesis Australian National University, Canberra.]
1989 'The impact of circular migration on a village economy', *Bulletin of Indonesian Economic Studies* 25:53-75.

Heyzer, N.
1982 'From rural subsistence to an industrial peripheral work force; An examination of female Malaysian migrants and capital accumulation in Singapore', in: L. Beneria (ed.), *Women and development; The sexual division of labour in rural societies; A study*, pp. 179-202. New York: Praeger.

Hirschfeld, L.A.
1979 'Notes on the Toba Batak (Sumatra)', *L'Homme* 19-1:141-4.

Hoddinott, J.
1992 'Rotten kids or manipulative parents; Are children old-age security in Western Kenya?', *Economic Development and Cultural Change* 40:545-67.

Hudson, A.B.
1967 *Padju Epat; The ethnography and social structure of a Ma'anjan Dajak group in Southeastern Borneo.* N.p.: n.n. [PhD thesis Cornell University, Ithaca.]

Hüsken, Franciscus A.M.
1988 *Een dorp op Java; Sociale differentiatie in een boerengemeenschap, 1850-1980.* Overveen: ACASEA. [PhD thesis Universiteit van Amsterdam.]

Hugo, Graeme J.
1975 *Population mobility in West Java, Indonesia.* [PhD thesis Australian National University, Canberra.]
1978 'Circulation in West Java, Indonesia', in: R.M. Prothero and M. Chapman (eds), *Circulation; Population movement in developing countries*, pp. 75-99. London: Routledge and Kegan Paul.
1979 'The impact of migration on villages in Java', in: R.J. Pryor (ed.), *Migration and development in South-East Asia; A demographic perspective*, pp. 204-11. Kuala Lumpur: Oxford University Press.

1985 'Structural change and labour mobility in rural Java', in: G. Standing (ed.), *Labour circulation and the labour process*, pp. 46-88. London/ Dover, N.H.: Croom Helm.
1993 'Migrant women in developing countries', *Internal migration of women in developing countries,* pp. 47-73. New York: United Nations.

Huston, P.
1979 *Third World women speak out; Interviews in six countries on change, development, and basic needs.* New York/London: Praeger. [Published in cooperation with the Overseas Development Council.]

Hutabarat, B.
1987 'Maduma antara makmur dan doa', *Kompas* 19-7-1987.
1988 'Tapanuli Utara memburu investasi', *Kompas* 2-10-1988.

Indonesische dorpsakten
1933 *Indonesische dorpsakten.* Vertaald en bewerkt door Rd. Tirtawinata and W.A. Muller. Batavia: Afdeeling Adatrecht van het Koninklijk Bataviaasch Genootschap van Kunsten en Wetenschappen.

Inglis, C.
1983 'The feminization of the teaching profession in Singapore', in: L. Manderson (ed.), *Women's work and women's roles; Economics and everyday life in Indonesia, Malaysia and Singapore*, pp. 217-38. Canberra: Australian National University.

Islam, M. and P. Ahmad
1984 'Bangladesh; Tradition reinforced', in: *Women in the villages, men in the towns*, pp. 21-75. Paris: UNESCO.

Iszaevich, A.
1974 'Emigrants, spinsters and priests; The dynamics of demography in Spanish peasant societies', *Journal of Peasant Studies* 2:292-312.

Izzard, W.
1985 'Migrants and mothers; Case-studies from Botswana', *Journal of Southern Africa Studies* 11:258-80.

Jansen, W.H.M.
1987 *Women without men; Gender and marginality in an Algerian town.* Leiden: Brill.

Janssen, C.W.
1924 'De Bataks als exploitanten van hun eigen gebied', *Koloniaal Tijdschrift* 13:353-75.

Jayawardena, C.
1977 'Women and kinship in Acheh Besar, northern Sumatra', *Ethnology* 16-1:21-38.
M 16

Jetley, S.
1984 'Eternal waiting', in: *Women in the villages, men in the towns*, pp. 75-147. Paris: UNESCO.

Jones, Gavin W. (ed.)
1984 *Women in the urban and industrial workforce; Southeast and South Asia.* Canberra: Australian National University.

Josephides, Lisette
1985   *The production of inequality; Gender and exchange among the Kewa.*
            London: Tavistock.
Joustra, M.
1910   *Batakspiegel.* Leiden: Van Doesburgh. [Uitgaven van het Bataksch
            Instituut 3.]
1912   *De Bataks, wie zij waren en wat wij, naar de opgedane ervaringen, van hen
            mogen verwachten; Een schets.* Leiden: Van Doesburgh. [Uitgaven van
            het Bataksch Instituut 7.]
1918   'Toekomst der Bataks', *De Gids* 22-1:282-315.
Junghuhn, Franz
1847   *Die Battaländer auf Sumatra.* Vol. 2. Berlin: Reimer.
Kahn, Joel S.
1980   *Minangkabau social formations; Indonesian peasants and the world economy.*
            Cambridge: Cambridge University Press.
Kandiyoti, D.
1988   'Bargaining with patriarchy', *Gender and Society* 2:274-90.
Kato, Tsuyoshi
1982   *Matriliny and migration; Evolving Minangkabau traditions in Indonesia.*
            Ithaca, N.Y./London: Cornell University Press.
Kearney, M.
1986   'From the invisible hand to visible feet; Anthropological studies of
            migration and development', *Annual Review of Anthropology* 15:331-61.
Kecamatan Muara dalam angka
1986   *Kecamatan Muara dalam angka.* N.p.: Mantis Kec. Muara, Tapanuli
            Utara.
Keuning, Johannes
1948   *Verwantschapsrecht en volksordening, huwelijksrecht en erfrecht in het
            Koeriagebied van Tapanoeli.* Leiden: IJdo. [PhD thesis Rijksuniversiteit
            Leiden.]
Khafagy, F.
1984   'One village in Egypt', *Merip Report* 14-5:17-22. [Special issue on
            Women and Labour Migration.]
Komter, A.
1989   'Hidden power in marriage', *Gender and Society* 3:187-216.
Kraemer, Hendrik
1958   *From missionfield to independent church; Report on a decisive decade in the
            growth of indigenous churches in Indonesia.* The Hague: Boekencentrum.
Krause, K.
1981   *Weisse Experten nicht gefragt; Selbsthilfe in indonesischen Dörfern Protokolle.* Reinbek: Rowohlt Taschenbuch Verlag.
Kruyt, A.C.
1946   'Het Christenvolk der Bataks', in: J. Poortenaar and W.P. Coolhaas
            (eds), *Onder palmen en waringins; Geest en godsdienst van Insulinde*,
            pp. 65-78. Naarden: In den Toren.

Laguerre, M.
1978   'The impact of migration on the Haitian family and household organization', in: A.F. Marks and R.A. Römer (eds), *Family and kinship in Middle America and the Caribbean*, pp. 446-81. Willemstad: University of the Netherlands Antilles, Leiden: Royal Institute of Linguistics and Anthropology.

Lando, Richard P.
1979   *The gift of land; Irrigation and social structure in a Toba Batak village*. [PhD thesis University of California.]

Langenberg, M. van
1977   'North Sumatra under Dutch colonial rule; Aspects of structural change', *Review of Indonesian and Malaysian Affairs* 11-1:74-110; 11-2:45-86.

Leacock, E.
1977   'Women in egalitarian societies', in: R. Bridenthal and C. Koonz (eds), *Becoming visible; Women in European history*, pp. 11-35. Boston: Houghton Mifflin.

Lee, E.
1966   'A theory of migration', *Demography* 3-1:47-57.

Leinbach, Thomas R. and Bambang Suwarno
1983   *Rural-urban mobility and employment; Indonesia; A final report to the International Development Research Centre, Ottawa*. N.p.: n.n.

Lev, D.S.
1972   'Judicial institutions and legal culture in Indonesia', in: C. Holt, with the assistance of B.R.O'G. Anderson and J. Siegel (eds), *Culture and politics in Indonesia*, pp. 246-318. Ithaca/London: Cornell University Press.

Lévi-Strauss, Claude
1969   *The elementary structures of kinship*. Revised edition. Translated from the French by J.H. Bell et al. (eds). London: Eyre and Spottiswoode. [Original title: *Les structures élémentaires de la parenté*, 1949.]

Liddle, R.W.
1967   *Politics in Simalungun; A study in political integration*. N.p.: n.n. [PhD thesis Yale University.]

Lim, L.L.
1991   'The structural determinants of female migration', *Internal migration of women in developing countries*. New York: United Nations.

Lineton, J.A.
1975   'Pasompe' Ugi'; Bugis migrants and wanderers', *Archipel* 10:173-201.

Lipton, M.
1982   'Migration from rural areas of poor countries; The impact on rural productivity and income distribution', in: R.H. Sabot (ed.), *Migration and the labor market in developing countries*, pp. 191-228. Boulder: Westview.

Loeb, E.M.
1933   'Patrilineal and matrilineal organization in Sumatra; The Batak and the Minangkabau', *American Anthropologist* 35:16-50.

1935   *Sumatra; Its history and people.* Wien: Verlag des Institutes für Völkerkunde der Universität Wien.

MacGaffey, J.
1983   'The effect of rural-urban ties, kinship and marriage on household structure in a Kongo village', *Canadian Journal of African Studies* 17-1:69-84.

McNicoll, G.
1968   'Internal migration in Indonesia; Descriptive notes', *Indonesia* 5:29-92.

Manderson, L.
1978   'The development and direction of female education in Peninsular Malaysia', *Journal of the Malaysian Branch of the Royal Asiatic Society* 51-2:100-22.

Mantra, Ida B.
1981   *Population movement in wet rice communities; A case study of two dukuh in Yogyakarta special region.* Yogyakarta: Gadjah Mada University.

Margolies, L. and M.M. Suarez
1978   'The peasant family in the Venezuelan Andes', in: A.F. Marks and R.A. Romer (eds), *Family and kinship in Middle America and the Caribbean*, pp. 382-404. Willemstad: University of the Netherlands Antilles, Leiden: Royal Institute of Linguistics and Anthropology.

Marsden, W.
1811   *The history of Sumatra, containing an account of the government, laws, customs, and manners of the native inhabitants, with a description of the natural productions, and a relation of the ancient political state of that island.* Third edition. London: Longman. [First edition 1783.]

Mascarenhas-Keyes, S.
1990   'Migration, "progressive motherhood" and female autonomy; Catholic women in Goa', in: L. Dube and R. Palriwala (eds), *Structures and strategies; Women, work and family*, pp. 255-73. New Delhi: Sage.

Massiah, J.
1986   'Work in the lives of Caribbean women', *Social and Economic Studies* 35-2:177-239.

Mather, C.
1985   'Rather than make trouble, it's better just to leave; Behind the lack of industrial strife in the Tangerang region of West Java', in: H. Afshar (ed.), *Women, work, and ideology in the Third World*, pp. 153-80. London: Tavistock.

Maude, A.M.
1979   'Intervillage differences in out-migration from West Sumatra', *Journal of Tropical Geography* 49:41-54.

Meillassoux, C.
1981   *Maidens, meal and money; Capitalism and the domestic community.* Cambridge: Cambridge University Press. [Original title: *Femmes, greniers et capitaux*, 1975.]

Menon, G.
1989   'The impact of migration on the work and status of tribal women in Orissa', in: *Women and seasonal labour migration in rural India; Research report*, pp. 71-217. Amsterdam: University of Amsterdam, Indo-Dutch Programma on Alternatives in Development. 2 Vols.

Meulen, Daniel van der
1977   *Hoort gij de donder niet? Begin van het einde der Nederlandse gezagvoering in Indië; Een persoonlijke terugblik.* Franeker: Wever.

Michaelson, E. and W. Goldschmidt
1971   'Female roles and male dominance among peasants', *Southwestern Journal of Anthropology* 27:330-52.

Middendorp, W.
1913   Memorie van Overgave van de onderafdeeling Samosir, afdeeling Bataklanden. [Unpublished typescript.]

Mitchell, J.C.
1985   'Towards a situational sociology of wage-labour circulation; The Indian scene', in: R.M. Prothero and M. Chapman (eds), *Circulation in Third World countries*, pp. 30-54. London: Routledge and Kegan Paul.

Momsen, J. Henshall
1987   'The feminization of agriculture in the Caribbean', in: J. Henshall Momsen and J. Townsend (eds), *Geography of gender in the Third World*, pp. 344-8. London: State University of New York Press.

Moore, H.L.
1988   *Feminism and anthropology.* Cambridge: Polity Press.

Morokvasic, M. (ed.)
1984   'Women in migration', *International Migration Review* 18:885-1314. [Special Issue.]

Mueller, M.
1977   'Women and men, power and powerlessness in Lesotho', *Signs* 3:154-66.

Murray, C.
1979   'The work of men, women and the ancestors; Social reproduction in the periphery of southern Africa', in: S. Wallman (ed.), *Social anthropology of work*, pp. 337-65. London: Academic Press.
1981   *Families divided; The impact of migrant labour in Lesotho.* Cambridge: Cambridge University Press.
1987   'Class, gender and the household; The developmental cycle in Southern Africa', *Development and Change* 18:235-49.

Muijzenberg, O.D. van den
1973   *Horizontale mobiliteit in Centraal Luzon; Kenmerken en achtergronden.* Amsterdam: Universiteit van Amsterdam. [Afdeling Zuid- en Zuidoost Azië, Universiteit van Amsterdam, Publikatie nr. 19.]

Myers, Muriel A.
1982   *Sacred shawls of the Toba Batak; 'Adat' in action.* N.p.: n.n. [PhD thesis University of California.]

Mijl, Jan P. van der
1988   *Atlas sosial-ekonomi Tapanuli Utara; Hasil baseline survey dalam tema dan peta*. Medan: Lembaga Penelitian Universitas HKBP Nommensen. [Makalah Sesewaktu 2.]

Myrdal, Gunnar
1972   *Asian drama; An inquiry into the poverty of nations*. Abridged version. New York: Vintage Books.

Naim, Mochtar
1971   *Merantau; Causes and effects of Minangkabau voluntary migration*. Singapore: Institute of Southeast Asian Studies. [Occasional Paper 5.]
1985   'Implications of merantau for social organization in Minangkabau', in: L. Thomas and F. von Benda-Beckmann (eds), *Change and continuity in Minangkabau; Local, regional, and historical perspectives on West Sumatra*, pp. 111-21. Athens: Ohio University.

Nasoetion, M.H.
1943   *De plaats van de vrouw in de Batakse maatschappij*. Utrecht: Kemink. [PhD thesis University of Utrecht.]

Nasution, J.S.
1987   'Tapanuli, wanita dan pembangunannya', *Waspada* 30-4-1987.

Neumann, J.B.
1887   'Het Pane en Bila-stroomgebied op het eiland Sumatra. (Studiën over Bataks en Bataksche landen)', *Tijdschrift van het Nederlandsch Aardrijkskundig Genootschap* Tweede Serie 3-2:217-314.

Niessen, S.A.
1985   *Motifs of life in Toba Batak texts and textiles*. Dordrecht/Cinnaminson: Foris. [KITLV, Verhandelingen 110.]

Oerlemans, L.J.
1937   *Memorie van Overgave betreffende de onderafdeeling Samosir*. [Available at the library of the Koninklijk Instituut voor de Tropen, Amsterdam.]

Oey, M.
1979   'Rising expectations but limited opportunities for women in Indonesia', in: R. Jahan and H. Papanek (eds), *Women and development; Perspectives from South and Southeast Asia*, pp. 233-52. Dacca: Bangladesh Institute of Law and International Affairs.

Oey-Gardiner, M.
1991   'Gender differences in schooling in Indonesia', *Bulletin of Indonesian Economic Studies* 21-1:57-79.

Ong, A.
1987   *Spirits of resistance and capitalist discipline; Factory women in Malaysia*. Albany: State University of New York Press.

Palmer, I.
1985   *The impact of male out-migration on women in farming*. West Hartford: Kumarian. [Women's Roles and Gender Differences in Development 7.]

Papanek, H.
1990 'To each less than she needs, from each more than she can do; Allocations, entitlements, and value', in: I. Tinker (ed.), *Persistent inequalities; Women and world development*, pp. 162-85. New York [etc.]: Oxford University Press.

Pedersen, Paul B.
1970 *Batak blood and Protestant soul; The development of national Batak churches in North Sumatra*. Grand Rapids: Eerdmans.

Pelly, Usman
1983 *Urban migration and adaptation in Indonesia; A case study of Minangkabau and Mandailing Batak migrants in Medan, North Sumatra*. N.p.: n.n. [PhD thesis University of Illinois.]
1992 'The role of the culture mission of migration', *Mizan* 1-5:8-16.

Pelzer, Karl J.
1958 'Preface', in: Clark E. Cunningham, *The postwar migration of the Toba-Bataks to East Sumatra*, pp. i-v. [New Haven]: Yale University.
1961 'Western impact on East Sumatra and North Tapanuli; The role of the planter and the missionary', *Journal of Southeast Asian History* 2-2:66-71.
1982 *Planters against peasants; The agrarian struggle in East Sumatra 1947-1958*. 's-Gravenhage: Nijhoff. [KITLV, Verhandelingen 97.]

Penduduk Indonesia
1990 *Penduduk Indonesia; Hasil sensus penduduk 1990/Population of Indonesia; Results of the 1990 population census*. Seri/Series: S2. Jakarta: Biro Pusat Statistik.

Penny, D.H. and M. Singarimbun
1973 *Population and poverty in rural Java: some economic arithmetic from Sriharjo*. Ithaca, N.Y.: Department of Agricultural Economics, New York State College of Agriculture and Life Sciences.

Pessar, P.R.
1982 *Kinship relations of production in the migration process; The case of Dominican emigration to the United States*. New York: New York University, Center for Latin American and Caribbean Studies. [Occasional Paper 32.]
1988 'The constraints on and release of female labour power; Dominican migration to the United States', in: D. Dwyer and J. Bruce (eds), *A home divided: Women and income in the Third World*, pp. 195-215. Stanford: Stanford University Press.

Philpott, S.B.
1970 'Some implications of migration for sending societies; Some theoretical considerations', in: R.F. Spencer (ed.), *Migration and anthropology*, pp. 9-20. Seattle: University of Washington.

Popkin, Samuel L.
1979 *The rational peasant; The political economy of rural society in Vietnam*. Berkeley/London: University of California Press.

Portes, A.
1981 'Unequal exchange and the urban informal sector', in: A. Portes and J. Walton (eds), *Labor, class, and the international system*, pp. 67-106. New York: Academic Press.

Portier, M.K. and H. Slaats
1987 'Women and the division of parental land in Karo society', in: R. Carle (ed.), *Cultures and societies of North Sumatra*, pp. 303-9. Berlin: Reimer.

Postel-Coster, Els
1985 *Het omheinde kweekbed; Machtsverhoudingen in de Minangkabause familieroman*. Delft: Eburon.

Pryor, Robin J.
1979 *Migration and development in Southeast Asia; A demographic perspective*. Kuala Lumpur: Oxford University Press.

Radcliffe, S.
1986 'Gender relations, peasant livelihood strategies and migration; A case-study from Cuzco, Peru', *Bulletin of Latin American Research* 5-2:29-47.
1990 'Between hearth and labour market; The recruitment of peasant women in the Andes', *International Migration Review* 24-2:229-49.

Raharjo, Y. and V. Hull
1984 'Employment patterns of educated women in Indonesian cities', in: G.W. Jones (ed.), *Women in the urban and industrial workforce; Southeast and East Asia*, pp. 101-26. Canberra: Australian National University.

Ravenstein, E.G.
1885 'The laws of migration', *Journal of the Royal Statistical Society* 48:167-235; 52:242-305.

Redclift, M.
1986 'Survival strategies in rural Europe; Continuity and change', *Sociologia Ruralis* 26-3/4.

Reenen, J. van
1987 'Labour migration and matrilineal patterns of land tenure; Some social impacts on a Minangkabau village community'. Paper for the Eighth Conference on Tropical Asia, Amsterdam.

Reid, Anthony
1979 *The blood of the people; Revolution and the end of traditional rule in northern Sumatra*. Kuala Lumpur/New York: Oxford University Press.
1983 (ed.) *Slavery, bondage and dependency in Southeast Asia*. St. Lucia: University of Queensland Press.

Renes-Boldingh, M.A.M.
1942 *Schaduw-schimmenspel*. Lochem: De Tijdstroom.

Riley, N.E. and R. Gardner
1993 'Migration decisions; The role of gender', *Internal migration of women in developing countries*, pp. 195-206. New York: United Nations.

Risseeuw, C.
1991 *Gender transformation, power and resistance among women in Sri Lanka; The fish don't talk about the water*. New Delhi: Manohar.

Rodenburg, J.
1993   'Emancipation or subordination? Consequences of female migration for migrants and their families', in: *Internal migration of women in developing countries*, pp. 273-89. New York: United Nations.

Rodgers, S.
1988   'Me and Toba; A childhood world in a Batak memoir', *Indonesia* 45:63-83.

Röll, W.
1984   'Ursachen, Erscheinungsformen und Folgen Interregionaler Migrationen aus dem Toba-Hochland; Untersuchungen zur raumlichen Mobilität der Bevölkerung in Nord-Sumatra'. Paper Universität Kassel.

Roldán, M.
1988   'Renegotiating the marital contract; Intra-household patterns of money allocation and women's subordination among domestic outworkers in Mexico City', in: D. Dwyer and J. Bruce (eds), *A home divided; Women and income in the Third World*, pp. 229-48. Stanford: Stanford University Press.

Ruychaver, M.J.
1936   Memorie van Overgave van de afdeeling Bataklanden. [Available at the library of the Koninklijk Instituut voor de Tropen, Amsterdam.]

Sahlins, M.
1972   *Stone Age economics*. Chicago: Aldine-Altherton.

Sarumpaet-Hutabarat, J.
1954   'De Batakse adat', *Zendingsblad Nederlands Hervormde Kerk* 8-9:4-9.

Schadee, W.
1920   *De uitbreiding van ons gezag in de Bataklanden*. Leiden: Van Doesburgh. [Uitgaven van het Bataksch Instituut 19.]

Schaik, Arthur van
1986   *Colonial control and peasant resources in Java; Agricultural involution reconsidered*. Amsterdam: Koninklijk Nederlands Aardrijkskundig Genootschap. [Nederlandse geografische studies 14.]

Schefold, R.
1988   'Hearthless house and painted concrete; Aspects of ethnicity among Sa'dan Toraja and Toba Batak (Indonesia)', in: Ph. Quarles van Ufford and M. Schoffeleers (eds), *Religion and development; Towards an integrated approach*, pp. 231-46. Amsterdam: Free University Press.

Schmink, M.
1984   'Household economic strategies; Review and research agenda', *Latin American Research Review* 19-3:87-101.

Schneider, D.M. and K. Gough
1961   *Matrilineal kinship*. Berkeley: University of California Press.

Scholz, U.
1983   *The natural regions of Sumatra and their agricultural production pattern; A regional analysis*. Vols I and II. Bogor: Central Research for Food Crops.

Schrijvers, J.Th.
1985   Mothers for life; Motherhood and marginalization in the north central province of Sri Lanka. Delft: Eburon.

Schwarz, A.
1992a   'Burning issue', Far Eastern Economic Review 12-3-1992:40.
1992b   'Monopoly under fire; Tommy's brashness turns attention on family', Far Eastern Economic Review 30-4-1992:58.

Scott, James C.
1976   The moral economy of the peasant; Rebellion and subsistence in Southeast Asia. New Haven: Yale University Press.
1985   Weapons of the weak; Everyday forms of peasant resistance. New Haven/London: Yale University Press.

Sen, A.K.
1976   'Famines as failures of exchange entitlements', Economic and Political Weekly 11:1273-80.
1990   'Gender and cooperative conflicts', in: I. Tinker (ed.), Persistent inequalities; Women and world development, pp. 123-50. New York: Oxford University Press.

Shaheed, F.
1981   Migration and its effects on women in the villages of provenance. Geneva: International Labour Organization.

Sherman, D. George
1990   Rice, rupees, and ritual; Economy and society among the Samosir Batak of Sumatra. Stanford: Stanford University Press.

Siahaan, S.M.
1983   'Kedukukan wanita dalam masyarakat Batak', Suara Indonesia Baru 29-1-1983.

Sibisi, H.
1977   'How African women cope with migrant labor in South Africa', Signs 3:167-77.

Siegel, J.
1969   The rope of God. Berkeley: University of California Press.

Simandjuntak, B.A.
1983   Sistem perpindahan penguasaan sawah pada masyarakat Batak Toba (Kasus Lumban Sibangun, Sipahutar). Medan: IKIP.

Simbolon, I.J.
1992   Who is violating whose laws? An analysis of the 'Sugapa Case' from legal, development, and gender perspectives. N.p.: n.n. [MA thesis Institute of Social Studies, The Hague.]
1994   'Women in a tug-of-war between traditional laws and national laws; Chances and problems of Batak-Toba women to obtain rights to land'. Paper for the Ninth INFID Conference on Good Governance in Regional Development, Paris, 22-24 April.

Sinaga, A.
1990   'Dari "Maduma" sampai "Martabe" keadaan tetap sama', Suara Pembaruan 13-10-1990.

Siregar, M.
1939 'Pandan; Dengan barang-barang anjamannja di Samosir', *Pandoe; Madjallah Opisil di Residentie Tapanoeli* 12:142.
Smale, M.
1980 *Women in Mauretania; The effects of drought and migration on their economic status and implications for development programs.* Washington: US Agency for International Development.
Snouck Hurgronje, C.
1906 *The Achehnese.* Translated by A.W.S. O'Sullivan. Leiden: Brill. 2 vols.
Speare, A.J.
1975 'Interpreting the migration data from the 1971 census', *Majalah Demografi Indonesia* 2:66-85.
Speare, A.J. and J. Harris
1986 'Education, earnings, and migration in Indonesia', *Economic Development and Cultural Change* 34-2:223-44.
Standing, G.
1983 'Preface', in C. Colfer, *On circular migration – from the distaff side; Women left behind in the forest of East Kalimantan*, pp. i-ii. Geneva: International Labour Office. [Population and Labour Policies Programme Working Paper 132.]
1985 (ed.) *Labour circulation and the labour process.* London/Dover: Croom Helm.
Stivens, M.
1981 'Women, kinship and capitalist development', in: K. Young, C. Wolkowitz and R. McCullagh (eds), *Of marriage and the market; Women's subordination in international perspective*, pp. 112-26. London: CSE Books.
1985 'The fate of women's land rights; Gender, matriliny, and capitalism in Rembau, Negeri Sembilan, Malaysia', in: H. Afshar (ed.), *Women, work, and ideology in the Third World*, pp. 3-36. London: Tavistock.
1991 'The evolution of kinship relations in Rembau, Negeri Sembilan, Malaysia', in: F. Hüsken and J. Kemp (eds), *Cognation and social organization in Southeast Asia*, pp. 193-201. Leiden: KITLV Press. [Verhandelingen 145.]
Strange, Heather
1978 'Education and employment patterns of rural Malay women, 1965-1975', *Journal of Asian and African Studies* 8-1/2:50-64.
1981 *Rural Malay women in tradition and transition.* New York: Praeger.
Strauch, J.
1984 'Women in rural–urban circulation networks; Implications for social structural change', in: J.T. Fawcett, Siew-Ean Khoo and Peter C. Smith (eds), *Women in the cities of Asia; Migration and urban adaptation*, pp. 60-79. Boulder: Westview.
Subarkah, A.W., D. Marsidi and E. Fadjari
1986 'Bawean Pulau Perempuan, tidak merantau bisa jadi alasan cerai', *Kompas* 27-4-1986:2.

SUPAS
1987   Survei penduduk antar sensus 1985: daftar SUPAS 85–S. Jakarta: Biro Pusat Statistik.

Swift, M.G.
1965   Malay peasant society in Jelebu. London/New York: Athlone. [Monographs on Social Anthropology 29.]

Tampubolon, Radja Patik
1964   Pustaha Tumbaga holing; Adat Batak - Patik Uhum. Pematang Siantar: n.n.

Tanner, N.
1974   'Matrifocality in Indonesia and Africa and among black Americans', in: M.Z. Rosaldo and L. Lamphere (eds), *Woman, culture, and society*, pp. 129-57. Stanford: Stanford University Press.

Tapanuli Utara
1986   Tapanuli Utara dalam angka 1985. Tarutung: Kantor Statistik Kabupaten Tapanuli Utara.

Tempo
1984   'Desa-desa yang kehilangan pria', *Tempo* 7-4-1984:37-41.

Tichelman, G.L.
1936   'Bataks arbeidsreservaat', *Koloniaal Tijdschrift* 25:399-403.

Tideman, J.
1922   *Simeloengoen; Het land der Timoer-Bataks in zijn vroegere isolatie en zijn ontwikkeling tot een deel van het cultuurgebied van de Oostkust van Sumatra*. Leiden: Becherer.
1934   Nota over Samosir. [Available at the library of the Koninklijk Instituut voor de Tropen, Amsterdam.]

Tobing, Ph.O.L.
1956   *The structure of the Toba-Batak belief in the high god*. Amsterdam: Van Campen.

Trager, Lillian
1984   'Migration and remittances; Urban income and rural households in the Philippines', *Journal of Developing Areas* 18:317-40.
1988   *The city connection; Migration and family interdependence in the Philippines*. Ann Arbor: University of Michigan Press.

UNICEF
1988   *Situation analysis of children and women in Indonesia*. [Jakarta]: Government of Indonesia/UNICEF.

Vatuk, S.
1972   *Kinship and urbanization; White collar migrants in North India*. Berkeley: University of California Press.

Velsen, J. van
1960   'Labour migration as a positive factor in the continuity of Tonga tribal society', *Economic Development and Cultural Change* 8-3:265-78.

Vergouwen, J.C.
1964 *The social organisation and customary law of the Toba-Batak of northern Sumatra*. The Hague: Nijhoff. [Translated by J. Scott-Kemball from *Het rechtsleven der Toba-Bataks*, 1933; KITLV, Translation Series 7.]

Verhoef, A.
1934 Memorie van Overgave van de onderafdeeling Toba Hoogvlakte. [Available at the library of the Koninklijk Instituut voor de Tropen, Amsterdam.]

Viner, A.C.
1979 'The changing Batak', *Journal of the Malaysian Branch of the Royal Asiatic Society* 52:84-112.

Volkstelling 1930
1933-36 *Volkstelling 1930*. Batavia: Landsdrukkerij.

Volz, W.
1899 'Zum Toba-see in Central-Sumatra', *Tijdschrift van het Koninklijk Nederlandsch Aardrijkskundig Genootschap* 16:415-85.

Vredenbregt, J.
1964 'Bawean migration', *Bijdragen tot de Taal-, Land- en Volkenkunde* 120:109-39.

Vuurmans, H.
1941 'Emigraties van Christen Toba-Bataks', *Zendingsblad* 3:38-40.

Weber, E.
1976 *Peasants into Frenchmen; The modernization of rural France, 1870-1914*. Stanford: Stanford University Press.

Weber, M.
1947 *The theory of social and economic organisation*. Translated and edited by T. Parsons. New York: Oxford University Press.

Welter, C.F.H.
1935 Memorie van Overgave betreffende de onderafdeeling Samosir. [Available at the library of the Koninklijk Instituut voor de Tropen, Amsterdam.]

Wertheim, W.F.
1969 *Indonesian society in transition; A study of social change*. The Hague: Van Hoeve. [First edition 1956.]

White, Benjamin N.F.
1977 *Production and reproduction in a Javanese village*. [PhD thesis Columbia University, New York.]
1980 'Rural household studies in anthropological perspective', in: H. Binswanger et al. (eds), *Rural household studies in Asia*, pp. 3-25. Singapore: Singapore University Press.
1983 'Agricultural involution and its critics; Twenty years after', *Bulletin of Concerned Asian Scholars* 15-2:18-31.

Whitehead, A.
1981 'I'm hungry, mum; The politics of domestic budgeting', in: K. Young, C. Wolkowitz and R. McCullagh (eds), *Of marriage and the market;*

Women's subordination in international perspective, pp. 88-112. London: CSE Books.

Wiest, R.E.
1973 'Wage-labor migration and the household in a Mexican town', *Journal of Anthropological Research* 29:180-209.

Wilkinson, C.
1987 'Women, migration and work in Lesotho', in: J.H. Momsen and J.G. Townsend (eds), *Geography of gender in the Third World*, pp. 225-40. London: State University of New York Press.

Wojno, M.G.
1986 *Staying behind but getting ahead; New economic roles for women in northern Portugal*. Michigan: Michigan State University. [Working Paper 132.]

Wolf, Diane L.
1986 'Linking women's labor with the global economy; Factory daughters and their families in rural Java'. Paper prepared for 'Gender, Race, and Labor in the World Economy' session, Annual Meeting of the American Sociological Association, New York.
1990 'Daughters, decisions and domination; An empirical and conceptual critique of household strategies', *Development and Change* 21:43-74.
1992 *Factory daughters; Gender, household dynamics, and rural industrialization in Java*. Berkeley: University of California Press.

Wolf, Erik R.
1966 *Peasants*. Englewood Cliffs, N.J.: Prentice Hall.

Wolfs, R.
1988 Groeten uit Padang; Een studie over circulaire arbeidsmigratie vanuit drie dorpsgemeenschappen in de provincie Noord-Sumatra, Indonesië. N.p.: n.n. [MA thesis Catholic University Nijmegen, Nijmegen.]

Wolters, W.
1991 'The political economy of kinship and marriage strategies in Java and Central Luzon', in: F. Hüsken and J. Kemp (eds), *Cognation and social organization in Southeast Asia*, pp. 169-82. Leiden: KITLV Press. [Verhandelingen 145.]

Wong, D.
1991 'Kinship and the domestic development cycle in a Kedah village, Malaysia', in: F. Hüsken and J. Kemp (eds), *Cognation and social organization in Southeast Asia*, pp. 193-203. Leiden: KITLV Press. [Verhandelingen 145.]

Wood, C.H.
1981 'Structural changes and household strategies; A conceptual framework for the study of rural migration', *Human Organization* 40:338-44.

Wood, C.H. and T.L. McCoy
1985 'Migration, remittances and development; A study of Caribbean cane cutters in Florida', *International Migration Review* 19-2:251-77.

Ypes, W.K.H.
1932   *Bijdrage tot de kennis van de stamverwantschap, de inheemsche rechtsgemeenschappen en het grondenrecht der Toba- en Dairibataks.* Leiden: Adatrechtstichting.

Zelinsky, W.
1971   'The hypothesis of mobility transition', *Geographical Review* 61:221-49.

Index

Aceh 105, 144, 167, 181-2, 190
   as migration destination, 53, 60
adat 39, 44, 67, 75, 77, 81, 96, 103,
   105-6, 133, 136, 144, 148, 176, 188,
   203, *see also* customary law
   – ceremonies 27, 41, 111
   – land 24, 115, 130
adolescent(s) 177, 189
   – as migrants 8, 45, 57, 141, 187,
   200, 202
   – as stayers 65, 170
affines *see* kinship
agency 4, 12, *see also* autonomy
agriculture 51, *see also* labour; farm(ing)
   – as main occupation 28, 31, 67, 179
   attitude to – 2, 8, 65, 69, 149-50,
   202
   division of labour in – 35, 93, 117,
   121, 139, 205
   investment in – 113, 128, 138
   intensification of – 115, 135, 180
   neglect of – 139-40, 191
   subsistence – 12, 139, 141
   women's contribution to – 12, 46,
   131, 135-6, 141, 175, 188, 195, 199,
   201-2, 205-6
Ambarita 37, 148
ancestor(s) 12, 21, 102
   – worship 33, 82, 99, 201
autonomy 9, 136, 199, 203

bargaining 10, 134, 173-4, 179, 181-2,
   186, 188-9, 191, 193-4, 197
Bemmelen, S.T. van 65, 77-8, 135, 146-9
bona ni pasogit 76, 96-7, 129, 134, 201
borrowing land 109, 111, 126
borrowing money 110, 113, 125, 138
Boserup, E. 134, 139, 160, 189

Bray, F.A. 112
bride-price 8, 78, 83-4, 193
brother(s) 2, 17, 78-9, 83, 91-2, 189-90
   – and education 155, 157, 159, 161,
   188
   – and migration 67, 79, 93-4, 126-7,
   133-4, 136, 138, 168, 171-2, 186-8,
   197, 202, 205
Bruner, E.M. 1, 22, 33, 46, 50, 54, 63,
   91, 95-6, 99, 146
Burton, R. 43-4, 135

cash 50, 59, 119-20, 174
   – economy 49, 51, 119, 141, 200
   – crops 28, 49, 112, 120, 135, 141
   – income 4, 62, 179-80
   women's access to – 186, 200, 206
Castles, L. 23, 43, 45, 48, 50, 52-3, 72,
   146
Chadwick, R.J. 101, 194
child(ren) 34, 75, *see also* daughters
   – and education 54, 143, 145-6, 150-
   2, 157, 162-4, 170-1, 193
   – and migration 4, 64-72, 90, 172,
   184, 190-1, 193-5
   – birth 23, 77, 85, 103-4
   – care 6-7, 12, 49, 57, 62, 148, 171-
   2, 184, 190, 194, 199-200, 202, 204
   – helping parents 117, 130, 137
   importance of – 79-84, 173, 182
   – mortality 23
childlessness 80, 99, 104, 106, 185,
   197, 203
Christian/Christianity 23, 27, 46-7, 52,
   61, 130, 143-4, 148, *see also* church,
   mission
   – and position of women 82, 107,
   182, 183
church 15, 18, 25-7, 32-3, 37, 39-40, 81,

189
HKBP 26-7, 32, 37, 163, 176
clan(s) 21, 25, 75-6, 99, 105, 180
    – as landholding corporation 43, 50, 101-2, 104, 109-12, 201
    – exogamy, 21, 76
    – identity, 15, 33, 149
    women's position within – 77-8, 147, 157
class 37, 97, 131
    – and education 21, 152, 156
    – differences between women 12, 18, 197
    land as indicator of – 53-4, 112-3, 115
Clauss, W. 19, 21-3, 52, 59, 164
colonial government 43, 46-9, 54, 146, 148, 150, *see also* Dutch
    – and educational policy 49, 149, 200
colonialism 18, 43, 46-50, 52, 54, 65
    effects on gender relations 6-7, 13, 47, 106, 134
    effects on infrastructure 22
conflict 44, 79, 91, 172-3, *see also* dispute
    – between spouses 78, 95, 181-2, 184-6, 204
    – within household 5, 11
    – over land 24, 91, 105, 127, 130, 201
    – over marriage choice 148
conjugal contract 181-3, 194
cooperation
    – between kin 6, 78, 97, 173, 201
    – between household members 4-5, 117, 172-4, 188
    – between women 117
    – in village 115, 118-9
cooperative conflict 172, 174, 188
Cunningham, C.E. 1, 21-3, 43, 52-3, 55, 103, 112, 117, 119, 130, 143-5, 156, 190
customary law 11, 44, *see also* adat

Dairi 21-2, 34, 51-3
    – as migration area 114, 135
dalihan na tolu 76, 130

daughters 171, 176
    – and education 12, 147-8, 151, 155-7, 159-60, 163, 166, 189
    – and migration 4, 17, 56-7, 65-7, 195, 203
    – compared to sons 65-9, 70-2, 83, 187, 189, 194-5, 203
    importance of – 57, 65, 78-80, 89, 95, 195
    responsibility of – 187-9
decision-making 3, 40, 95, 105, 157
    – among household members 5, 11-2, 41, 63, 123, 173, 201-3
    – of women 2, 6-10, 41, 123, 137, 139, 203, 205
    – within clan 104
descent 76, 85, 90, 95-6, 190
    patrilineal – 11, 21, 115
development 2, 24, 114
differentiation
    – based on migration 113, 204
    – by gender 6, 10, 206
    rural – 112-3, 115
dispute 44, 47-8, 174, *see also* conflict
    – over land 43
    – between agnates 78
divorce 11, 83-4, 104, 106, 182, 184-6, 203
domestic *see also* household
    – activities 159, 195, 203-4
    – group 13, 79, 84, 87, 89
    – servant(s) 68, 148
    – tensions 5, 191
Dutch 18, 22-3, 43, 45-50, 52-3, 134, 145-6, 149-50, 160
    – administration 49, 112, 143, 145, 184

East (Coast of) Sumatra 120-1, 144
    – as migration area 1, 22, 49-54, 59-60, 63, 69, 83, 93, 128, 168, 171, 180, 184-5
education 64, 143-70, *see also* school(ing)
    – and class status 145-6, 151, 170, 194, 197
    – and mission 47-8, 143-5, 148, 150
    differences by gender 10, 143, 146-8,

151, 155-7, 163, 170, 174, 187, 189
financing of – 62-3, 67-8, 111-2, 134, 138, 157, 162-6, 168, 188
– and employment 65, 143-6, 149, 157, 160, 166-7
– of women 49, 64-7, 141, 147-9, 157, 159-60, 163, 189, 195, 200, 204
– as a way to success 49, 54, 149, 151, 168-70, 193, 200, 202
environment 22, 55-6, 59, 138
 urban 1, 62-4, 97, 152, 167
ethnicity/ethnic 50, 54, 69, 83, 105, 147

factories/y 121, *see also* industrial(ization)
 rural-based – 24, 68
 urban-based – 67-9, 161, 168
family 62-4, 75-99, 200-1, *see also* household, kinship, marriage
 – defined 84
 extended – 40, 84, 88-9
 nuclear – 51, 84-5, 89, 199
 – relations 3, 5, 8, 11, 172-3, 189, 194, 205
 – values among Toba Batak 77, 96-7, 99, 146, 206 173-4, 177, 187-9, 194-5, 197
family planning 81-2, *see also* fertility
farm(ing) 27-8, 34, 36-7, 41, 44, 49, 51, 56, 59, 62, 67-9, 172, 176, 180, 186
 – area 124, 128, 130
 attitude to – 2, 23, 54, 65, 91, 141, 146, 150, 160, 201
 – management 127, 132, 134, 137-9, 175, 179, 202-3, *see also* agriculture, feminization
 – practices 113, 119, 137
 – size 107, 109
farmer(s) 28, 31, 35, 45, 56, 107, 114-5, 119-20
father(s) 1, 11, 36, 45, 50, 151, 156, 159-60, 162-3, 185, 190-1, 195, 203
 migrant 4, 57, 66, 152, 164, 171, 175, 184-5, 204
feminization of farming 131-2, 139-41, 205-6
(in)fertility

– of women 23, 28, 80, 104
– of land 23, 36, 109-10, 125, 139, 201
field work 15-7, 19, 21
firewood 41, 90, 117
fish(ing) 27, 35-6, 39, 99, 123
food 33, 36, 83, 112-3, 120, 139, 162, 165, 177
 women's responsibility for 7, 41, 85, 141, 180, 199, 202
forest 23, 110, 115, 120, 130
friend(ship) 60, 69
 female – 17, 65-6, 79
funeral 99, 175, 191

gambling 39, 140, 182-3
Geertz, C. 50, 95, 113
gender 3, 5, 10-1, 39, 47, 90, 154, 156, *see also* family; household; work; division of labour
 – complementarity 172, 176, 179, 197
 – differentiation 6, 10, 206
 – ideology 1, 8, 12, 136, 147-8, 157, 159, 182
 – inequality 5, 8, 49, 157, 173, 179, 187, 204
 – relations 10-1, 43, 141, 172, 190
 – roles 2, 9, 140
generation 5, 11, 25, 85, 93, 101, 104, 109, 155-6, 172, 191, 194, 199, 201
government 1, 22, 37, 40, 47-9, 52, 55, 69, 96, 176, *see also* colonial government; Netherlands Indies
 – and agrarian change 105, 114-5, 121, 130
 – and village improvement 15, 36-7
 – officials 47-8, 54, 130
 – service 48, 65, 69
Greenhalgh, S. 166, 194
Green Revolution 114, *see also* agriculture

Hart, G. 10, 18, 203
hawk(ing) 1, 63, 83, 93-5, 171, 174, 180-1, 185, 191, 193
hawker 60-3, 72
health 10, 23, 25, 36-7, 81, 90, 112,

146, 149, 161, 171
Hetler, C.B. 9, 97
house(s) 16-7, 33, 39, 41, 77, 91, 105, 151, 162, 165, 168-9, 197, 203
  traditional 25, 27, 40, 75, 80, 84, 91, 93-4, 97
  – building 27-8, 33, 45, 60, 78, 97, 120, 163, 180, 185, 191, 197
household(s) 1-6, 87, 156-7, 161, see also family; decision-making; cooperation
  activities of – 18, 172
  – census 17, 19, 28, 34-5
  class status of – 51, 54, 112, 124-5, 163-4, 168-70, 197
  concept of – 3, 5, 84, 87
  division of labour in – 94, 147, 172, 186, 188, 195, 199
  effect of migration on – 56-7, 59-60, 62-4, 136-7
  female-headed – 9-10, 60, 89-90
  position of women in – 76, 79-80, 84, 164, 171, 190, 201, 203-4
  male head of – 9, 12, 16, 39, 47, 49, 56, 141, 186
  migrants' contribution to – 4, 8-9, 159, 166, 179, 181, 194, 201
  – organization 9, 57, 177, 179, 188, 201, 203
  relations between – 4, 11, 78, 99, 118, 165
  relations beyond – 5-6, 40, 176
  relations within – 3-4, 5, 11, 19, 47, 77, 90, 172-4, 186, 188
  – size and composition 21, 86-90, 112-3
household development cycle 112, 175
household strategy 4-5, 174, 179, 194, 201
Hüsken, F. 40, 109, 112
Hugo, G.J. 57, 60, 63, 66, 72, 155, 182, 184
husband(s) 2, 8-10, 12-3, 75-6, 78-80, 82-5, 89-90, 156, 162, 168, 179, 195, 197, 203, 205
  – as migrant 1, 8, 12, 16-8, 36, 57-9, 60-4, 72, 76, 81, 83-4, 87, 90, 93-5, 130, 135-9, 164, 171-7, 179-84, 185- 6, 190-1, 193, 197, 199-200, 203-6
  authority of – 18, 41, 87, 157, 203

income 11, 19, 22, 33, 36, 39, 89-90, 165, 172-3, 179, 181, 187
  – and class 125, 162-3, 202
  – from agriculture 2, 7, 12, 19, 36, 51, 62, 113, 123, 127, 129, 179-80, 201
  – from migration 3-4, 7, 19, 61, 63, 137, 142, 171, 176, 179-80, 182
  – of women 2, 35, 157, 159, 180, 204
  – pooling 4, 87, 89, 159
independence
  – of husbands 182, 185
  – of women 2, 6, 8-9, 89, 174, 180, 203-4
  political – 23, 99, 149-51, 160
industrial(ization) 24, 150
inherit(ance) 5, 11
  – and women 67, 103, 105-7, 134, 203
  – of land 75, 91, 93, 96, 99, 102-3, 106-7, 112, 126-7, 130, 136, 168, 191, 193, 200-1
invest(ment) 37, 54, 202
  – in agriculture 67, 113, 120, 128-9, 138, 140, 179
  – in education 57, 128, 138, 143, 147, 157, 159, 162-3, 165-6, 168-9, 188, 194, 197, 201-2
  – in *tugu* 99
irrigation 24-5, 34, 114-5, 119, 139

Jakarta, as migration destination 60, 69, 72, 93, 124, 127, 155, 166, 168, 187, 189
Jambi, as migration destination 60, 93, 133, 171, 188
Java 7, 97, 107, 109, 112, 115, 139
  – as migration destination 53, 56, 63, 69
Jayawardena, C. 9, 181-2
jobs (non-agricultural) 2, 7, 60, 67, 97, 143, 145, 149-51, 155, 157, 160-7, 169-70, 187, 189, 194, 197, 202, see also labour
  – for women 7, 65, 67, 118, 147,

149, 160-1, 163, 167, 187, 189, 195, 197, 204
white-collar – 54, 67, 69
Joustra, M. 43, 47-8, 53, 146, 150

Kato, T. 7-8, 53, 64, 94, 96-7, 129
kinship 3, 5, 9, 11-2, 83, 105, 161, 204, *see also* family, inheritance, marriage, patriliny
– and position of women 7, 105, 132, 157, 182, 186-7, 190, 200, 203
– and solidarity 79, 95-7
– as economic and political structure 48, 50, 91, 99
– cooperation 173, 203
– obligations 191, 197, 201
patrilineal – 2, 11, 166, 173, 187, 190, 200
– relations 5-6, 63, 67, 201
Krause, K. 39, 44, 83, 99, 105, 135, 179, 184

labour 5, 7, 9, 50, 150-1, 169, 176, 179, 181, *see also* agriculture; household; wage labour; jobs
agricultural – 8, 56, 59, 61-2, 109, 113, 117-8, 120-1, 123, 131-2, 135, 137, 172, 195, 203
allocation of – 4, 6, 90, 187, 191, 195, 201
– market 3, 6-7, 49, 57, 68, 145, 161-2, 169, 189
– of women 2, 48, 51, 57, 78, 82, 85, 147, 149, 161, 187-8, 195, 203
lack of – 7, 77, 124, 128, 135, 139
land 180, 185, *see also* inherit(ance)
access to – 75, 77, 85, 99, 101-2, 106-7, 110, 124, 126, 186, 201
ancestral – 107, 127, 129-30, 134
– as a gift 77, 85, 103-4, 107, 133, 159, 164
caretakers of – 93, 96, 126, 141, 171, 175, 188, 191, 197, 200-1, 205-6
control over – 2, 44, 50, 103, 106, 110, 173, 205
cultural value of – 201, 205
distribution of – 101, 107, 112, 126, 174

economic value of – 63, 76, 111, 129, 164, 177, 201
fallow – 93, 11, 128, 130, 140
pawning of – 108-1, 126-7, 129, 138, 164, 168
women's access to – 6, 45, 75, 79, 82, 93, 95, 103, 106-7, 132-3, 164, 176, 182, 185, 197, 201-2, 205
land colonization 47, 51-2, 68-9
land fragmentation 11, 91, 112, 126, 202, 205
landlessness 54, 66, 102, 109, 111, 123-4, 126
land ownership 43, 50, 77, 99, 103, 105, 107, 109, 111-2, 124-6, 129-30, 133, 162-4, 170, 174, 189, 200
land quality 23, 110, 113-4, 125, 129
land scarcity 36, 43, 52, 55-6, 109, 11, 125, 151, 170, 201
land tenure 107-9, 111-2
land transaction(s) 78, 130, 138, 176
Lineton, J.A. 55, 95-6, 184-5
Lipton, M. 17, 123, 128, 162, 194
literacy 144, 155
– and access to jobs 43, 54
– of females, 149, 164, 175
Loeb, E.M. 21, 77, 83

management 12, 181
– of agricultural land 9, 127, 132, 134, 137-9, 179
– of household 9, 85, 89-90, 94, 179, 204
marital alliance(s) 77-8, 80, 148
market 96, 204, *see also* labour market
place 12, 18, 24-5, 27, 30, 33, 35, 39, 41, 45, 49-50, 64, 115, 119, 123
marriage 39, 75-7, 79-80, 82-4, 89, 95, 97, 147, 157, 160, 164, 175-6, 181, 186, 195, 203, *see also* bride-price; divorce; family; inheritance; kinship; reproduction
– age 34, 81
– and position of women 11, 78, 84, 106, 181, 186-7, 200
– and migration 66, 68
– and property 103, 109
arranged – 66, 77-8, 82

cross cousin – 77, 79
daughter's choice in – 65
– relations 183-5
traditional practices of – 83, 85, 90-1, 94
Marsden, W. 44, 135
matrifocality 190
matriliny/matrilineal 7, 9, 84, 133, 190
matrilocality 76, 95, 105, 181
Medan 27, 33, 165
– as migration destination 1, 16, 18-9, 60, 67-9, 72, 109, 124, 137, 152, 155, 159-61, 163, 167-8, 176, 185, 187, 189, 197
method(ology) *see* field work
migrant(s)/migration 13, 15-9, 21-4, 28, 34
– and education 63, 145, 155, 160, 162, 169
– and stayers 1-2, 10-1, 171, 174-6, 194, 197, 199, 201, 204
approaches to gender and – 6-12
– as household strategy 4-6, 176, 179, 186, 190, 194, 201
circular – 7, 8-9, 16, 19, 34, 50, 56-7, 60, 64, 90, 93-4, 174, 199-200
female – 1-3, 6, 31, 51, 65-6, 94, 147, 159, 195, 160, 200
household affected by – 87, 90, 96, 172, 174, 179, 181, 186, 191, 199, 201-2, 206
impact on land 119, 123-30
male and female compared 53, 67
occupations of – 1, 50, 59, 61, 67-8, 160
parents' reaction to – 90, 187, 193
permanent – 34, 56-7, 200-1
preconditions for – 1, 3, 7, 10, 12, 172, 184-5, 199
reasons for – 4, 8, 54-7, 65-6
return 63-4, 128
rural support of – 2, 24, 62, 72, 172, 201, 203
white-collar – 1, 54
migration destinations 58, 69-72
Minangkabau 21, 46, 53, 63, 94, 129
– woman's position in society 40, 84, 182, 190, 194

mission(aries) 22-3, 43, 45-9, 52-3, *see also* education
mobility 10, 34, 49, 55-6, 151, 160, *see also* migration
female – 47, 60, 67, 91, 174, 189, 202
male – 1, 6, 9, 28, 44-6, 49
social – 49, 55, 200, 202
Moore, H.L. 6, 12, 78, 131
moral (economy) 95-7, 203-4
mother(s) 1, 10, 23, 34, 41, 106, 133, 164, 171, 173-4, 181, 185-7, 189-91, 193-5, 197, 199, 203-4
– of migrants 65, 72, 134, 141
motherhood 80-2, 190-5, *see also* marriage; kinship
Murray, C. 5-6, 8-9, 99, 131, 199

Naim, M. 46, 57, 63, 94, 182, 184
Nasoetion, M.H. 41, 79, 104, 106-7, 136
negotiation(s) 117, 173, 176, 179, 181, 193, 204, *see also* bargaining
Netherlands (East) Indies 22, 45-6, 53, 146
network 173
– between migrants and stayers 56, 125
kin-based – 3, 11, 60, 72, 76, 83, 96, 189
– in village 79, 83, 99, 199
New Order *see* government
Niessen, S. 75-6, 78

occupation 17, 33-5, 56, 67-9, *see also* job
– of land 23, 52
– of women 31, 47, 68, 147
– of men 31, 44, 63, 68, 160, 186-7
Oey-Gardiner, M. 144, 156, 165
old age 63, 69, 81-2, 85, 109, 176, 191, 193, 195

Pangururan 25, 34-5, 37, 60-1, 67, 94, 147, 151
Padang 94, 176, 180, 189, 191
– as migration destination 60, 62, 66
Palembang 97, 195

– as migration destination 59, 66
Papanek, H. 187
parents 17, 21, 67, 95, 161, 165-8, 171, 185-6, 194, *see also* old age
– and attitude to education 8, 67-8, 147-8, 152, 155-7, 160, 162-4, 168
– and migrated children 64
– and migrated daughters 160, 189, 195
– and migrated sons 45, 160, 187, 191, 193-5
daughters controlled by – 65, 160, 167, 187-8
patriarchy 2, 11, 102, 105, 181, 201
patriliny 11, 21, 102, 147, 166, 173
– and position of women 2, 11, 133-4, 173, 182, 186-7, 190
patrilocal(ity) 21, 75-6, 82, 93, 182
pauseang 103-4, 105, 107, 134, 164
peddling 56, 63, 152, 164, 175, *see also* hawking
Pedersen, P.B. 22, 27, 144-5, 148-50
Pelzer, K.J. 46, 52-3, 143, 150
perceived interest 172, 174, 205
plantation 22, 24, 43, 50-1, 120, 150, 184, 200
– recruitment 7, 47, 49
politics 6, 11, 21, 39-40, 148, 166
polygamy 112, 183
population 29, 75, 91, 97, 149, 156, 172
– census 23, 31, 34, 87
– density 4, 22-4, 28, 120
– distribution 23, 28
– growth 10, 23, 24, 28, 34, 50, 53, 69, 113
– pressure 107, 124
postal orders 162, 149, 169, *see also* remittances
power 5, 11-2, 144-5, 172, 177, 190, 203-5
bargaining – 10, 173-4, 186, 188-9, 193, 204
concept of – 11-2, 204
– of men 44, 47, 203
– of women 9, 12, 40-1, 134, 202-5
powerlessness 5, 12, 177
production/productive 5-7, 24, 62, 169, 172, 175, 182, 190, 199, 202-5
agricultural – 33, 44, 57, 112-5, 120, 123, 128, 131, 137, 139-40
property 62, 96, 103, 105, 127, 130, 133, *see also* family; household; marriage; *pauseang*
male – 45, 57, 62, 77, 91, 93, 106, 126, 138, 187-9, 191, 195, 201, 204
– of couple 84, 103, 181, 203
– of women 103, 133, 181
public 27, 39-40, 44, 205
– sector 67, 125, 152, 166-7
Pusuk Buhit 21, 101

Radcliffe, S. 3, 6-7, 57
Reenen, J. van 137, 162
remittances 17-9, 137, 159, 166, 173
– allocated to education 57, 128-9, 138, 163
– from husbands 137, 141, 175, 181-2, 185, 202
– to parents 90, 163, 166, 168, 193-5, 197
Renes-Boldingh, M.A.M. 82-3
reproduction/reproductive 7, 11, 13, 46, 78, 80, 82-3, 113, 172-3, 191, 199, 203
– and production 3, 5, 85, 175, 190
Riley, N.E. 9, 105
ritual(s) 44, 48, 79, 91, 95, 97, 190
clan – 15, 18, 105, 140, 180
life-cycle – 112
road(s) 22, 25, 27-8, 33-4, 36, 39, 114, 145, 167, 200
– construction 47, 49, 134
Robertson, A.F. 112
Roldán, M. 5, 11, 173, 181

savings 9, 37, 61, 164-5, 177, 183, *see also* education
Schefold, R. 33, 99
school 26, 40, 143, 149, 151, 155, 159-60, 162, 164-8, *see also* education
attended by boys 49
attended by women 68, 147-8, 150-1, 156-7, 163, 170
government – 145-6, 150
mission – 144-8, 150

schooling
- and migration 57, 62, 65, 67, 69, 72, 186, 200
attitude to – 54, 143, 149, 150-1, 168-9, 186, 195
- of women 49, 66, 138
Schrijvers, J.Th. 8, 11, 190, 204
Scott, J.C. 49, 96, 110
security 40, 110
- for migrant men 63, 130, 199
- for parents 75, 165, 168, 191
- for women 8, 79-82, 84-5, 104, 106
Sen, A.K. 157, 172-3, 179, 182
settlement 11, 17, 22, 24-5, 33, 79, 101-2, 112, *see also* patrilocal(ity)
matrilocal – 181
- of migrants 43, 52-3
sharecrop(ping) 107-9, 111-2, 124, 127-8, 133-7, 168
Sherman, D.G. 1, 23, 31, 41, 44, 76, 89, 110-1, 119, 135, 166, 186, 188
Siborong-borong 25, 28, 47, 152, 168
Siegel, J. 46, 105, 181-2, 190
Silindung 22-3, 52, 102, 135, 143-4
Simalungun 19, 34-5, 164
- as migration destination 51-3, 59, 69
Simbolon, I.J. 24, 77, 104, 107, 109, 111, 130
socialization 94, 174, 199
Standing, G. 3, 202
state 37, 47-8, 63, 84, 96, 146, 161, 165, 180, *see also* (colonial) government
status 78, 90, 96, 148, 173, 175, 189-91
- and job 160-1, 165
- enhanced by migration 56, 65
marital – 3, 12, 17, 132
- of women 8-9, 49, 77, 80, 85, 131, 199, 202, 206
stayer(s) 5-8, 68, 138, 171-2
- as actors 8, 12
benefits for – 2, 127, 197
- dependent on migrants 8, 180
household contribution by – 180, 201
migrants compared to – 2, 11, 91, 130, 153-5, 174, 197, 199

perception of – 2, 177, 188, 193
Stivens, M. 90, 96, 104, 133, 139-40
stratification *see* class
subsistence 12, 22, 35-6, 48, 51, 113-4, 121, 128, 135, 139, 141, 179, 199, 205
- crops 113, 119

Tanner, N. 40, 190, 194
Tarutung 15, 24, 28, 47, 145
tax 7, 18, 23, 40
- raised by colonial government 47, 49-50, 54, 135
technology (in agriculture) 7, 43, 114, 119
Tichelman, G.L. 50-2, 54, 111
Tideman, J. 34 , 51-2, 56
tomb 96-8, *see also tugu*
tourist 24-5, 33, 36, 123
trade 1, 6-7, 9, 22, 93-4, 171, 176, 183-7, 189, 191
trader(s) 3, 9, 24, 35-6, 45, 51, 60-2, 68, 78, 93, 193
female – 28, 33, 35, 46, 49, 66, 68, 179, 189
transport(ation) 22, 24, 27, 54, 66-7, 114, 121
tugu 26, 32-3, 97, 99-100, 201, *see also* tomb

university 57, 123-5, 130, 150, 152, 155, 159, 161-2, 164-8, 171, 180, 185, 193

Vergouwen, J.C. 11, 45, 48, 50, 76, 77-9, 82, 85, 91, 101-3, 106, 109, 130, 177, 182-5
Volkstelling 1930 22, 53, 72, 83, 89, 135-6
Vredenbregt, J. 46, 65, 139

wage labour 9, 47, 56, 67, 113, 128
- in village 115, 118, 134, 137-8, 140, 162-3, 203
- on plantations 49, 51
wages 25, 50, 59, 61, 113, 131, 139, 165
- of women 51, 117
Ward, N.M. 43-4, 135

water 22, 25, 28, 34, 36-7, 39, 115, 118, 120, 179, 197
water works 48-9, 115, *see also* irrigation
weaving 11, 35, 134, 148, 160, 164, 181
wedding 27, 40, 77, 79, 99, 191, *see also* marriage; ritual
West Sumatra 1, 7, 94, 96-7, 137, 149, 162, 182, 194
– as migration destination 60
widow/widower 11, 31, 60, 75, 79, 82-3, 89, 94, 104, 106, 109, 111, 118, 132, 134, 136, 175
wife giver(s)/receiver(s) 11, 76, 79, 94, 102
wife/wives (of migrants) 1, 7-10, 12, 51, 57, 59, 61-2, 72, 137-8, 140-1, 148, 164, 170-1, 176-7, 179, 186-7, 191, 193, 199, 202-5
Wolf, D.L. 3, 5, 68, 87

Ypes, W.K. 48, 101-2, 106-7, 111, 136